DRAMATHERAPY AND AUTISM

Using extensive examples from practice with a range of client groups, *Dramatherapy and Autism* confronts the assumption that people with autism are not able to function within the metaphorical realms of the imagination and creativity. It demonstrates not only that people who function along the spectrum are capable of engaging in creative exploration, but also that, through encountering these processes in the clinical context of dramatherapy, people with autism can make changes that are life enhancing.

Bringing in cutting-edge research and practice on dramatherapy, *Dramatherapy and Autism* aims to contribute to developing the theory and practice of creative arts therapies interventions with clients with autism. The book is part of the series Dramatherapy: approaches, relationships, critical ideas, in which leading practitioners and researchers in the field develop the knowledge base of this unique discipline, whilst contextualising and acknowledging its relationship with other arts and therapeutic practices.

Dramatherapy and Autism will be of interest to a broad spectrum of readers, such as dramatherapists in practice and training, arts practitioners, and academic researchers engaged in multidisciplinary enquiry.

Deborah Haythorne is a founder and director of Roundabout, the largest dramatherapy charity in the UK. She is a trainer and supervisor for student dramatherapists, as well as for experienced practitioners.

Anna Seymour is Senior Lecturer in Dramatherapy at the University of Roehampton, London, Editor of *Dramatherapy: Journal of the British Association of Dramatherapists* and an international trainer.

Dramatherapy: approaches, relationships, critical ideas
Series Editor: Dr Anna Seymour

This series brings together leading practitioners and researchers in the field of Dramatherapy to explore the practices, thinking and evidence base for Dramatherapy.

Each volume focuses on a particular aspect of Dramatherapy practice, its application with a specific client group, an exploration of a particular methodology or approach, or the relationship between Dramatherapy and related field(s) of practice, all informed by ongoing critical analysis of existing and emergent theoretical ideas.

This series will be essential reading to trainee dramatherapists, arts practitioners, and academic researchers engaged in multidisciplinary enquiry.

In this series:

Dramatherapy and Autism
Edited by Deborah Haythorne and Anna Seymour

DRAMATHERAPY AND AUTISM

Edited by Deborah Haythorne and Anna Seymour

Routledge
Taylor & Francis Group

LONDON AND NEW YORK

First published 2017
by Routledge
2 Park Square, Milton Park, Abingdon, Oxon OX14 4RN

and by Routledge
711 Third Avenue, New York, NY 10017

Routledge is an imprint of the Taylor & Francis Group, an informa business

© 2017 selection and editorial matter, Anna Seymour and Deborah Haythorne; individual chapters, the contributors

British Library Cataloguing in Publication Data
A catalogue record for this book is available from the British Library

Library of Congress Cataloging in Publication Data
Names: Haythorne, Deborah, editor. | Seymour, Anna, editor.
Title: Dramatherapy and autism / edited by Deborah Haythorne and
    Anna Seymour.
Description: Milton Park, Abingdon, Oxon; New York, NY: Routledge,
    2016.
Identifiers: LCCN 2015040532| ISBN 9781138827165 (hardback) |
    ISBN 9781138827172 (pbk.)
Subjects: LCSH: Autism—Treatment. | Drama—Therapeutic use.
Classification: LCC RC553.A88 D73 2016 | DDC 616.85/88206—dc23
LC record available at http://lccn.loc.gov/2015040532

ISBN: 978-1-138-82716-5 (hbk)
ISBN: 978-1-138-82717-2 (pbk)
ISBN: 978-1-315-73383-8 (ebk)

Typeset in Bembo
by Swales & Willis, Exeter, Devon, UK

This book is dedicated to all of the children, young people, adults and their families represented in case studies and vignettes in this book – thank you.

CONTENTS

Contributors   *ix*
Foreword   *xii*
Acknowledgements   *xiv*

1 Introduction   1
  Anna Seymour and Deborah Haythorne

2 Dramatherapy and autism   4
  Deborah Haythorne and Anna Seymour

3 Entering Colourland: working with metaphor with
  high-functioning autistic children   16
  Rosalind Davidson

4 Do you believe in Peter Pan?   29
  Helen Ridlington-White

5 Dramatherapy, autism and metaphor: meeting
  The Silky Stranger   41
  Jeannie Lewis

6 Supporting agency, choice making and the expression
  of 'voice' with Kate: dramatherapy in a mainstream
  primary school setting with a 9-year-old girl diagnosed
  with ASD and ADHD   53
  Emma Ramsden

7 Becoming visible: identifying and empowering girls on
the autistic spectrum through dramatherapy   66
Ann Dix

8 Introversion, mindfulness and dramatherapy:
working with young people with autism   81
Jeni Treves

9 Mother, son and then some: on autism, dramatic
reality and relationship   93
Maria Hodermarska

10 Being men: men, Asperger's and dramatherapy   106
Adrian Benbow

11 'Remember me': dramatherapy with adults who have
autism and complex needs and are non-verbal   121
Adrian Benbow and Jane Jackson

12 Assessing the impact of dramatherapy on the
early social behaviour of young children
on the autistic spectrum   137
Roya Dooman

13 An exploration of the impact of dramatherapy
on the whole system supporting children and
young people on the autistic spectrum   156
Emma Godfrey and Deborah Haythorne

Index   *170*

CONTRIBUTORS

Adrian Benbow has been working as a full-time HCPC registered dramatherapist for over nineteen years. He has worked with a broad range of client groups, which has always included people on the autistic spectrum, as well as learning disability and mainstream schools. He has worked in freelance and employed situations, with Roundabout Dramatherapy, and he also has a private clinical supervision practice.

Rosalind Davidson has an MA in Dramatherapy (Roehampton University), Diploma in Acting (Birmingham School of Acting), and MA in Theatre, Film and Television Studies (Glasgow University). Rosalind is a freelance dramatherapist currently working with children and young people with learning difficulties and ASD, LAC, and children with emotional/behavioural difficulties in SEN secondary schools and mainstream primary schools.

Ann Dix is a dramatherapist, supervisor and trainer who has worked as a therapist with children and families for over twenty years in community, CAMHS and school settings. Ann currently works in a cluster team where she receives referrals from schools and GPs; she is also a school counsellor with Leeds Counselling, working in schools in Inner City Leeds. In her private practice she offers dramatherapy, supervision and training. Ann has a number of publications on her work with children.

Roya Dooman has worked for over twenty-five years as a dramatherapist, with adults, children and families for social services, and in education both in the UK and abroad. In 1998 she co-founded dramatherapy groups for children with Autistic Spectrum Conditions for the charity Signal in South London. She taught for seven years at Greenwich University. Currently Roya works as a dramatherapist in an inner city school and has a private practice offering training and supervision. She has a number of publications on her work with children and families.

Emma Godfrey, PhD, is a lecturer in Psychology at King's College London and is registered with the HCPC as a Health Psychologist and Dramatherapist. She trained as a dramatherapist at Roehampton Institute in 1994 and then completed a PhD in Psychology in 2004. Emma is an experienced published researcher and practitioner who specialises in developing new ways to capture, analyse and present the evaluation of therapy. She is particularly interested in building the research base for dramatherapy and developing client-centred outcome measures. She has collaborated with Roundabout Dramatherapy for many years and with them has developed PSYCHLOPS Kids, a highly sensitive client-generated measure of change.

Deborah Haythorne is a dramatherapist, supervisor and trainer. She is co-founder and co-director of Roundabout, the largest dramatherapy charity in the UK. Deborah qualified as a dramatherapist in 1985 and completed her MA research on Dramatherapy with children on the autistic spectrum in 1996. Deborah is a member of The British Association of Dramatherapists and is registered with the Health and Care Professions Council. Deborah has had a number of articles published about the work of Roundabout.

Maria Hodermarska, MA, RDT-BCT, CASAC, LCAT, is a master teacher of Drama Therapy at New York University. She is Supervisor of creative arts therapies for Project Common Bond, an international symposium for young people who have lost a family member to an act of terror, armed or inter-religious conflict, and she has published widely on dramatherapy theory and practice.

Jane Jackson, MA, is a dramatherapist and clinical supervisor. She has worked with many client groups but has specialised in working with people who have autism, older people including those with dementia, and adults with all levels of learning disability, in a variety of settings. Jane is a freelance practitioner, who also works with the dramatherapy charity Roundabout, and was also for many years within the NHS. She has published her research into self-harm by people who have severe to profound learning disability.

Jeannie Lewis has gained BA Hons Drama, Manchester University, PGCE Drama, Institute of Education, and MA Dramatherapy, Roehampton University. She studied acting with Philippe Gaulier and Monika Pagneaux, and at the Drama Studio. Jeannie has worked as a teacher in mainstream, further education and special school settings. As a dramatherapist, Jeannie has worked with early years, primary- and secondary-aged children in mainstream and special schools, adults with enduring mental health difficulties, and men with challenging behaviour in low secure forensic and rehab NHS settings. Jeannie currently works as a dramatherapist in private practice and with Roundabout Dramatherapy, specialising in working with children and young adults on the autistic spectrum. She is a clinical supervisor registered with the British Association of Dramatherapists and has published on her work.

Emma Ramsden, PhD, works with children and adults in educational settings, in the NHS, and in private practice as an HCPC registered dramatherapist and BADth approved clinical supervisor. In addition, she is a member of staff at Leeds Beckett University in the School of Education, and is currently an associate tutor at the Institute of Education. Emma's research interests focus on the ethics of consent for clients in vulnerable communities and she has a number of publications on her work with children.

Helen Ridlington-White graduated with PG Dip (1995) and MA (2001) Drama and Movement Therapy, Royal Central School of Speech and Drama, and MA Psychotherapy and Healing (2004), Society of Psychology and Healing, Middlesex University. Helen has extensive experience working with children on the autistic spectrum and with children in mainstream primary education. From 2002 Helen worked in the NHS as a counsellor in GP surgeries and now has a private practice. She supervises dramatherapy students and arts therapy professionals and was a Laban Movement tutor for The Royal Central School of Speech and Drama (Sesame) for five years.

Anna Seymour, PhD, is a dramatherapist, supervisor and international trainer. She teaches at the University of Roehampton and is a Principal Fellow of the Higher Education Academy. She has delivered keynote conference papers, master-classes and training workshops in Europe, the US and Russia. Anna has published on both Theatre and Dramatherapy. She is the Editor of the British Association of Dramatherapists' peer-reviewed journal *Dramatherapy* and Series Editor of Dramatherapy: approaches, relationships, critical ideas, Routledge.

Jeni Treves is an HCPC registered dramatherapist and BADth registered supervisor. She qualified as a dramatherapist in 1985 and taught on the Drama and Movement Therapy training at The Royal Central School of Speech and Drama in London; currently she is a placement supervisor. She has extensive experience with many client groups, specialising in work with children and adolescents who have emotional and behavioural difficulties. She has a private supervision and therapy practice too. Also trained as a body-centred psychotherapist, Jeni runs myth and voice workshops, bringing Jungian theory, psychodrama and myth enactment together.

FOREWORD

This fascinating and much-needed book brings to the reader the rigour and passion of innovators who are telling us new stories of how change can happen and be accounted for in relation to dramatherapy and clients on the autistic spectrum. It sets a high standard for enquiry in the field and creates agendas for future research.

The book holds up processes such as play, story, role or improvisation and sees how therapist and client use the space, form and relationships within dramatherapy to create opportunities for change in areas ranging from social, communication and learning skills to emotional wellbeing and creativity. The different chapters offer insights into individual situations and are alive with the detail of how specific encounters between therapist and client create change. Their accounts help us see how dramatherapists and clients have worked with their rich, contextual, individual encounters – but they do so in ways that tell us much more. The chapters have been written and edited to give us understanding of broader processes at work in order to help illuminate how drama as a therapy functions. As the dramatherapist takes the lived encounter and reflects upon and communicates it, they situate it in relation to knowledge from other texts and accounts and help us build field knowledge of how and why dramatherapy can be a therapy of high quality for clients on the autistic spectrum.

Any effective account of therapy needs to be alert to the learning the client offers the therapist not only about their own individual practice but also, more broadly, about the form of therapy they are engaging with. Each chapter can be considered on its own, but, having read the book as a whole, I can vouch for the way it builds to give deep insights across chapters to help us understand what clients are teaching us about the potency of dramatherapy as a field. In addition, the book offers insights into the ways in which different research methodologies can be brought to explore the meaning and impact of dramatherapy, with fascinating examples ranging from adaptations of formal methods of evaluating outcome to arts-based enquiry into change.

This is an exciting book that asks what it is to be a person on the autistic spectrum, what it is to be a dramatherapist, and how meetings between the two within the dramatherapy space can create rich opportunities for change.

Professor Phil Jones
University College London, Institute of Education

ACKNOWLEDGEMENTS

Many thanks are due as we arrive at the completion of this book.

The editors would like to extend their gratitude to Dr George Taylor for astute editorial advice and support.

We are grateful also to Lynn Cedar, who shared the original inspiration for the book, and to the entire team at Roundabout, who are continuously supportive.

The editors would like to thank their partners and families for their kindness and forbearance as we prepared the book.

To our Commissioning Editor at Routledge, Joanne Forshaw, thank you for your consistent encouragement; and to Kirsten Buchanan, thanks for all your assistance with the details of publication.

To the authors: thank you for your hard work and dedication and for enabling a voice for people with autism, who cannot always speak for themselves. We have been inspired by your practice and we are grateful for your commitment.

Deborah Haythorne and Anna Seymour

1

INTRODUCTION

Anna Seymour and Deborah Haythorne

This book has long been anticipated. Over the last thirty years and more, dramatherapists have been working in the field of autism providing dedicated service and achieving life-changing outcomes with their clients, but little of this work has been published. This book reverses that trend and celebrates the practice and research of dramatherapists working with people with autism in a whole range of settings, with clients representing different demographics, ages, genders and sexualities.

The book gives voice to both clients and practitioners whose voices have not been heard before. In doing so, it profiles innovative practice in the field.

We provide evidence for the effectivity of dramatherapy as a clinical intervention with people with autism and also as a way of conceiving the performative aspects of dramatherapy as ongoing metaphors that improve and support daily life for people living with the challenges of being autistic, in an often unsympathetic world.

We intend, therefore, that this book should be a resource for practitioners, researchers, students and carers.

The book is dedicated to *dramatherapy* praxis rather than attempting to embrace the other creative arts therapies or discuss joint work. This deliberate choice acknowledges that more needs to be published across the arts therapies and respects the work that colleagues are doing in related fields.

Following this chapter, Chapter 2 consists of an introduction to dramatherapy and autism authored by the editors of this book, Deborah Haythorne and Anna Seymour. In this chapter we look briefly at the origins of dramatherapy and the core elements of its theory and practice. We recognise that there are variations in practice depending on the particular orientation of the therapist and in each chapter this is spelled out by the author to locate their individual practice within the field. We then describe features of autism and reference critical literature and current thinking about diagnosis and dramatherapy clinical practice.

Chapter 3, 'Entering Colourland: working with metaphor with high functioning autistic children' by Rosalind Davidson, presents a case study with two 10-year-old boys. In this chapter she describes detailed case material that charts how the therapist was able to enter into the clients' world in contrast to the daily challenge they face of adapting to fit the world around them.

In Chapter 4, 'Do you believe in Peter Pan?', Helen Ridlington-White draws on her extensive experience of working with non-verbal clients. We follow the therapist's reflective process as she records patiently waiting for the client's story to emerge and the rewards that this brings.

Referencing current research, in Chapter 5, 'Dramatherapy, autism and metaphor: meeting *The Silky Stranger*', Jeannie Lewis recounts using verbal and non-verbal processes to create a metaphorical 'character' with her client, a boy making the transition to secondary school.

In Chapter 6, Emma Ramsden examines her work with a girl returning to mainstream education after a period of home schooling, in 'Supporting agency, choice making and the expression of "voice" with Kate: dramatherapy in a mainstream primary school setting with a 9-year-old girl diagnosed with ASD and ADHD'. The chapter looks at how this school incorporates dramatherapy into a holistic approach to serving children's emotional and behavioural needs, and highlights the importance of empowerment through dramatherapy.

Turning the focus onto issues of gender, Ann Dix in Chapter 7, 'Becoming visible: identifying and empowering girls on the autistic spectrum through dramatherapy', discusses how girls on the ASD spectrum often learn neurotypical behaviours in order to fit in and thus go undiagnosed. The implications are that because of gender stereotyping they miss out on support when early intervention could have prevented later anxieties.

Jeni Treves in Chapter 8, 'Introversion, mindfulness and dramatherapy: working with young people with autism', shifts our attention to male perspectives, offering detailed reflections from three former clients looking back on their therapy. In particular she discusses introversion and how her practice of mindfulness incorporated into dramatherapy has been effective.

Maria Hodermarska in Chapter 9, 'Mother, son and then some: on autism, dramatic reality and relationship', writes from the perspective of a dramatherapist who is also the mother of a 21-year-old son on the autistic spectrum. She describes how dramatic roles have been integral to developing his sense of self.

Exploration of masculinity continues in Adrian Benbow's Chapter 10, with 'Being men: men, Asperger's and dramatherapy'. Here, Benbow explores the difficult transition to manhood and the particular challenges facing his clients with Asperger's syndrome as they explore male identity.

In Chapter 11, Adrian Benbow and Jane Jackson share their investigative study into the therapeutic practice of dramatherapists working with adults in '"Remember me": dramatherapy with adults who have autism and complex needs and are non-verbal'.

Social Stories — About 1 thing
        ↳ Task + the slide

↳ Use positive examples to teach

(App)

Differences. Everyone has difficulties

Ask what we find difficult or easy

Comprehension — doing mind map

↳ Meta-comprehension (having time, your
                        thinking process)

Contact foyer

make a deal

photograph the 3 point scale to show
progress

talk about good dream

Bullet point the process — needs it visually

processing speed slower

"I don't feel panicked"

subtle ??? ??? but ??? ??? ??? ??? ???

Alexithimia — physical / emotions

Adse or Autistic

Finally, there are two chapters on research. Chapter 12, 'Assessing the impact of dramatherapy on the early social behaviour of young children on the autistic spectrum' by Roya Dooman, offers accessible pre- and post-therapy outcome measures and the results of her findings. Emma Godfrey and Deborah Haythorne's concluding Chapter 13, 'An exploration of the impact of dramatherapy on the whole system supporting children and young people on the autistic spectrum', provides an evaluation of post-therapy outcomes through the use of audio-recorded semi-structured interviews that have been subjected to thematic analysis. In each of these chapters, wholly positive results confirm the effectivity of the dramatherapy interventions with ASD clients in schools.

A note on the use of terminology

The authors have used a range of terminology to refer to people with autism. We have purposely embraced this in order to reflect current research into the preferred used of terminology as identified by people with autism, professionals, parents, carers and friends. Extensive research into the use of terminology was carried out by the National Autistic Society (NAS), the Royal College of GPs and the UCL Institute of Education, and the findings are based on the preferences expressed from people on the autism spectrum, their families, friends and professionals. The results evidence no preference for a specific term and clearly show a shift towards more positive and assertive language. 'There is likely to remain, therefore, a wide and understandable plurality of perspectives when it comes to talking about autism for years to come, not as the result of any error or false perception but as the result of divergent experiences and ranging points of view' (Kenny et al., 2015, p.18)

A final note

As editors we have been at turns informed, impressed and moved by the work contained in these pages. We are grateful for the generosity with which the authors, clients, professionals, families and carers have shared their experiences, and we feel inspired and honoured to be able to present their work.

Reference

Kenny, L., Hattersley, C., Molins, B., Buckley, C., Povey, C. and Pellicano, E. (2015), 'Which terms should be used to describe autism? Perspectives from the UK autism community', *Autism: The International Journal of Research and Practice*, 19:5, 1–21, at http://aut.sagepub.com/content/early/2015/06/10/1362361315588200.full.pdf+html [accessed 25 July 2015].

2

DRAMATHERAPY AND AUTISM

Deborah Haythorne and Anna Seymour

This book sets out to examine the use of drama as a *clinical* intervention in dramatherapy and how it can support clients on the autistic spectrum.

Drama and theatre arts are practised in a whole range of settings, from drama classes in schools, to putting on plays, and in forms variously titled Applied Theatre, (Nicholson, 2005; Prendergast and Saxton, 2009), Arts in Health (Brodzinski, 2010) or Social Theatre (Seymour, 2009, pp.27–37). Activities take place in theatres, community, educational and health settings, with the intention of improving well-being and sometimes encouraging behavioural change.

In each of these contexts the fundamental idea is that, by taking part in drama-based activities, people can feel better and make positive changes in their lives. Sometimes the sheer exposure to theatre can be deeply affecting, when being part of an audience enables identification with the plight of a character, a story or a situation. In his book *Nine Ways the Theatre Affects Our Lives* (2013), dramatherapist Roger Grainger examines different roles that the theatre can play, concluding with a chapter on 'Healing theatre' (Grainger, 2013, pp.147–165).

But what does this mean? If it is possible for someone to experience 'therapeusis' or a 'therapeutic effect' because they have taken part in drama activities per se, how is dramatherapy different from the other uses of drama we have referred to?

What is dramatherapy?

Dramatherapy grew out of a movement that began in the late 1970s, which, responding to the changing political climate, sought to explore new possibilities in the theatre by taking it out of theatre buildings and into communities. In this period the existing formal aesthetics of theatre practice were challenged in every way, from the content of plays to the ways they were produced. The bourgeois theatre became an artistic medium for everyone – a functional expressive art form to be put to use for learning (theatre in education), for political activism (community theatre), for aesthetic exploration (alternative theatre) and for healing (dramatherapy).

The core principle emerging from this work was that theatre can be used to deepen our understanding of the human condition and that the skills and means of making theatre can be flexible, mobile and inestimable in their scope. This also coincided with an expanded, liberatory view of whose story could be told in the theatre, valuing voices that had not been heard before. In dramatherapy the client learns that their 'voice' is respected and valued and the therapist is the kindly audience or 'witness' to what they want to show. Many of our clients have suffered vilification for their incapacities, so the straightforward acceptance of who they are, in the present moment, can of itself be reparative. The theme of empowerment runs through all of the work described in this book, so that dramatherapy as a clinical practice may be justifiably associated with a tradition of theatre for change.

In order to understand why we believe that dramatherapy can be an effective therapeutic intervention for people with autism, it is important to recognise its unique features.

A significant and broad starting point is provided by the definition used by dramatherapists' professional body:

> Dramatherapy has as its main focus the intentional use of healing aspects of drama and theatre as the therapeutic process. It is a method of working and playing that uses action methods to facilitate creativity, imagination, learning, insight and growth. (British Association of Dramatherapists (BADth) website)

Dramatherapists use drama and theatre arts *intentionally* as *the therapeutic process*. This process rests on two fundamental premises about the nature of drama:

1. Drama is part of being a human being.
2. *Metaphor* in drama is a way of encapsulating human experience that is accessible to everyone because, to paraphrase Lakoff and Johnson (1980), we 'live by' metaphors.

So drama is regarded as an implicit function within human development and as part of the metaphorical vocabulary through which human beings express their thoughts and feelings.

Both Sue Jennings' and Marian Lindkvist's work in the 1970s was foundational in instituting dramatherapy training and practice. Lindkvist created the 'Sesame Method' based on an oblique approach to using arts-based therapeutic interventions. Her commitment to the power of using 'Movement and Touch' in the work, led to the earliest research of dramatherapy with children with autism, published in the late 1970s (Lindkvist, 1977).

At the same time, Sue Jennings was developing her groundbreaking EPR (embodiment–projection–role) paradigm, which has become a core principle of dramatherapy (Jennings, 1992). This model regards human development as an essentially *dramatic process* whereby the individual's growth can be understood through metaphors derived from the theatre process. The earliest stage of sensory experience (embodiment) is analogous with the material presence of the actor.

The ensuing projective phase involves the separation from primary carer to establish what is 'me and not me' in relation to a material external world. It also marks the capacity to make choices of how to be in that world, to separate aspects of the self and allow objects to symbolically hold those parts. This process enables both projection into the imaginative realm as well as active bodily engagement, when the child can begin to fashion and influence the world about them. In this phase, what can be explained through object relations (Winnicott, 1980, 1991) can also be envisioned as the child constructing their own mise-en-scène whilst at the same time inhabiting a world constructed by the adults around them. In play, the child recreates what they have learned and experienced but is able to explore difference and other possibilities. The paradoxical nature of this process is one that will be further developed in later chapters. The dramatherapists presenting their work in this book explore how they act simultaneously as companion and guide to their clients, as they attempt to be 'alongside' them in the therapeutic relationship.

The final stage involves the fullest sense of projection in the taking on of roles, dressing up and imagining to be someone else. This process is the beginning of what dramatherapist Robert Landy has theorised as the 'role repertoire' (Landy, 1993). The capacity to adopt roles is conditioned by multiple factors, from social environment to learning ability. The potential 'to act' may be encouraged or restrained. In the dramatherapy process, the client is invited to be 'on the stage' of their own life.

In summary, we are actors in our lives with the potential to form early primary attachment, to separate and operate independently, to negotiate space and relationship to an objective and relational universe, and to form independent attachments of different orders. We propose that, even though the capacity to achieve these goals is impaired for many people with autism, dramatherapy works on the principle of discovering and building the power of the creative self in whatever form that is manifest, in the knowledge that this process has the capacity for healing and change.

Because dramatherapy is a clinical intervention, it adopts formal assessment procedures. These identify whether or not the client may be able to benefit from dramatherapy's creative processes and if so they establish appropriate starting points from which to build a shared 'vocabulary' with the therapist. In this book, there are countless examples of where the therapist patiently endeavours to be 'alongside' the client. A delicate balance is required, where firm containing structures need to be in place to establish safety and trust and, at the same time, to allow the client to explore and enact chaotic and difficult feelings. Within the aesthetic boundaries of metaphor, further layers of containment are offered whereby the client is supported to enter into an imaginative world working with metaphor arising out of the therapeutic encounter.

Dramatherapy has a long and established history of being practised with people with autism. The earliest published works on dramatherapy and autism include

Lindkvist's (1977) 'Movement and drama with autistic children' and Jones' (1984) 'Therapeutic storymaking and autism'.

Dramatherapists have continued to be drawn to this client group, believing that dramatherapy has real relevance for people on the autistic spectrum. Practitioners have begun to build an evidence base of the impact and outcomes of dramatherapy interventions. For example, Chasen (2011, pp.307–308) shows that, through the 'Process Reflective Enactment' model of dramatherapy he uses in his work with children and young people on the autistic spectrum, they are 'empowered to address personal and social challenges . . . . Group members become more fluent with perceiving themselves, perceiving others, perceiving themselves as others and perceiving others as themselves.' In other words, dramatherapy can enable people with autism to develop a stronger sense of self and identity for the inside out and the outside in. Greene (2012) evaluates the impact of dramatherapy on children's social behaviour and adjustment in school and the community. The study demonstrates children with autism reporting that they were more able to stay calm when dealing with problems after dramatherapy, and parents reporting that they saw a significant improvement in their children's empathy and problem behaviours. Brown (2012) proposes that dramatherapy can help autistic children with their capacity to manage their anxieties and 'internalize a more stable container to moderate greater levels of anxiety' (p.169).

Godfrey and Haythorne (2013) highlight five areas of change as identified by parents, carers and teachers of children with autism, in their thematic analysis of feedback from dramatherapy interventions. Dramatherapy is seen as a positive intervention that facilitated emotional development, peer relationships and social skills, reducing anxiety through its structure and clear boundaries, and also helping to support the wider family and social system around the child. The development of this study, detailed in Chapter 13 along with other chapters in this book, highlights that the processes of the dramatherapy interventions link strongly to areas identified as causing particular difficulty for people on the autistic spectrum, such as high levels of anxiety, difficulty in making relationships, and poor social skills.

The aims and objectives of Andersen-Warren's (2013) investigation were to gather information about the settings where dramatherapy with children and young people with ASD takes place, the assessment and outcome measures used in this work, the range of difficulties experienced by the children and young people, and the range of the dramatherapy interventions used by the dramatherapists. The study found that dramatherapy practitioners were working with people of all ages on the autistic spectrum. The work was taking place in schools, after school provision, in colleges, in day centres and at home, and was both one-to-one and group work.

Given this interest by the dramatherapy community, there is surprisingly little published about the practice in the UK. This book begins the much-needed process of addressing the lack of published work. By highlighting and exploring the dramatherapy approach, primarily through case study, a broad spectrum of current practice is shared.

What is autism?

The National Autistic Society (NAS) website (2014) describes autism as 'a lifelong developmental disability that affects how a person communicates with, and relates to, other people. It also affects how they make sense of the world around them.' The NAS describes autism as a spectrum disorder, encompassing people who are affected in different ways. Difficulties with social interaction, social communication and imagination, known as the Triad of Impairments (Wing and Gould, 1979), are widely accepted as the basis for diagnosis and definition. There is a wide variability in the degree to which these difficulties manifest themselves, leading to the use of the term 'autism spectrum disorders' (ASD) (Wing and Gould, 1979).

In 1911 Eugen Bleuler first used the term *autismus* (English translation *autism*) to describe defining symptoms of schizophrenia. He derived it from the Greek word *autos*, meaning self, in relation to morbid self-admiration. In 1938 Hans Asperger, of Vienna Hospital University, adopted Bleuler's terminology when talking about autistic psychopaths in a lecture about child psychology.

Leo Kanner (1943) referred to *early infantile autism* in his 1943 published paper, 'Autistic disturbances of affective contact', in the journal *Nervous Child*, where he identified patterns of behaviour in 11 children, including a lack of empathy and poor ability to form friendships, poor communication, and special interest. In 1994, Hans Asperger was also noticing that children referred to his clinic were displaying certain personality traits and behaviour. He observed social difficulties, impairments in verbal and non-verbal communication and conversation, difficulty in expressing and controlling emotions, a poor sense of empathy, special interests, and other traits including clumsiness of gait and sensitivity to sound, taste and touch. He was unable to find a description or explanation for his observations and so coined the term 'autistic psychopathy'. Lorna Wing, a pioneer in childhood development, illuminated key aspects of autism and coined the term 'Asperger's syndrome' in 1981.

In the UK, two main diagnostic classification systems are used for autism, the *Diagnostic and Statistical Manual of Mental Disorders* (DSM-5) (2013) and the World Health Organization's *International Classification of Diseases* (ICD-10 Version 2010). According to the NAS, the DSM is influential; however, the main set of criteria used is ICD-10 Version 2010:

> A type of pervasive developmental disorder that is defined by: (a) the presence of abnormal or impaired development that is manifest before the age of three years, and (b) the characteristic type of abnormal functioning in all the three areas of psychopathology: reciprocal social interaction, communication, and restricted, stereotyped, repetitive behaviour. In addition to these specific diagnostic features, a range of other nonspecific problems [is] common, such as phobias, sleeping and eating disturbances, temper tantrums, and (self-directed) aggression. (World Health Organization website)

DSM-5 has now gathered the three separate disorders of autistic disorder, Asperger's disorder and childhood disintegrative disorder, and the catch-all diagnosis of pervasive developmental disorder not otherwise specified from DSM-IV, into one diagnosis of Autistic Spectrum Disorder (ASD). Under DSM-5 criteria, individuals with ASD must show symptoms from early childhood, even if those symptoms are not recognised until later. This criteria change encourages earlier diagnosis of ASD. According to DSM-5, people with autism tend to have communication deficits and difficulty building friendships; they may be dependent on routines, highly sensitive to changes in their environment, or intensely focused on a subject or object of interest. These criteria strongly echo the work of the early pioneers in this field. The DSM-5 proposes that people with ASD fall into a continuum, with some being affected mildly and others having much more severe symptoms. According to the NAS website, the latest prevalence studies of autism indicate that 1.1 per cent of the population in the UK – that is, over 695,000 people – may have autism (using the 2011 census). The NAS proposes that *social interaction* is the most important part of the triad (NAS website). Alongside the triad of social impairments, lack of 'Theory of Mind' is seen as a core deficit for people with autism, this being the capacity to understand the thoughts, emotions and points of view or intentions of others (Baron-Cohen, Leslie and Frith, 1985).

People with autism, and parents, carers, professionals and researchers, are increasingly questioning and reframing the 'deficits' presented in diagnostic criteria and the impact this has on the lives and possibilities for people with autism (Bogdashina, 2005; Dunne, 2009). Books like *The Reason I Jump* (2013), written when he was 13 by Naoki Higashida, who is severely autistic, demonstrate imagination, humour and empathy. In the introduction to the book, David Mitchell writes, '*The Reason I Jump* unwittingly discredits the doomiest item of received wisdom about autism – that people with autism are antisocial loners who lack empathy with others' (p.9). Higashida himself writes, 'True compassion is about not bruising the other person's self-respect' (p.30). Other writers, such as Grandin (2005 with Scariano, 2006, 2014 with Panek), Williams (1996, 1998, 1998b, 2008) and Tammet (2007, 2009), have also welcomed the reader into their worldview and life experiences, providing challenging and enlightening insights from the perspective of a person with autism calling for acceptance of diversity. Grandin and Panek (2014) challenge the broad labelling of people with autism under current criteria, advocating a focus on the uniqueness of the individual.

Dramatherapy and autism

We suggest that dramatherapy can reach out to people on the autistic spectrum by recognising difference and individuality, and through a broad range of techniques it can support people to express their feelings and imagination and to develop their communication and social skills. It might seem that the creative medium of drama is inaccessible and perhaps confrontational to people who are struggling with the triad of social impairments. However, in this book we want to explore whether dramatherapy can support people with autism to develop 'theory of mind' and to find ways to explore the experiences of others through Jennings' EPR model (1992), through taking on roles, through working with metaphor and symbol, pretence and the imagination, through embodied experience, through acting 'as if' (Pearson, Smail and Watts, 2013; Friedman and Leslie, 2007) and through entering into a world of 'make believe' (Griffin, 1984; Lewis and Banerjee, 2013). There is a strong precedence for this premise, as Hans Asperger created an educational programme for the boys he was treating that actually involved drama alongside speech therapy and physical education (Attwood, 1998).

Sherratt and Peter (2002) suggest that drama can support social and emotional development and that children with autism respond well to drama-play-based interventions. They propose that, through entering into make-believe scenarios, children with autism are offered the opportunity to explore why people think and behave as they do, and so can begin to 'mind read':

> Drama can explicitly teach about empathy and emotions; it directly targets as its core content aspects of citizenship and the development of children's personal, social and emotional understanding . . . . Drama can be instrumental for children with autism developing good relationships and respecting differences between people. (Sherratt and Peter, 2002, p.90)

Gallo-Lopez (2012) proposes that dramatherapy 'provides a purposeful intervention that affords a unique opportunity to address many of the significant areas of need via a single medium' (p.103). Lord (1997), a head teacher (not a dramatherapist) specialising in working with drama with children with autism, emphasises that the focus for children with autism should be on each child establishing a sense of 'self' to explore their creativity and imagination, and that through movement, touch, drama and dance, one can begin to reach and work with the children.

We believe that some of the key methods of dramatherapeutic practice, such as embodiment and movement, projection, aesthetic distance and dramatic distance, adaptability, improvisation, working with symbol and metaphor, puppet and mask work, role, character work, story making and enactment (Andersen-Warren, 2013; Tricomi and Gallo-Lopez, 2012) support people of all ages with autism to develop a greater sense of self and other alongside outcomes such as building confidence and self-esteem. In dramatherapy, these methods are presented in ways that are specially adapted to address accessibility and relevance for people with autism, such as focusing on the client–therapist relationship as well as supporting relationships with peers within a dramatherapy group, exploring safety and challenge within the therapy space, encouraging group support and interaction, creating clear and repeatable structures within the sessions, and being aware of the group process (Andersen-Warren, 2013). Many of these concepts and practice methods are explored in this book.

Dramatherapy practice is also client led and as such is a suitable approach to take with people with autism (Jordan and Powell, 1995; Gallo-Lopez, 2012). Jordan and Powell (1995) emphasise working in this way with children with autism within an educational framework: 'The important point is not to try to impose one's own agenda but rather to follow the lead of the child; he or she has to learn what an interaction is as well as what a particular interacting means' (p.22).

Prevezer (1990) highlights the importance of using the communication offered by the children she works with through sounds, words and movements as the starting point for developing relationships. She adds, 'Meanwhile, we are also letting the child know that his own contributions are valuable, helping him to build self-esteem' (p.2). Bogdashina (2005) invites her readers to learn the communication systems, the 'language' in its broadest sense, of autistic people, rather than expecting them to learn the language and culture of the neurotypical.

Previous publications by dramatherapy practitioners have begun the process of identifying how and why dramatherapy can be a relevant and accessible form of creative therapy. Gallo-Lopez (2012) sends out a strong argument in favour of dramatic play through dramatherapy intervention as a catalyst for moving from the self, a solitary state, a reference to *autos*, the Greek root of the word autism, to a world of connectivity. She focuses on two case studies and suggests that dramatherapy encompasses the developmental and social aspects of autism as explored through a dramatic play continuum, similar to Jennings' (2005) EPR model of dramatherapy, Landy's (1993) Role Theory and Method model, and Chasen's (2011) Process Reflective Enactment 30-week programme. Beginning with sensory play, the autistic child may move on to symbolic play and then to projective play, with the aim of moving finally into sociodramatic play. This is where there is movement from 'monologue', with the child absorbed in solitary play expressing little interest in others, to 'dialogue', as the child builds relationships and chooses to interact.

Lewis and Banerjee (2013) research the use of story in dramatherapy as a way to practise social skills as well as process personal experiences with regard to emotional, psychological and social development. Through three case studies they propose that dramatherapy can support young people with autism to reflect on real-life experiences and to learn about the differences between play and reality (Winnicott, 1980/1991), something that many people with autism struggle with (Rogers, Cook and Meryl, 2005).

Researching a dramatherapy programme for a group of young people with Asperger's over an academic year, Wilmer-Barbrook (2013) reports improvements in areas of self-confidence, self-esteem, communication skills, social skills and ability to co-operate, and ability to express emotions. The dramatherapy medium utilised in the project included improvisation, role-play, story, myth and movement.

Carrette (1992) supports a non-verbal dramatherapeutic approach starting with movement and song, focusing on relationship building, communication and the meeting of experiences in a shared space. Carrette correlates these four concepts of creative expressing with developmental areas affected by people with autism, indicating that dramatherapy can offer an opportunity to explore identify areas of difficulty for a client with autism.

Discussing her 'Developmental Drama' practice with people with profound or severe multiple learning disabilities, including autism, dramatherapist Mary Booker (2011) claims that outcomes of this form of dramatherapy practice include, 'An increase in intentional communication . . . . A greater sense of self . . . . Developments in emotional literacy . . . . Improved narrative sequencing . . . . More awareness of, tolerance of and interaction with their peers . . . . Pleasure, laughter, excitement and surprise!' (pp.120–121).

Jones (1984) describes a project with a group of three young people exploring personal experiences by working with stories. Jones (1996) also describes action research carried out with a group of young people with autism, focusing on developing relationships and communication skills through projected work with puppets with a view to these skills transferring into other social contexts. Tytherleigh and Karkou (2010) also focus on the opportunity to build relationships through a short programme of group dramatherapy sessions. They suggest that the participants developed their capacity to relate to one another through embodiment play, projective work and role.

Chasen (2011, 2014) has written extensively on his Process Reflective Enactment dramatherapy model based on neurobiology and mirror neuron research and believes that dramatic enactment promotes a stronger social connection and a clearer sense of self-identity, 'perhaps more significantly for this particular population, [it] integrates processes that support competence with the manual shifting of gears between perception of and pragmatic response to self and other' (2011, p.69).

In the conclusion to her article examining dramatherapists' practice with children and young people who have autistic spectrum disorders, Andersen-Warren (2013) calls for more studies to 'examine how generic and dramatherapy based methods can inform each other and, if combined with client reported outcomes, provide a comprehensive view of the potential effectivity of dramatherapy' (p. 18).

Dramatherapy and Autism takes up this challenge and does indeed bring together a broad base of current practice that demonstrates the 'effectivity of dramatherapy' with people with autism. However, we believe that it goes beyond this. Through the voices of the clients, alongside those of parents, carers and professionals, we gain a unique insight into the transformative power of working in a therapeutic relationship through the language and communication of drama. We hope that this book will inspire other dramatherapists to work with people with autism, to share their knowledge and experiences, and most importantly we hope it will encourage more people with autism to consider engaging with dramatherapy.

References

Andersen-Warren, M. (2013) 'Dramatherapy with children and young people who have autistic spectrum disorders: an examination of dramatherapists' practices', *Dramatherapy*, 35:1, 3–19.

Attwood, T. (1998) *Asperger's Syndrome: A Guide for Parents and Professionals*. London: Jessica Kingsley Publishers.

Baron-Cohen, S., Leslie, A. M. and Frith, U. (1985) 'Does the autistic child have "theory of mind"?', *Cognition*, 21:1, 37–46.

Bogdashina, O. (2005) *Communication Issues in Autism and Asperger Syndrome*. London: Jessica Kingsley Publishers.

Booker, M. (2011) *Developmental Drama: Dramatherapy Approaches for People with Profound or Severe Multiple Disabilities, Including Sensory Impairment*. London: Jessica Kingsley Publishers.

Brodzinski, E. (2010) *Theatre in Health and Care*. Basingstoke: Palgrave Macmillan.

Brown, T. (2012) 'Play and reality in child psychosis: how psychoanalytical dramatherapy can open the door to the world of make believe', in Leigh, L., Gersch, I., Dix, A. and Haythorne, D. (eds), *Dramatherapy with Children, Young People and Schools*. London: Routledge.

Carrette, J. (1992) 'Autism and dramatherapy', *Dramatherapy: The Journal of the British Association for Dramatherapists*, 14:2, 17–20.

Chasen, L. R. (2011) *Social Skills, Emotional Growth and Drama Therapy*. London: Jessica Kingsley Publishers.

Chasen, L. R. (2014) *Engaging Mirror Neurons to Inspire Connection and Social Emotional Development in Children and Teens on the Autism Spectrum*. London: Jessica Kingsley Publishers.

Dunne, L. M. (2009) 'Playing for real: drama therapy, autism and an eight-year-old boy', in Brooke, S. L. (ed.), *The Use of Creative Therapies with Autism Spectrum Disorders*. Springfield, IL: Charles C Thomas Publishers Ltd.

Friedman, O. and Leslie, A. M. (2007) 'The conceptual underpinnings of pretense: pretending is not "behaving-as-if"', *Cognition*, 105:1, 104–106.

Gallo-Lopez, L. (2012) 'From monologue to dialogue', in Gallo-Lopez, L. and Rubin, L. C. (eds), *Play-Based Interventions for Children and Adolescents with Autism Spectrum Disorders*, New York: Routledge.

Godfrey, E. and Haythorne, D. (2013) 'Benefits of dramatherapy for Autism Spectrum Disorder: a qualitative analysis of feedback from parents and teachers of clients attending Roundabout dramatherapy sessions in schools', *Dramatherapy*, 35:1, 20–28.

Grainger, R. (2013) *Nine Ways the Theatre Affects Our Lives*. Lampeter: Edward Mellen Press.

Grandin, T. (2006) *Thinking in Pictures*. London: Bloomsbury Publishing plc.

Grandin, T. and Panek, R. (2014) *The Autistic Brain: Exploring the Strength of a Different Kind of Mind*. London: Rider Books.

Grandin, T. and Scariano, M. M. (2005) *Emergence: Labeled Autistic*. New York: Grand Central Publishing.

Greene, J. (2012) 'An educational psychology service evaluation of a dramatherapy intervention for children with additional needs in primary school', in Leigh, L., Gersch, I., Dix, A. and Haythorne, D. (eds), *Dramatherapy with Children, Young People and Schools*. London: Routledge.

Griffin, H. (1984) 'The coordination of meaning in the creation of a shared make-believe reality', in Bretherton, I. (ed.), *Symbolic Play: The Development of Social Understanding*. New York: Academic Press Inc.

Higashida, N. (2013) *The Reason I Jump*. London: Hodder & Stoughton.

Jennings, S. (1992) *Dramatherapy with Families, Groups and Individuals: Waiting in the Wings*. London and Philadelphia, PA: Jessica Kingsley Publishers.

Jennings, S. (2005) 'Embodiment–Project–Role: a developmental model for the play therapy method', in Shaefer, C., McCormick, J. and Ohnogi, A. (eds), *International Handbook of Play Therapy: Advances in Assessment, Theory, Research, and Practice*. Lanham, MD: Rowman & Littlefield Publishers.

Jones, P. (1984) 'Therapeutic storymaking and autism', in Dubowski, J. (ed.), *Art Therapy as a Psychotherapy with the Mentally Handicapped*. Conference Proceedings, Hertfordshire College of Art and Design.

Jones, P. (1996) *Drama as Therapy: Theatre as Living*. London: Routledge.

Jordan, R. and Powell, S. (1995) *Understanding and Teaching Children with Autism*. London: Wiley.

Kanner, L. (1943) 'Autistic disturbances of affective contact', *Nervous Child*, 2, 217–250.

Lakoff, G. and Johnson, M. (1980) *Metaphors We Live By*. Chicago, IL and London: University of Chicago Press.

Landy, R. (1993) *Persona and Performance: The Meaning of Role in Drama, Therapy, and Everyday Life*. New York: Guilford Press.

Lewis, J. and Banerjee, S. (2013) 'An investigation of the therapeutic potential of stories in Dramatherapy with young people with autistic spectrum disorder', *Dramatherapy*, 35:1, 29–42.

Lindkvist, M. R. (1977) 'Movement and drama with autistic children', in Shatner, G. and Courtney, R. (eds), *Drama in Therapy, Vol. 1: Children*. New York: Drama Book Specialists.

Lord, S. (1997) 'Dance and drama', in Jordan, R. and Powell, S. (eds), *Autism and Learning: A Guide to Good Practice*. London: David Fulton Publishers.

Nicholson, H. (2005) *Applied Drama: The Gift of Theatre*. Basingstoke: Palgrave Macmillan.

Pearson, J., Smail, M. and Watts, P. (2013) *The Golden Stories of Sesame*. London: Jessica Kingsley Publishers.

Prendergast, M. and Saxton, J. (2009) *Applied Theatre: International Case Studies and Challenges for Practice*. Bristol and Chicago, IL: Intellect.

Prevezer, W. (1990) 'Strategies for tuning into autism', *Therapy Weekly, London*, p.2.

Rogers, S. J., Cook, I. and Meryl, A. (2005) 'Imitation and play in autism', in Volkmar, F. R., Paul, R., Klin, A. and Cohen, D. (eds), *Handbook of Autism and Pervasive Development Disorders*. London: John Wiley & Sons, Inc.

Seymour, A. (2009) 'Dramatherapy and social theatre: a question of boundaries', in Jennings, S. (ed.), *Dramatherapy and Social Theatre: Necessary Dialogues*. London and New York: Routledge.

Sherratt, D. and Peter, M. (2002) *Developing Play and Drama in Children with Autistic Spectrum Disorders*. London: David Fulton Publishers.

Tammet, D. (2007) *Born on a Blue Day: The Gift of an Extraordinary Mind*. London: Hodder & Stoughton Paperbacks.

Tammet, D. (2009) *Embracing the Wide Sky: A Tour across the Horizons of the Human Mind*. London: Hodder & Stoughton.

Tricomi, L. P. and Gallo-Lopez, L. (2012) 'The ACT project: enhancing social competence through drama therapy and performance', in Gallo-Lopez, L. and Rubin, L. C. (eds), *Play-Based Interventions for Children and Adolescents with Autism Spectrum Disorders*. New York: Routledge.

Tytherleigh, L. and Karkou, V. (2010) 'Dramatherapy, autism and relationship building: a case study', in Karkou, V. (ed.), *Arts Therapies in Schools: Research and Practice*. London: Jessica Kingsley Publishers.

Williams, D. (1996) *Autism: An Inside-Out Approach*. London: Jessica Kingsley Publishers.

Williams, D. (1998a) *Nobody Nowhere: The Remarkable Autobiography of an Autistic Girl*. London: Jessica Kingsley Publishers.

Williams, D. (1998b) *Somebody Somewhere: Breaking Free from the World of Autism*. London: Jessica Kingsley Publishers.

Williams, D. (2008) *The Jumbled Jigsaw: An Insider's Approach to the Treatment of Autistic Spectrum 'Fruit Salads'*. London: Jessica Kingsley Publishers.

Wilmer-Barbrook, C. (2013) 'Adolescence, Asperger's and acting: can dramatherapy improve social and communication skills for young people with Asperger's syndrome?', *Dramatherapy*, 35:1, 43–56.

Wing, L. (1996) *The Autistic Spectrum: A Guide for Parents and Professionals*. London: Robinson.

Wing, L. and Gould, J. (1979) 'Severe impairments of social interaction and associated abnormalities in children: epidemiology and classification', *Journal of Autism and Developmental Disorders*, 9:1, 11–29.

Winnicott, D.W. (1980, 1991) *Playing and Reality*, London and New York: Routledge.

Websites

British Association of Dramatherapists (BADth), at https://badth.org.uk/ (accessed September 2014).

Diagnostic and Statistical Manual of Mental Disorders *(DSM-5)*, at https://www.autismspeaks.org/what-autism/diagnosis/dsm-5-diagnostic-criteria (accessed September 2014).

National Autistic Society, at http://www.autism.org.uk (accessed September 2014).

World Health Organization, International Classification of Diseases (ICD-10 Version 2010), at http://apps.who.int/classifications/icd10/browse/2015/en#/F84.0 (accessed September 2014).

3

ENTERING COLOURLAND

Working with metaphor with high-functioning autistic children

Rosalind Davidson

Introduction

Many writers on autism talk about the autistic mind being 'unable' to work in metaphor and symbol: 'Although a few pupils with autism will acquire the rudiments of symbolic or pretend play . . . it is very often stereotyped and fails to develop in any creative way' (Jordan & Powell, 1995, p.124). However, I have found that autistic clients *can* engage with metaphor and symbol. Dramatherapy offers a unique opportunity for an embodied experience through the use of 'dramatic metaphor': 'The "embodied metaphor" offers a larger number of possibilities for therapeutic and communicative use than the "verbal metaphor"' (Milioni, 2007, p.5). I believe that this embodied experience is one of the reasons why dramatherapy is a successful intervention with autistic children who often find creative expression difficult.

Swanepoel (2011) explains that the dramatherapist may engage with metaphor and symbol in a number of ways, through verbal expression, projective exercises (drawings, images and stories) or through expression in the body (gesture, sound and actions, in improvisations and enactments). This allows for a somatic response and an experience of feelings that can break habitual or repetitive behaviours. Symbolic representations are particularly important as they allow the autistic child an opportunity to practise the 'switching of gears' necessary to take them between the polarised concepts of the literal to the metaphorical. 'By projecting qualities of emotion and story onto otherwise inanimate play objects, autistic children are able to break perseverative patterns and increase their ability to interact' (Chasen, 2011, p.85).

Baron-Cohen describes children with ASD as having a developmental delay of Theory of Mind or 'mindblindness' that makes it difficult to comprehend their own emotional struggles and understand the world around them. '[They] may be puzzled by other people's actions, or anxious because other people's behaviour seems unpredictable, precisely because they cannot use a ToM (Theory of

Mind) to interpret or anticipate what others are doing or are going to do' (Baron-Cohen, 2008, p.57). As dramatherapy supports the exploration of complex feelings through the use of character and role, when the client enters into role they can examine their own struggles through embodying a character: 'Role-reversal can be employed as a technique to help individuals recognise another point of view' (Landy, 2008, p.8). In this chapter I explore whether this creative practice and experience of relationship dynamics allows the autistic child to address their struggles with 'mindblindness'. Hodermarska (2013) suggests that autistic individuals can begin to develop a Theory of Mind by using character and role to explore their experiences. Winnicott (1971, 2010) describes that in 'normal' child development it is through 'playing' that children begin to understand the perspectives of others. This development is initiated through a 'transitional object' that allows for early symbolisation. For example, a teddy bear is always soft and 'exists in the external world in a concrete way, but is creatively endowed by the child with significance from its inner world' (Jennings et al., 1993, p.116). However, in the developmental stages of an autistic child Tustin (1980) describes the use of the 'autistic object' that is usually hard, for example the wheels of a toy car used for spinning: 'Autistic objects are not played with, nor are they endowed with imaginary qualities in the way normal children treat toys in their games' (Spensley, 1995, p.65). The autistic object inhibits development; it is not used as an exploration of the external world but rather, 'the absolute elimination of all that is unknown and unpredictable' (Spensley, 1995, p.66). This early lack of symbolisation and disengagement from the external world may be a factor in the autistic child's struggle to work with metaphor and symbol: 'Such a child has missed the "practicing" stage of normal infancy . . . . In short, they have missed the early learning experiences associated with play' (Tustin, 1980, p.32). I wanted to explore whether dramatherapy could introduce the autistic child to a 'transitional space' in which to explore symbolisation that may not have occurred during early developmental stages. 'The therapeutic space in dramatherapy . . . is also "transitional", operating as a bridge between inner and outer worlds' (Jennings et al., 1993, p.116).

Recent research has confirmed what I experienced in my own work, that '71% of children with autism have at least one co-occurring mental health problem, while 40% have two or more' (Madders, 2010, p.7). I questioned whether autistic children experiencing emotional trauma may not have the expressive tools with which to manage these experiences. Could dramatherapy practices help these children express difficult feelings through metaphor and symbol?

Containment and ritual in the session structure

'Dramatic structure . . . is the container in which the practice can be adapted for meeting the needs of young people with autistic spectrum disorders' (Andersen-Warren, 2013, p.17). Dramatherapy sessions take place in a predictable space and have strong containing rituals, which allow the autistic child to feel safe enough to begin to explore and make connections. 'By providing dramatic rituals for defining space, time and other boundaries that guide appropriate enactment, these self-soothing rituals of autistic children are able to spontaneously transform from isolated events into something new, a shared experience representing authentic connection with other people' (Chasen, 2011, p.80).

In order to build confidence and lessen anxiety for my two clients, I held sessions at the same time and place each week in a room always set up in the same manner. Every session began with the client checking in with a heart-shaped cushion and a drum. Whilst holding the cushion, they could talk about anything 'good' or 'not so good' that had been happening in their lives. The drum provided an opportunity for non-verbal expression of emotions, as the client was encouraged to play out their feelings. The check-out at the end of the session mirrored the start, giving time for reflection and closure. The clients ticked off each session on their individual wall calendars to keep track of progress.

When preparing to enter the 'creative space', the clients crossed a metaphorical threshold, which they imagined and created for themselves each week. During the work in the 'creative space', they accessed a number of transitional objects. As they engaged with them, I followed their lead, making additional offers and initiating dialogue. When the work was finished, the clients returned over an imagined threshold – which may be different to the one originally crossed. This supported the de-rolling process allowing them to re-connect with their everyday identity.

The thresholds served a dual purpose: to provide a containing ritual to the work and to give metaphorical insight into how the client felt on that particular day. They decide not only how they would cross the threshold but also how I should cross, so as to enter their worlds on their terms.

Client/therapist relationship

The world of an autistic child is often separate to 'the world around them'. Isolation can occur through feelings of being different or not being understood. Working in a child-led way enables the possibility of the therapist entering into 'their world' and meeting the child in their own contextual environment, without forcing the child to alter or adapt their behaviour. For autistic children, constantly trying to fit in to a world that works differently to them, this can be a great relief. The therapist and client can explore a trusting holding relationship that mirrors a 'secure attachment' (Bowlby, 1977).

The following vignette explores the development of the client/therapist relationship between myself and Joey, a 10-year-old boy with high-functioning autism attending a mainstream school. His referral described a boy isolated from his peers, with challenging familial relationships. His class teacher described him by saying he, '*has a skewed understanding of "fairness" in that things are only fair if they work in his favour. He doesn't empathise with the needs of others.*' At the point of referral, Joey was at risk of exclusion due to his behaviour in school. The sessions took place over one school term in an Autistic Spectrum Disorder (ASD) service. Please note that the pseudonyms used in this chapter were chosen by the clients themselves.

Joey and mutuality

Joey was drawn to the percussion instruments in the room, regularly choosing an instrument to play and one for me to play alongside him. On one early occasion, we both finished playing at exactly the same moment. Joey was thrilled with this and thereafter always looked for us to complete our improvisation at the same point. Sometimes this would occur spontaneously and sometimes Joey would signal the end of our improvisation through eye contact. I felt transference of his need for mutuality. This same need began to impact his work in the creative space.

Joey had created an entire world and a story with many characters. Up to this point I had been placed by Joey in the role of 'active witness'. I use this term as, whilst he would engage in dramatic projection with the objects and take on all the characters, it was still an isolated play. I would participate by asking him questions in character, but I was not invited to engage in his story as an active participant. For many sessions Joey seemed comfortable with this and it was important I went at his pace. My role as active witness seemed to have two reasons. First, Joey did not naturally know how to play with others, and I was quite literally 'bearing witness' to his struggles. Second, I was to remain in this role until Joey trusted our relationship enough to invite me to fully interact and engage in his world.

Once Joey started to feel mutuality, he shifted my role to that of a character who had my real name, 'Roz'. 'Roz' seemed to be a bridge between my role as witness and therapist and an active role in the story. Joey appeared to project aspirational or heroic qualities onto the character of 'Roz'. At key moments in the story, he instructed me to intervene in a specific way. This was always the 'positive' action, saving a character from death or 'doing the right thing'. In later reflections Joey would comment on the actions that he had instructed me to do – 'I am glad you saved the Dark Witch', for example. This progressively built towards a significant moment in session 9.

The 'hero' of Joey's story was Sir Stretchyman (a blue rubber man), a character who battled with the Dark Witch (a beaded doll). Sir Stretchyman had a friend called Butterfree (a soft butterfly cushion). At the beginning of the story, Sir Stretchyman and Butterfree could not have any physical contact as the Dark Witch had cast a spell creating an opposing magnetic field that held them apart. This was a source of great sadness to both characters, as they could not touch or be together. By session 9 the story had progressed and the spell had been counteracted; they could enjoy closeness again. Joey proceeded to have a direct conversation with Sir Stretchyman, switching between himself and the character:

Sir Stretchyman: *'I have a secret, but I can't tell anyone.'*
Joey: *'You should tell Roz.'*
Sir Stretchyman: *'I can't; I'm scared.'*
Joey: *'Don't worry; you can trust Roz.'*

Sir Stretchyman climbed up my arm and whispered in my ear, 'I am in love with Butterfree and have been for six years.'

In role, Sir Stretchyman then asked 'Roz' whether he should tell Butterfree. I looked at Joey, who nodded 'yes', and I advised Sir Stretchyman to share his feelings.

Butterfree responded that she too loved Sir Stretchyman. Joey took both objects and enacted a beautiful scene where the two characters flew through Colourland together, leading and following and supporting each other.

In session 10, the Dark Witch stole all of the 'power objects' that enabled characters to have different powers. Sir Stretchyman had to retrieve them. As 'Roz', I was entrusted to hold the objects and keep them safe until they were all collected. Once they had been retrieved, Butterfree returned them safely to the object box. Joey reflected that, although Butterfree could feel the power of the objects, she was able to resist and not let them overwhelm her. Sir Stretchyman did not have the strength to do this on his own and needed 'Roz' and Butterfree to provide him with that support.

Discussion of vignette

I reviewed these episodes in detail in supervision, confirming my sense that Joey was exploring the client/therapist relationship through his enactment with Sir Stretchyman and Butterfree. Their relationship seemed to mirror 'our' relationship and he seemed to be exploring and expressing his deep desire to be understood and accepted. 'The drama engaged then is both healing and set within a context of healing, within a triple boundary of metaphor, client therapist relationship, and dramatherapy space' (Mann, 1996, p.5).

The character of 'Roz' enabled Joey to project his desires, to be helped to achieve his goals through doing 'the right thing'. This was something Joey struggled with in his day-to-day life. Integrating this character within the story created a bridge between reality and metaphor.

The 'power objects' seemed to symbolise the 'power' that Joey believed he held and other people tried to destroy. He often referred to having '*something inside me that no one can touch*'. These objects appeared to represent Joey's autism and how that made him both different and special. They all had different functions and effects upon the characters, which represented both the positive aspects of Joey's ASD and the shadow elements.

In the musical improvisations and the story, we had found a way to engage and communicate in a language that Joey understood and could access: 'Establishing communication and understanding between any two people with different experiences and perceptions involves developing a common language' (Bogdashina, 2005, p.85). Being attuned to his inner states (as opposed to just mirroring the outer states) allowed Joey the sense that others could share his feelings. The reciprocation of the feelings from Butterfree seemed to demonstrate Joey's acknowledgement that another person could encounter him and communicate with him in a language that he understood.

Developmental stages: Theory of Mind

The lack of development of a Theory of Mind is often referred to in 'explaining' the behaviour of autistic children; it results in what Baron-Cohen (1997) refers to as 'mindblindness'. Dramatherapy allows for emotional reciprocity, an opportunity to relate to the feelings of another person. I wanted to investigate whether this opportunity to 'rehearse' 'mindreading' could allow the autistic child the time and space through which to develop a theory of mind. 'It is logical to suppose that a failure to understand about mental states . . . would lead to people seeming confusing and frightening and this in turn could lead to withdrawal and a failure to engage with people' (Jordan & Powell, 1995, p.32).

Agro, a 10-year-old boy with a diagnosis of ASD and the second client in this piece of work, clearly had difficulty with understanding the perspectives and actions of those around him. Agro was referred due to difficult family issues, having become more tearful and having threatened to kill himself. He had been school refusing and there were serious concerns over his mental health. Agro was unable to recognise and express his own emotions. This was apparent from the initial assessment session and from his referral. Agro was on the surface a very placid boy, but he was prone to angry outbursts, when he would smash windows and hit out (he later described this as feeling like the Incredible Hulk) He appeared to have no control over his outbursts. He could not anticipate their eruption by reading his own feelings, as there were no signifiers he could recognise.

This vignette explores my stepping stones with Agro towards his accessing an emotional vocabulary to make sense of his own feelings and beginning to empathise with others' feelings and reactions.

Reading emotions

Initially we worked with hand puppets with differing facial expressions, marked with named emotions on the reverse (happy, sad, angry, worried, etc.). I invited Agro to name the emotion on each puppet's face and to experiment with replicating it with his own face, looking in a mirror. He struggled particularly with the 'negative' or 'complex' emotions. I then invited him to describe a situation where he had experienced these emotions. Agro had a close bond with his dog and could understand these emotions in relation to how he felt about his dog. 'I am happy when I am with my dog'; 'I would be worried if I was away from my dog.' Recognising when these emotions were felt was an initial step towards understanding his emotions. We also worked with OH cards, selecting a word card in relation to a particular feeling or event and a picture card to support this (from www.ohcards.com). Agro seemed to find that picture cards could encompass feelings that were difficult to express verbally. In session 3, Agro selected a word card of 'laughter' and attached a picture of a group of people with one person standing on the side. He explained that the individual 'doesn't understand what they are laughing at'. He said he often felt like an outsider who is unsure as to 'what is going on with other people'. As his confidence with naming emotions grew, Agro began to bring his concerns and worries into the therapy space.

He described feeling worried that his dog was going to be taken away. Neighbours had been complaining about the noise and his mum said the dog might have to be given away. I asked him whether he had shared these concerns with his mum. He responded that he didn't know how to. I invited him to enter into a role play with me playing his mum, so that he could rehearse telling her how he felt. It quickly became clear that he was unable to do this as he quite literally did not know what to say. We reversed roles and I modelled how he might express his fears and he listened and responded in the role of Mum. We then reverted to our original casting and Agro was able to express his feelings and rehearse telling Mum how he felt.

Discussion of vignette

Working in small and achievable stages towards recognising and contextualising emotions seemed to give Agro confidence. Attitudes towards autism often describe a 'lack' of emotions. However, this may derive from a struggle to reference and express what is being felt and therefore be able to recognise and empathise with these feelings in others. 'People with autism may not show emotions in a traditional way, but this does not mean they have no emotions' (Bogdashina, 2005, p.87).

Through building emotional vocabulary an autistic child may enter into the developmental stage of theory of mind, which may have been delayed or not developed in childhood. Towards the end of the course of therapy there was a major shift in Agro, as he began to speak regularly at length about his feelings. He spoke of feeling upset as *'Mum has said we can't afford Christmas this year'*. He was able to express how he could not discuss it with Mum, as he imagined that she must already be feeling *'stressed about it'*. This ability to express himself and to 'mindread' how his Mum might be feeling showed a marked shift in Agro's ability to anticipate how others might feel, potentially developing a Theory of Mind

Entering their world

Meeting the client on their own terms presents an opportunity for the therapist to be invited to experience 'their world'. One of the defining characteristics of autism is 'rigid ritualistic interests'. Many people with autism have obsessions or detailed knowledge of narrow fields of interest. Allowing these interests to have voice, and exploring them in the dramatherapy session, enables communication. The principle is to acknowledge and support what the clients bring to sessions. 'We need to first embrace and align with who they are, rather than merely rejecting and extinguishing behaviour, if we are to guide them toward more effective perspective shifting, emotional adaptation and enhanced functioning' (Chasen, 2011, p.52).

In conjunction with the work on emotional literacy, described in the previous vignette, I was keen to engage with Agro through character and role. During the initial assessment session, Agro struggled to engage. He responded with monosyllabic answers and little eye contact. His mother and school had spoken of his isolation and inability to engage with others. Agro was fixated with Pokémon and brought this into the assessment session. He became animated, making eye contact and giving in-depth explanation of the Pokémon world. The following vignette is focused on the development of Agro's own Pokémon character.

Pokémon

I invited Agro to create his own Pokémon character. He enthusiastically drew a character called 'Voltage', which he then described. Voltage held great strength and power and was able to motivate change. Agro created a sculpt of Voltage and then walked around the room in character. He then created a 'Six-part Story' (Lahad, 1992), with Voltage as the main character. In his story Agro drew an identical twin Voltage, who assisted Voltage in carrying out his task. This metaphor carried across much of the work with Agro. He showed a need and desire for friendship with someone 'like him', and he wished to be supported and understood by someone who experienced the world as he did. I was intrigued that the 'obstacle that stands in the way' was an unnamed character that Agro was unable to describe. In later sessions, this character was called 'Bob'. Bob was drawn as a stick man with a sad face.

In the second session, Agro turned up with his Pokémon collection and we used this as a starting point from which to create his own card for Voltage. First, Agro created the world of Voltage in the therapy space. He was hesitant and unsure as he dressed himself as Voltage to explore the world he had created. He clearly stated he was not ready to enter the dark cave he had created as Voltage's home: 'not yet'. Agro maintained control over the pace and the depth of his therapeutic process. He had started to take small steps without feeling overwhelmed.

In the next session, Agro wanted to create another Pokémon character. He created 'Mew-Three', who was psychic with an ability to read the minds of others. Agro integrated Voltage into Mew-Three's story to assist him in his task. Again, it was the unnamed and un-described character of Bob that was the obstacle that stands in the way.

Over the next few sessions, we began to investigate the character of Bob. Agro explained that Bob was sad and lonely because nobody liked him. I invited Agro to create masks for his characters, focusing on their emotions. He made one for Voltage ('happy'), one for Mew-Three ('somewhere in the middle') and one for Bob ('sad'). Agro then tried the masks on and looked at himself in the mirror. I invited Agro to speak and answer questions as each of the characters. This was the most verbally engaged that I had seen Agro. The masks appeared to act as an additional container that allowed him to feel safe enough to express himself in role. He reflected afterwards that he had felt sad playing Bob. I asked if he could give Bob any advice and I put on the 'Bob mask'. Agro advised Bob that he 'should tell people how you are feeling'.

In session 6, Agro chose to create the world of Bob and take on this role. The world had a house and a bed in it. Bob had nightmares as he slept; his bed was uncomfortable. He sat in his room alone all day with no one to play with and nothing in his room; he felt lonely. Agro cast me in the role of Voltage, who came to visit Bob. Bob could not show Voltage around his house, as his brother and sister might shout at them. When reflecting after the enactment, Agro commented that he had felt sad being Bob, because he had nothing to offer Voltage.

Discussion of vignette

I used Agro's fixation with Pokémon as a means to communicate on a level and in a context that he would understand: 'it is possible to use a child's particular obsession or stereotyped actions as a legitimate starting point . . . one has to engage with whatever is engaging the child whatever that may be' (Jordan & Powell, 1995, p.23). By encouraging him to create his own characters, he was able to work with his own unconscious material and begin to look at the world through the eyes of the characters. It had become apparent that Agro saw himself as Bob. Through this character, he explored and expressed his loneliness and isolation. The character of Voltage seemed to encompass Agro's desire to reach out and connect with others. Through the role of Mew-Three, he metaphorically explored his desire to be able to 'mindread'.

Working in metaphor

The dramatic metaphors in Joey's Colourland story appeared to be symbolic of his real-life experiences: they worked as a container, giving Joey a distance through which he could safely explore and express these experiences. As the process of therapy continued, some of Joey's feelings began to move from the unconscious to the conscious and the story itself became more literal as he started to make connections between what was taking place in the creative space and his reality. The language of reality began to creep into the metaphor and reflected his movement into a more conscious way of working.

The following vignette demonstrates the potential for the autistic child to fully engage in working with metaphor and symbol in the dramatherapy space and highlights the impact upon Joey's personal process.

Colourland

Joey's story took place in a world called Colourland, situated adjacent to Darkland, where the Dark Witch reigned. Historically there were battles between the two lands and a barrier had been built to keep the dark from infiltrating Colourland. Joey described that Sir Stretchyman had been turned into rubber by a spell, cast by the Dark Witch. She had thought she was punishing him by turning him into rubber, 'but it had actually been a good thing'. When reflecting on this afterwards, Joey commented that, 'the wrong done to Sir Stretchyman only makes him stronger.'

In session 2, I invited Joey to create the world of Colourland in the therapy room, using fabrics and other items. He created a visceral landscape with mountains, the cave of the Dark Witch, and a protective barrier between Colourland and Darkland made from a series of drums. Joey embodied Sir Stretchyman and gave me a tour of Colourland. He explained that the Dark Witch had to live there now as she had destroyed Darkland.

In session 3, Joey wanted to re-create the Colourland landscape. He did this, but without the barrier between the two lands. When I questioned its removal, he commented that 'it is not needed anymore'. The session continued with a battle between Sir

Stretchyman and the Dark Witch until a truce was reached. When reflecting after leaving the creative space, Joey explained, 'Colourland cannot exist without the Dark Witch, as she gives things their black outline. A white pencil will only show up on dark paper. So without the Dark Witch you would not be able to see any of the colours in Colourland.'

In session 6, Sir Stretchyman sought out the Dark Witch and beat her till she was almost dead. He came out of role and invited me as 'Roz' to give her the 'heart power object' that would restore her to life. Joey then returned into role as Sir Stretchyman and told me he was angry that I had healed the Dark Witch. After the enactment, Joey reflected that I had shown 'affection to the Dark Witch' by restoring her health. I mentioned that Sir Stretchyman had been angry; Joey responded that I had done what was 'the right thing to do'.

In session 7, Joey enacted a scene between the Dark Witch and the Dark Witch's Mum (a larger version of the beaded doll). He came out of role and commented that, 'The Mum causes the Dark Witch to be evil as she shouts at her when she has done nothing wrong. She sits in her room and watches Jeremy Kyle *and this is why the Dark Witch's Dad left.' He discussed that the Dark Witch feels lonely because no one listens to her 'except Roz'. He then engaged me in the scene, getting me to stop the Dark Witch's Mum from hurting her. Joey then involved himself in the scene and fought, as himself, with the Dark Witch's Mum and threw her back into the object box.*

Discussion of vignette

Through the complex metaphors of Colourland, Joey was able to externalise his preoccupations and anxieties. Much of the work with Joey centred on his adjusting and accepting the 'dark' things that had taken place in his past, an acceptance that these things had found space in his psyche. The negotiation between Colourland and Darkland, and the Dark Witch and Sir Stretchyman, seemed to be an embodiment of this struggle: 'In this role play, he not only activated a Theory of Mind but he was able to embody the complexities of . . . both hero and villain, role and counter-role' (Hodermarska, 2013, p.69). Joey had begun to unite the characters of the Dark Witch and Sir Stretchyman and find ways in which they could exist and work alongside each other as part of the whole self.

In the last session, I invited Joey to re-visit the 'key moments' of the story and I offered the creation of a ritual ending. Joey did this by re-visiting the main characters and lining up all the objects around the object box. He separated them into three categories of 'main characters', 'extras' and 'power objects', and one by one returned them to the object box. He closed the box and invited me to join him in a ritual dance. Joey then moved the box to another space in the room and took my hand and bowed to the box. He said, '*They are no longer characters; they are now just objects in a box.*' I was deeply moved by Joey's creation of his ritual ending. It seemed to demonstrate a clear and instinctive understanding of the process of dramatherapy and a powerful ability to work in symbol and metaphor. Rather than being unable to work in metaphor due to his autism, Joey clearly demonstrated that this was a language that he understood and connected with.

Outcomes: Joey

Both Joey's school and his mum reported a shift in his behaviour and his ability to express himself – and the threat of exclusion from school was removed. Joey's ability to work in metaphor and symbol challenges the common conception that autistic children cannot engage in this way. I believe that dramatherapy demonstrates huge possibilities for high-functioning autistic children at risk of mental health issues: 'Dramatherapy using stories presents a real and exciting set of possibilities for engaging young people with ASD in a positive therapy, likely to benefit their emotional, psychological and social development' (Lewis & Banerjee, 2013, p.29).

Joey's ability to express and examine his issues using dramatic metaphor appeared to have had a direct impact on his day-to-day life. His mum reported, *'He has enjoyed every session and comes out very happy and calm. He seems much more understanding of people's feelings, or at least shows more of an interest in people's feelings. There have been no major incidents or issues at school since therapy began. He seems less anxious in situations that he would normally find very difficult and is overall just generally happier and less worried.'* His relationship with his father, which had been a source of some concern at the point of referral, also improved during this period: *'His father has also noticed a change in the last few weeks in that he has not been as defiant and [is] generally happier when he is there (he hated going to his dad's before).'*

Outcomes: Agro

> The Dramatherapy session content and structure works for children and young people with ASD, reducing anxiety and building confidence.
>
> *(Godfrey & Haythorne, 2013, p.26)*

Part of Agro's referral was that he was frequently refusing school, causing serious concerns and risk of exclusion. Agro responded well to the regularity and structure of the sessions, turning up early for sessions eager to enter the space, even attending on days when he had refused to go to school. By session 10, Agro told me that he had received a certificate from school celebrating his consistent attendance over two weeks.

Both the school and Agro's mum reflected that the only difference at this time was his attending dramatherapy sessions. Whilst we never worked directly with his school refusal, the child-led dramatherapy had achieved this improvement indirectly. I had discussed with his mum, at the outset, that his attendance of dramatherapy should not be used as a bargaining tool or an option that may be removed as a punishment. In this way, the dramatherapy sessions were always available to Agro as a consistently safe space.

Agro's mum reported she felt that dramatherapy, *'has helped Agro with confidence and he has really enjoyed going to sessions. Agro finds it difficult to talk about emotions; I find dramatherapy does help him cope better.'*

After the 13th session, for the first time in many years, Agro invited a friend to his house to play. This had not happened previously due to concerns about his behaviour and his difficulties in making friends. This felt like a major shift for Agro.

Conclusion

This chapter demonstrates that dramatherapy sessions enable the autistic child to engage with their issues through dramatic metaphor. The containment and ritual within the session structure creates a secure environment in which the client can begin to explore and make connections. The development of a trusting and holding client/therapist relationship supports exploration through mutuality and respect.

Dramatherapy sessions offer a 'transitional space' in which to explore symbolisations that may have not have occurred during early developmental stages and help to build an emotional vocabulary.

The 'mindblindness' of autistic children can be examined through character and role, allowing the client to work with feelings and experience the world from others' perspectives.

Working *with* autism rather than against it through the autistic child's obsessions or fixations allows an opportunity to 'enter into their world' using dramatic metaphor.

The vignettes show that Joey and Agro were able to engage in symbolic play and work metaphorically, and that they could use this way of working to express and explore difficult feelings.

The outcomes demonstrate that the opportunity to work with their own issues through the embodied experience of dramatic metaphor can effect positive changes and assist better integration into the day-to-day lives of this client group. They offer exciting possibilities for further work with children with ASD at risk of mental health issues to explore and develop their capacity to manage their emotions.

References

Andersen-Warren, M. (2013) 'Dramatherapy with children and young people who have autistic spectrum disorders: an examination of dramatherapists' practices', *Dramatherapy*, 35:1, 3–19.

Baron-Cohen, S. (1997) *Mindblindness: An Essay on Autism and Theory of Mind*. London: The MIT Press.

Baron-Cohen, S. (2008) *Autism and Asperger Syndrome: The Facts*. Oxford: Oxford University Press.

Bogdashina, O. (2005) *Theory of Mind and the Triad of Perspectives on Autism and Asperger Syndrome: A View from the Bridge*. London: Jessica Kingsley Publishers.

Bowlby, J. (1977) 'The making and breaking of affectional bonds. I. Aetiology and psychopathology in the light of attachment theory', an expanded version of the Fiftieth Maudsley Lecture, delivered before the Royal College of Psychiatrists, 19 November 1976, *The British Journal of Psychiatry*, 130: 201–210.

Chasen, L. (2011) *Social Skills, Emotional Growth and Drama Therapy: Inspiring Connection on the Autism Spectrum*. London: Jessica Kingsley Publishers.

Godfrey, E. & Haythorne, D. (2013) 'Benefits of dramatherapy for Autism Spectrum Disorder: a qualitative analysis of feedback from parents and teachers of clients attending Roundabout dramatherapy sessions in schools', *Dramatherapy*, 35:1, 20–28.

Hodermarska, M. (2013) 'Autism as performance', *Dramatherapy*, 35:1, 64–76.

Jennings, S., Cattanach, A., Mitchell, S., Chesner, A. & Meldrum, B. (1993) *The Handbook of Dramatherapy*. London: Routledge.

Jordan, R. & Powell, S. (1995) *Understanding and Teaching Children with Autism*. New York: John Wiley & Sons.

Lahad, M. (1992) 'Story-making in assessment method for coping with stress: six-piece story-making and BASIC Ph', in: S. Jennings, ed., *Dramatherapy: Theory and Practice 2*, pp.150–163. London & New York: Routledge.

Landy, R. (2008) 'The dramatic world view revisited: reflections on the roles taken and played by young children and adolescents', *Dramatherapy*, 30:2, 3–13.

Lewis, J. & Banerjee, S. (2013) 'An investigation of the therapeutic potential of stories in Dramatherapy with young people with autistic spectrum disorder', *Dramatherapy*, 35:1, 29–42.

Madders, T. (2010) *You Need to Know*. London: The National Autistic Society.

Mann, S. (1996) 'Metaphor, symbol and the healing process in Dramatherapy', *The Journal of the British Association of Dramatherapists*, 18:2, 2–5.

Milioni, D. (2007) 'Embodiment and metaphor in Dramatherapy: a discursive approach to the extra-discursive', *Dramatherapy*, 29:3, 3–8.

Spensley, S. (1995) *Frances Tustin*. London & New York: Routledge.

Swanepoel, M. (2011) 'Meeting with the metaphor: the impact of the dramatic metaphor on the therapeutic relationship', *Dramatherapy*, 33:2, 101–113.

Tustin, F. (1980) 'Autistic objects', *The International Review of Psycho-Analysis*, 7, 27–39.

Winnicott, D.W. (1971/2010) *Playing and Reality*. London & New York: Routledge.

4

DO YOU BELIEVE IN PETER PAN?

Helen Ridlington-White

Introduction

This chapter will be based on my extensive experience of working with non-verbal clients with autistic spectrum disorder. Although my account is based on one particular client, whom I will call 'Cathy', certain observations will draw on working with a wide number of clients, as much of my own expertise in practice comes from my clients and their personal stories, as well as those who have written or talked about their experience of having an autistic condition. I chose the name Cathy because my client reminded me of Cathy from Emily Brontë's *Wuthering Heights*, with her free-spiritedness. She was twelve years old, tall, vibrant and pretty. She had little verbal language. At the time of the referral, Cathy's high spirits were often expressed destructively in unpredictable emotional and violent outbursts, which were dangerous to herself and others. She was referred to me to support her engagement with school, both academically and socially. Consent has been obtained to write about our work and confidentiality will be maintained.

Background

My dramatherapy practice combines an integrative approach including Carl Jung's (1964) psychoanalytical theories and his understandings of unconscious and collective unconscious aspects of humankind. Central to this is the individuation process and Jung's idea that the unconscious is the connection to the soul, that each individual has a possibility to find their own meaning through bringing into consciousness forgotten or repressed material: 'It is vital for each living being to become its own entelechia and to grow into that which it was from the very beginning' (Dunne, 2000, p.6). From this comes my belief that within each client there is a source of symbolic wisdom, and it is possible, through dramatherapy work with metaphor, movement, dreams, creative expression and play, that this wisdom may become inte-grated. Developmental theories also inform my work, including Winnicott's concept of the 'True Self': 'Where there is a high degree of split between the True Self and the False Self which hides the True Self, there is found a poor capacity for using symbols, and poverty of cultural living' (Winnicott, 2002a, p.150).

The true self is dependent on early life experiences and the mother/environment's ego-supportive function. When there has been damage or disruption, dramatherapy can provide reparative creative possibilities, to re-member and re-find lost or buried elements of the self to a degree that depends on the wounds of the inner child. There is psychobiological evidence that early dysregulatory functions operating in adult clients may be addressed in the dyadic psychotherapeutic treatment, through recog-nition and transformation of infantile non-verbal defences and early shame (Schore, 2003). For a client, psychobiological structural change is the outcome of long-term psychological treatment, involving 'rewiring the connections of the right frontolimbic cortex and the consequent replacement of toxic with more benign internal repre-sentations of the self' (Schore, 2003, p.78).

In my practice, the diversity of the therapeutic relationship is contained in examining counter-transference through thoughts, feelings and ideas associated with a client, including investigating how I myself react somatically to non-verbal energetic expression. Transference from the client may evoke a variety of states, including motherly feelings, hate or rage, tiredness or protectiveness. These are explored in supervision and generally craft the way I am session to session. Petrushka Clarkson's (1990) 5 relationship model helps define transference through her five intersubjective therapist–client phases within therapy work: the begin-ning working alliance phase building upon the therapy contract; the transference/counter-transference phase deep-rooted in the *presenting past* and consequential projections; the reparative corrective phase where the therapist becomes the *good enough other* carer figure; the person-to-person phase dependent on human con-nection built through trust; and the transpersonal relationship where the spiritual dimension of healing can include an expansion of consciousness. All these phases manifested in my work with Cathy.

In this chapter I include a feature from the story of Peter Pan, as the client chose this particular book herself, and the way in which she energetically engaged with the fairy tale enabled meaningful communication between us. Although she responded to specific images from the story, I am drawn to use it as a metaphor for her development during dramatherapy. At the start of the fairy tale, Peter Pan is looking for his lost shadow, as he feels he is missing something; he finds it with the help of Wendy, who sews it back on for him. Perhaps, like Wendy, I helped Cathy to find something she felt was lost (Barrie, 1911).

Preparation

School referred Cathy to dramatherapy to gain a better understanding of her needs and her problems with communication. They also hoped the sessions might help her engaging with school. Before I carried out my assessment, I read Cathy's notes in order to gain an understanding of her self-presentation in a variety of settings, including school, home, after-school clubs and respite care. I also hoped to gain insight into any possible triggers linked to Cathy's occasionally extreme incidents. Cathy mainly had a loving relationship with her parents, though they were exhausted by having to constantly review ways of coping as Cathy's specific developmental and emotional needs changed. At the time of the referral, they had decided to give her a certain amount of freedom at home. Eventually, the family were able to employ a nanny, which provided them with some respite and meant their time with Cathy could be more enjoyable.

Cathy's destructive emotional outbursts were exhibited mainly at school, and her lack of verbal language compounded her frustrations at not being able to express clearly what she needed or how she felt. An outburst might manifest biting and head banging, hitting and kicking herself, or others or objects, and throughout Cathy would scream and cry. Naoki Higashida, a non-verbal 13-year-old boy with autism, explains, 'If a person without autism is going through a hard time, he or she can talk it over with someone . . . but in our case, that's not an option. My guess is the despair we're feeling has nowhere to go and fills up our bodies making our senses more and more confused' (Higashida, 2013, p.86).

In our sessions I wanted to be prepared for any of Cathy's sudden and unexpected emotional outbursts and contain them safely. I decided to seek extra support for containing strategies in case they were needed. We agreed that Cathy should attend therapy with her one-to-one teaching assistant, as a familiar adult who might provide security for her in a new environment. As a therapist, I wanted sessions to be calm and inviting, and, most of all, safe. I explained to the teaching assistant that I did not need her to do anything except be there in a calm, relaxed and non-intrusive way. I would initially assess Cathy without putting particular demands on her, except to abide by the working agreement of not hurting ourselves or others. I thought carefully about how I might move and present myself in a sustained, grounded manner, as sudden movements at the beginning stage might trigger a fright response from Cathy. From my reading about her, I knew Cathy could go rapidly into panic mode, and I wanted to prevent any anti-therapeutic (unsafe) experiences for her. I needed Cathy to trust me so she could immerse herself in the creative process. If she had an outburst, we agreed that I would not physically intervene in any restraint procedures, as it might damage my relationship with Cathy. My presence and manner would remain calm and reassuring.

I had chosen some objects to have in the therapy room every week: a few books, some light-coloured cloth, a blanket and a soft bouncy ball. I hoped that Cathy would be more secure and relaxed in relating to me through working with familiar objects. Winnicott reflects that 'a need for a specific object (transitional object) or a behaviour pattern that started at a very early age may reappear at a later age when deprivation threatens' (Winnicott, 2002b, p.xvii) In this case, deprivation came in the form of something new and unfamiliar, therefore depriving the child of familiarity. Initially everything about the session would be a new experience for Cathy, change being a challenging process for many on the spectrum in its unpredictability and sense of a loss of control. As time proceeded, familiar objects would provide reassurance and an underpinning platform of security. Furthermore the object may become an extension of self-expression and enhance a relationship avoiding direct touch. Donna Williams has written about her difficult experiences of growing up with high-functioning autism: 'For me, when the directedness of relating is too great, the walls go up' (Williams, 1992, p.1).

First phase of therapy

'Help me'

Now I felt ready to provide Cathy with dramatherapy, the first session began. As Cathy entered the therapy room for the first time, I sensed strongly that the message coming from her was: 'help me'. She appeared very wary and her body movements were frozen and tense. I felt a counter-transference of anxiety in my abdomen, and I felt what Cathy needed was for me to be non-threatening, so she could have a chance to visually assess who I might be, and what was in the therapy space – as well as have time to regulate herself. After ten minutes I initiated the working alliance with a few simple words: '*Welcome, Cathy, to dramatherapy. This is a space just for you to be and play in. We don't hurt each other or ourselves, and if we want to go out we can find a way to ask.*' I spoke gently and clearly, looking occasionally towards, but not obviously at, Cathy. I felt that this information needed to be taken in, without me expecting eye contact, or indeed any response, from Cathy. Williams suggests a hint for working with those on the autistic spectrum: 'The best way I could have been able to listen to someone, was for them to speak to themselves about me out loud or about someone like me. Indirect contact, such as looking out of the window whilst talking, would have been best' (Williams, 1992, p.182). I wished to assure Cathy there could be a hopeful chance for creativity, relating and understanding. 'The Neverland is an island children visit in their dreams, where anything can happen. To reach it, you have to fly' (Barrie, 1911, p.2).

A school teacher once asked me, 'Do you work with the autism or the child?' 'I work with the whole child, their unique personality as well as their specialisms,' I replied, 'and I meet them in their world first to make a connection.' Dr Violet Oaklander, psychologist and therapist, writes in *Windows to Our Children* of a colleague working with a child with autism:

> Instead of insisting that he come to her, she went to him, sat by the mirror without a word, and watched as he looked at himself . . . she realised he was actually SEEING himself. Suddenly he noticed that her reflection was in the mirror as well, and he was so delighted and excited that he settled right down into her lap. (Oaklander, 1988, p.274)

My acceptance and affirmation of Cathy's uniqueness, along with my sensitive and respectful manner, would, I hoped, enable me to *fly* to her world so I could meet and grow in my understanding of her.

Building trust

For several weeks, Cathy entered the therapy space excited, but very cautiously. She preferred to sit at a distance from me and the atmosphere felt thick with visceral intensity. I felt relaxed yet on high alert. Metaphorically, it was as if we were in the desert, curious but very wary, unable to know what the other was like, two different species moving a little closer as trust was built through the consistency of providing the same weekly space, and in my continued aim of not yet challenging Cathy in this first phase of dramatherapy. In these weeks I too sat on the ground, mainly still and non-verbal, aiming to be an open and friendly recipient to Cathy's presence, however that might be. The tension in the room eventually began to soften, and week by week the spatial distance lessened as Cathy crept closer to me, until one day she laid her head on my lap. In that tender moment, I sensed that Cathy experienced a letting go – into a childlike state of being. My therapeutic *waiting* had been rewarded with a gift of trust from Cathy. I felt that from this moment she would start being able to play with me alongside.

Winnicott developed the Spatula Strategy test as an initial assessment tool with mother and baby. The spatula was placed on a table and without prompting the baby Winnicott watched to see how the baby explored the spatula or not. Stage 1 is the usual first period of hesitation, when the baby holds his body still but with security from the mother; in stage 2 he 'gradually becomes brave enough to let his feelings develop, and then the picture changes quickly . . . instead of expectancy and stillness there now develops self-confidence, and there is free bodily movement' (Winnicott, 2002b, p.232). From this first phase of therapy providing a consistent and non-threatening creative environment, Cathy was eventually secure enough to begin to engage in exploring objects.

Middle phase of dramatherapy

'I'm all tied up'

In the story of Peter Pan, there are two domains: Wendy's earthly world, with mothers and fathers who look after children and go to work, and Neverland, where fairies exist and where children who never grow up live together. As human beings, simplistically speaking, the playful curiosity of our child-self and the rounded wisdom and responsibilities of our adult-self are held in a healthy balance. Evolving children need attentive and unselfish adults to tend to their ego development and psychological health:

> The baby's temperament or genetic make-up inevitably has an impact on
> the caregiver, who has his or her own personality style too. The point is,

however, that the outcome depends far more on the mother and father than on the baby. Researchers have found even the most difficult and irritable babies do fine with responsive parents who adapt their needs. (Gerhardt, 2015, p.35)

As a dramatherapist I adopted the reparative parent role, and, as such, I was mindful of Cathy's playful expressive child-self, often expressed in ways much younger than her chronological age. I continued to have the familiar objects in the therapy room, including a simple Ladybird picture book version of *Peter Pan*. Cathy was drawn to this particular little book and liked to sit close to me, side by side, flicking through the pages. Cathy would take a sideways glance from time to time to check me, eventually happy to look longer into my eyes with a contented giggle. I engaged in a non-judgemental, affirming and accepting way during these exchanges, and I felt instinctively – and reflected analytically – that these moments were very significant.

Neuroscientific research provides evidence that in these moments of non-judgemental, accepting positive therapeutic regard, social neural pathways are built and according to Allan Schore, 'looking at faces has an even more powerful role to play in human life. Especially in infancy, these looks and smiles actually help the brain to grow . . . it is positive looks which are the most vital stimulus to the growth of the social, emotionally intellectual brain' (Gerhardt, 2015, p.59). The MIFNE model of early intervention was developed in Israel by Hanna Alonim with babies and toddlers showing signs of autism. The method focuses on using eye contact as a starting point to motivate babies to communicate; they then move on to touch through reciprocal play therapy. All the interaction is done in a very low key and relaxed environment, responding to the baby on their terms. 'A 5 year follow up of babies who have been treated at the Mifne Center revealed they were neuro-typically developing children, and an evaluation of the program by the Schneider Children's Medical Center showed that the children improved on 2 scales: the Childhood Autism Rating Scale (CARS) and the Social Behavior Rating Scale (SBRS)' (Wagner, 2012). Although 12-year-old Cathy was not a baby, I still thought that using eye contact and reciprocal relational experiences would be enriching and could improve her social development.

For many weeks Cathy went straight to the same page in the Peter Pan book, '"Tie her to the Mast!" Hook shouted' (Barrie, 1911, p.43). Far from home, in Neverland, Wendy is captured by Hook and faces walking the plank into the sea. In Jungian symbolic concepts the sea represents the unconscious, and in metaphysical terms our earliest home. The image of Wendy tied up in rope took on symbolic and metaphoric meaning and Cathy desired to share it with me. I reflected in simple empathic words what was happening in the picture, so that she felt I truly understood its importance. Exploring my own somatic responses to Cathy's energy around this image, it felt constrained, tied up. There was a sense of waiting, and I detected an unconscious desire by Cathy to absorb what this meant. Any dream, or archetypal symbol, enables a self-regulatory process to take place and Cathy's search through this fairy story needed time. I decided we could not take too big a leap to enact the image in Cathy's present introverted state, as it may well invite distracting sensory stimuli, which might interfere with the inner process. We should, rather, 'sit in a process of osmosis until symbolic meaning became clear; if we understand the ways in which the unconscious of the child makes use of imagery we are greatly helped in our task in guiding him in the integration of these forces' (Wickes, 1977, p.190).

In my work with children on the autistic spectrum who have a lack of verbal language, I have observed that they can communicate through metaphor. 'Call this speaking through objects or use of visual symbols, it is a way of communicating' (Williams, 1992, p.190). Using metaphor as a language has the same challenges as the puzzle of dream-language and our interpretations of them. However, by my paying great attention, especially to the repeated use of a metaphor or symbolic representation, I attempt to use words to help communicate what might be being expressed by non-verbal children. Often, by engaging my non-verbal self, mind, body and spirit, the essence of the message falls into place like a light turning on. Young children and babies express themselves through play, metaphor and imagination, and the adult interprets and makes meaning as to what the child is expressing and also helps the child self-regulate, as their mechanism to do so is still developing. In the case of autistic children this can be an on-going challenge and the outer world needs to understand and support them: 'in forming an attachment bond of somatically expressed emotional communications, the mother is synchronising and resonating with the rhythms of the infant's dynamic internal states and then regulating the arousal level of these negative and positive states' (Schore, 2003, p.135). As dramatherapists, we continually use this circular way of relating, particularly important for trauma work with non-verbal clients and indeed in the individuation journey of the self, where connections between the verbal and non-verbal self support self-awareness and psychological growth. 'Good regulation depends on feelings flowing freely through the body, while having the mental capacity to notice and reflect on them, and to choose whether or not to act on them' (Gerhardt, 2015, p.227).

I needed to maintain the mother/caregiver alertness as a way of being fully present with Cathy, whilst communicating with the school as to what was happening in the work. The emergent theme of the therapy was that Cathy was feeling restricted and captured and had previously felt lost and alone with those feelings. Within the dramatherapy process, Cathy had found a way to express how she had been feeling internally. Her internal state of constraint had been expressed at school by emotional eruptions when she was unable to hold in the feelings any longer, and then the school's existing coping responses of further restrictions and 'consequences' had reaffirmed her internal state of rage and frustration, thus creating a vicious self-perpetuating cycle.

My therapist's capacity to understand what was being presented symbolically and psychologically, led me to offer the school what I thought was important information about the themes taking place in therapy. The school agreed to provide a consistent space for free play during the school day and to allow Cathy time to self-regulate and have some positive, fun school experiences.

Last phase of therapy

'See me'

The next phase of therapy emerged when Cathy was ready, that is, after we had waited long enough for the symbol to reach some conscious recognition. In dramatherapy we had spent time being with the active image symbol and learnt something important about Cathy. In the next and last phase of dramatherapy, Cathy was ready to leave this symbol behind to find something new. It was possible the cycle could be changed. It was decided that Cathy's one-to-one support worker need not stay in the session room, but be nearby if any emergencies or toilet needs arose.

Finding artistic freedom

The little Peter Pan book was left behind, and Cathy began to explore the room and its contents through a variety of play, movements and sounds. Her use of space broadened to encompass the whole room. Her physical movements were relaxed, effortless and more physically expressive: for example, Cathy running to a soft ball, picking it up, throwing it in the air and then letting it fall whilst laughing and looking at me. In these moments she demonstrated her need for someone to witness and affirm her play. By engaging me in eye contact, and sometimes direct contact by throwing a ball or object to me, Cathy demonstrated her relationships were not solely confined to objects; she invited a two-way interactive dialogue with a person. Cathy's purposeful open-hearted intention to include me in her play showed her propensity, and need, for a warm shared relationship.

Dramatherapy reflection

Upon reflection it felt that in moments of shared play I had become more of an equal, more of a play mate in relationship terms. This was an important assessment that I fed back to school – perhaps Cathy could attend small group sessions to build friendships and enhance her sense of belonging to others. It was also important that I witnessed Cathy's potential to play, and mirrored this back to her so she could feel good and joyful about herself. In these moments my therapeutic relationship was like a nurturing parent, enabling free play and encouraging Cathy's ability to communicate and relate. Her range of expressions was significantly amplified; eye contact was often and openly shared, laughter and warmth were exchanged in facial expressions and physical gestures, spontaneous vocalisations and sounds emerged, and her variety of movements increased. This experience of a fuller range of self-expression seemed to give Cathy a sense of satisfaction and happiness. I too felt that the true nature of Cathy and her creativity had been revealed during this period of dramatherapy. With her more positive energy, it seemed that solutions and greater options were going to be available to her as a person and within school.

Ending

Week after week, Cathy continued to enjoy herself and much of the process revolved around being creative, enjoying play and then sharing that with the other. It was important to have enough time in this period of dramatherapy so that Cathy could assimilate her own goodness and self-worth, as well as her growing ability to communicate and relate. By evoking a positive response from the therapist, Cathy gained a more positive sense of herself, like an infant who shows delight when noticed by the other. Eventually, after consultation with the school and my supervisor, it was decided to end our sessions. Cathy had used dramatherapy extremely well and now seemed more balanced and grounded. The school confirmed this was evident outside.

I spoke about the ending with Cathy, reviewing her process over the weeks and how she seemed more able to cope generally. As Cathy listened, she looked at me and met my eyes more seriously than usual, as though to let me know she understood. As part of the ending, we created a map of Cathy's journey in dramatherapy. Cathy participated, creating expressive coloured lines on paper, then mirroring them spontaneously in movement, as I followed her lead. Cathy had used her body as an expressive tool naturally throughout, but the ending process introduced the use of art, pen to paper, as another means of expression. That Cathy was open to this was something useful to pass on to school. The last ten sessions were counted down on a written timetable, marking off each session until the final week. In that last week there was a strong underlying sense of sadness; I felt the sadness in my abdomen, exactly where I had felt anxiety at the beginning of the work. Despite the sadness, I wanted to celebrate our sessions and I thanked Cathy for her commitment to exploring herself and all that she had shared with me. The last session was playful, but Cathy wanted to be close to me. I accepted this and sensed Cathy's insecurity in her clinginess. I assured her that in our sessions she had shown creativity, that journey had given her a more grounded sense of her own potential – which she was now more able to communicate.

Conclusion and outcome

'Do I believe?'

How does the therapy process, and client's development, transfer to the outside world? In this case, as often with younger children, part of my work is to enhance others' understanding so as to support that child systemically. I do this on a weekly basis, though if major issues arise I arrange a meeting with the parent or professional concerned. I feed-back the themes and the child's moods to teachers or parents and carers so they can understand how that child might be directly after therapy and generally in themselves. Therapeutic processes can be baffling for untrained staff and caregivers; therefore I choose my words considerately and carefully to help them support the child outside therapy. Cathy's one-to-one support had witnessed her transformation and seen a new side of Cathy. However, there were times when Cathy's one-to-one questioned what I was doing by allowing Cathy so much free reign – was it over-indulgent? This is a question I am often asked! I point out the boundaries in dramatherapy, reiterating that my aims are different from school aims, in that the therapist works with the process of the child within therapeutic boundaries.

Perhaps, as she settled into school, the more positive side of Cathy would have emerged in time, but I believe the therapy intervention helped prevent Cathy from being further misunderstood, compounding the school's inability to provide her with a safe learning environment. If the negative cycle had not changed, it may have led to Cathy's exclusion. The dramatherapy worked effectively with school by facilitating Cathy to unravel and communicate what she had been unable to say before. 'Here the child works out certain problems and draws up into his/her own personality the desired traits' (Wickes, 1977, p.190).

Through my work I got to know Cathy as a delightful, playful and loving child who needed others' affirmation. 'The survival of living organisms depends upon the maintenance of a harmonious equilibrium or homeostasis in the face of constant challenge by intrinsic forces or stressors' (Schore, 2003, p.437). Cathy had found a balance within herself through the therapeutic process, resulting in the emergence of the previously lost naturally playful child. School reported that Cathy was more settled and connected to others, she had adapted to change, and she actually enjoyed being at school. Mostly she stayed in lessons and although at times old patterns were triggered, the school reported that Cathy was more consistently receptive and that they understood her better now from their discussions with myself.

Role of therapy and the therapist

My work is about waiting for the client to find something of herself: for Cathy, first, security and creative potential in the therapy room as a place of trust; second, from the period of being with the symbol of Wendy being tied up, a potent symbol of her own feelings of futility and inability to escape or make right choices, followed by decoding her image to retrieve energy that had been subdued elsewhere; and, third, the eventual emergence of the free, playful and interactive Cathy.

I hope that the transformation that Cathy experienced on our journey through Neverland continues to be integrated in her life, and that what she found in dramatherapy will help her to connect more with others in school and beyond. Donna Williams writes of her own autism,

I believe that autism is the case where some sort of mechanism which controls emotion does not function properly, leaving an otherwise normal body and a normal mind unable to express itself with the depth that it would otherwise be capable of. . . . Without this, perhaps the child creates within itself what it perceives as missing and in effect becomes a world with itself to which all else is simply irrelevant, external and redundant . . . until the child begins to be imposed upon by a world which expects it (interaction) and the (child's) desire to learn and be part of things which usually springs from emotional attachment and belonging. (Williams, 1992, p.182)

Children on the autistic spectrum, each one unique, need sensitive perceptive therapeutic attention at difficult times. A lack of connection to anyone or anything, can lead to despair, depression, self-harming, aggression, suicide and a whole range of expressions that cry out for help. But with understanding and knowledge we can all help autistic children and adults achieve their full potential and place in the world. Some previous clients and ex-pupils with ASC now live independently, getting married, driving, having jobs, writing, creating amazing art, their lives full of contentment and meaning. With the dedicated help from his father, 13-year-old Naoki managed to write a book by pointing to letters on a cardboard keyboard. He wrote:

What am I going to be, if autism can ever be cured? When I was little, this question was always a big, big worry. I used to be afraid that as long as I was autistic, I'd never be able to live properly as a human being. There were many things I couldn't do like other people, and having to apologize day in, day out totally drained me of hope. . . . However hard an autistic life, so long as there's hope we can stick at it. And when the light of hope shines on all this world, then our future will be connected with your future. That's what I want, above all. (Higashida, 2013, p.180)

As dramatherapists, I believe we have the tools to aid both hope and connection, which increase each client's sense of self and being in the world. Entering Cathy's world was vital to my role as her therapist, as was my communication to Cathy's support system on her behalf. I often reflect how much Cathy taught me about dramatherapy, how enriching metaphor and symbol can be in the world of the autistic condition, and how, by finding a relationship with Cathy's unconscious, transformation occurred.

Peter did come back one day to Wendy's house. Mrs Darling let Wendy go back to Neverland once a year to help Peter with the spring cleaning. As Peter never grew up, one year Wendy's daughter was the one who went. And so it will go on, as long as there are children, and Neverland and Peter Pan. (Barrie, 1911, p.51)

References

Barrie, J. M. (1911) *Peter Pan*, retold in simple language by Joan Collins, Loughborough: Ladybird Books.

Clarkson, P. (1990) 'A multiplicity of psychotherapeutic relationships', *British Journal of Psychotherapy*, 7(2): 148–163.

Dunne, C. (2000) *Carl Jung: Wounded Healer of the Soul*, New York: Parabola Books.

Gerhardt, S. (2015) *Why Love Matters: How Affection Shapes a Baby's Brain*, London: Routledge.

Higashida, N. (2013) *The Reason I Jump*, London: Hodder & Stoughton.

Jung, C. G. (1964) *Man and His Symbols*, Aldus Books; reprinted 1990, London: Arkana, Penguin Group.

Wagner, M. (2012) *The MIFNE Model of Early Intervention: Early Signs of Autism*, http://www.earlysignsofautism.com/the-mifne-model-of-early-intervention/, accessed July 2015.

Oaklander, V. (1988) *Windows to Our Children*, Gouldsboro, ME: The Gestalt Journal Press.

Schore, A. (2003) *Affect Dysregulation and Disorders of the Self*, New York: W.W. Norton & Company.

Wickes, F. (1977) *The Inner World of Childhood*, London: G. Conventure.

Williams, D. (1992) *Nobody Nowhere*, Reading: Cox & Wyman.

Winnicott, D. W. (2002a) *The Maturational Process and the Facilitating Environment*, London: Karnac Books.

Winnicott, D. W. (2002b) *Through Paediatrics to Psychoanalysis Collected Papers*, London: Karnac Books.

5

DRAMATHERAPY, AUTISM AND METAPHOR

Meeting *The Silky Stranger*

Jeannie Lewis

Metaphors are lies.

Mark Haddon, The Curious Incident of the
Dog in the Night-Time

Introduction

One of the cardinal features of Autistic Spectrum Disorder (ASD) is held to
be an impairment in the ability to think metaphorically and to work imaginatively (Happé, 1993, 1995; Rundblad and Annaz, 2010). However, clinical
experience and emerging research suggest that this impairment may not be as
absolute as it was once believed (Kasirer and Mashal, 2014). These data support the potential of people with ASD to generate and use metaphor and other
imaginative structures. In this chapter I will consider the evidence on use of
imagination and metaphor in ASD and illustrate these themes using the case of
The Silky Stranger.

The Silky Stranger was a character created in dramatherapy by an 11-year-old
boy with ASD who was approaching a challenging transition from primary to
secondary school. The co-production (with the therapist) of the imaginative
construct of *The Silky Stranger* enabled him to successfully negotiate this profoundly stressful time. In this chapter *The Silky Stranger* is used as an exemplar of
the potential that exists in young people with ASD to use their imagination in
dramatherapy to create meaningful metaphors and narratives that can help them to
solve their own problems. The chapter investigates the potential for metaphor in
dramatherapy to work therapeutically with, and develop the imaginative resources
of, young people with ASD.

Metaphor and psychotherapy

The *Oxford English Dictionary* defines metaphor as:

> A figure of speech in which a name or descriptive word or phrase is transferred to an object or action different from, but analogous to, that to which it is literally applicable.

Metaphor is everywhere. Garner (2005) has estimated that the average English-speaker uses four metaphors per minute, amounting to over 3,000 metaphors per week in everyday conversation. Bruyn (1966, p.133) writes: 'A metaphor is . . . so much a part of language we hardly notice it; for example, the "leg" of a table, or the "face" of a clock.' The ability to understand metaphors appears to be fundamental to language comprehension and communication. Seen in this way, an inability to understand metaphor is likely to be detrimental to social functioning.

The non-literal transfer of attribution to enable understanding, and the language of metaphor, is deeply embedded in psychoanalysis and psychotherapy. Metaphor is used not just as a bridge to the unconscious mind but as the way that theorists and practitioners communicate about the unconscious mind and enable their clients to derive therapeutic understanding and benefit. Freud (1923, 1960, p.21) talked in terms of 'thinking in pictures' being 'nearer to unconscious processes than . . . thinking in words'. So 'thinking in pictures', or the use of metaphor, can enable access to and discussion of emotional material. Nash (1962, pp.26–27), reviewing Freud's use of metaphor, states that, 'Challenged by a great variety of clinical problems, he produced a multiplicity of metaphors, each a special conceptual tool for handling a given problem'.

It is striking that Freud's whole model of the human mind is itself a metaphor. There are no anatomic or functional structures within the brain that are the *super-ego*, *ego* or *id*. These terms are simply metaphors to aid understanding and therapy. The same is true for Jung's 'iceberg' model of the *conscious*, *subconscious* and *collective unconscious*. Carveth (1984) notes that this was acknowledged explicitly right at the start of the development of psychoanalysis in *Studies on Hysteria* (Breuer and Freud, 1895, 1955), in which Breuer wrote:

> It is only too easy to fall into a habit of thought which assumes that every substantive has a substance behind it – which gradually comes to regard 'consciousness' as standing for some actual thing; and when we have become accustomed to make use metaphorically of spatial relations, as in the term 'sub-consciousness,' we find as time goes on that we have actually formed an idea which has lost its metaphorical nature . . . . (pp.227–228)

The perceived inability of people with ASD to engage in metaphor is perhaps one of the reasons why traditional forms of psychotherapy, such as psychoanalysis, have not been influential in conceptualisation and therapy in ASD. It may also explain the profound negativity of some analytic formulations of autism such as Bettleheim's punitive 'refrigerator mother' theory. In this he holds that autism is psychogenic, caused by 'refrigerator' mothers as a child's defence mechanism against cold, emotionless and detached mothers (Gardner, 2000). Given this attitude, it is perhaps not surprising that other forms of therapy have been sought and developed to try to help people with ASD and their families.

An early example of this was Hans Asperger's own paediatric ward in Vienna in the 1920s. It eschewed psychoanalysis for a daily programme of play and lessons directed by the nurse Sister Viktorine Zac (who Asperger described as 'a genius'), whose regime included daily PE 'using rhythm and music' and 'dramatic enactments of events and songs' (Frith, 1991, p.9). These can be seen as precursors to the current interventions by play and arts therapists, including dramatherapists, which are increasingly used with young people with ASD.

Happé (1993) illustrated difficulties in imagination and metaphor in ASD in terms of deficits in Theory of Mind. Theory of Mind can be defined as the ability to appreciate the mental states of others (Baron-Cohen, 2000). Two orders of Theory of Mind ability have been described (Baron-Cohen et al., 1995): first-order Theory of Mind refers to inferring the thoughts of another person; and second-order Theory of Mind, to reasoning what one person (other than the self) thinks about another person's thoughts. Happé (1993) found that, in autism in general, first-order Theory of Mind was necessary to understand metaphor, but similes could be processed by individuals who were not able to pass first-order Theory of Mind tasks. This was explained in terms of not needing to understand speaker intention to understand similes, e.g. 'The room was like an oven', because the expressions are literally true. However, metaphors, e.g. 'The room was an oven', are not literally true, and inference as to the speaker's intention is needed so the statement can be interpreted in a non-literal fashion.

These studies are helpful in illuminating the specific difficulties encountered by people with ASD. However, it has become increasingly clear that there is considerable heterogeneity in terms of abilities and deficits in the presentation and experience of people with ASD. Research has shown that many with ASD have Theory of Mind and are able to pass tests such as the Sally–Anne and Smarties tests described below. Even in the first test of the hypothesis (Baron-Cohen et al., 1985), 20 per cent of the children with autism tested passed the Sally–Anne task. Equally, some who have first-order Theory of Mind have deficits in metaphoric comprehension and this may be caused more by receptive language disorder than by Theory of Mind; Norbury (2005) concluded:

> Only those individuals with autism who had concomitant structural language deficits were impaired on the metaphor task and they were indistinguishable from children with language impairment who did not have clinically significant autistic features. This finding suggests that at least some of the pragmatic deficits characteristic of autism may be attributable to lower level linguistic deficits. (p.396)

The stability of these deficits has also been challenged. Persicke et al. (2012), in a small interventional case series of three children, concluded that the ability to understand metaphorical language is teachable to children with ASD. In this study the researchers used a behavioural intervention, 'multiple exemplar training'. This consisted of sessions containing four stories: two previously trained stories and two novel stories. During each training session, the experimenter read the story, asked observing response questions, and then presented metaphor questions. They reported that all participants demonstrated generalisation of the ability to understand metaphorical language to multiple spontaneous metaphors. Accurate responding persisted after feedback was discontinued in the post-training phase. One of the children started to generate novel metaphors.

Other recent case studies have also yielded encouraging findings. Mashal and Kasirer (2011) examined the ability of 20 children with ASD and 20 children with learning disabilities to improve their metaphoric competence by an intervention programme using 'thinking maps'. Both groups improved their metaphoric comprehension of items learned during the intervention. Whyte et al. (2013) attempted to improve idiomatic comprehension in ten 7–12-year-old children with ASD, using a 2-week group intervention. The children were able to learn and remember the meaning of idiomatic phrases better than untrained controls. In a fascinating study of adults with ASD, Kasirer et al. (2014) reported that adults with ASD demonstrated no difficulties in comprehension of conventional and novel metaphors compared with age-matched typically developed controls. Counterintuitively, the adults with ASD showed higher levels of verbal creativity, outperforming the controls in new metaphor generation. The ASD group was assessed to have produced more original and creative metaphors than the typically developed control group. These findings show the emerging evidence on the abilities of people with ASD to use and generate metaphor, thus clearly lending support for the potential for dramatherapy to assist metaphoric understanding, communication and function in people with ASD.

Dramatherapy, autism and metaphor

Much has been written about the use of metaphor in dramatherapy. The British Association of Dramatherapists describes this in terms of the use of an 'indirect approach' and the creation of 'aesthetic distance' from which to explore painful experiences or overwhelming emotions:

> The Dramatherapist will work with the client to create their own unique imaginary story . . . to create a special form of fictional reality, which is the client's own story retold in a different way and will thus assist the client to resolve or come to terms with areas of emotional or psychological discomfort or distress . . . . In a fictional reality, we can allow ourselves to feel things without having to deny their presence because we know fiction protects us but allows us to be involved. (British Association of Dramatherapists website)

Dramatherapy provides the means, through its core processes of metaphor and a distanced approach, for participants to explore their internal world. In the following case study I will demonstrate how these core processes and action-based methods enable personal psychological material to be processed, and a challenging scenario managed, by an individual with ASD.

This case study contributes to the growing evidence that supports the value of dramatherapy, with its highly personalised, playful, imaginative, sensory interaction between therapist and client, as a working approach to enhance the emotional wellbeing and communication of people with ASD.

The Silky Stranger

As described in the introduction to this chapter, *The Silky Stranger* was created in dramatherapy by an 11-year-old boy with ASD whom I will call Adam. Adam was approaching a challenging transition from primary to secondary school. The primary school was his first and only school and he was the only student moving on to his chosen secondary school. Adam had been with one peer group since the start of school. As his dramatherapist, I was a new person to Adam and the individual dramatherapy sessions offered a new and different way of working.

Adam had been diagnosed with ASD at the age of 4 and had no other medical conditions. He was referred for a brief dramatherapy intervention in order to explore his anxious feelings. In the referral Adam was described as having receptive language difficulties. He also had difficulties with peer social interactions, which included sometimes being too aggressive in his play and having difficulty observing other people's spatial boundaries.

Adam had an ability to concentrate on activities of his own choice, sometimes to the exclusion of outside influences. His ability to focus on directed activities was variable depending on whether he liked the task. Sometimes Adam appeared to be absorbed by his own thoughts and was difficult to engage. The variance in his ability to focus seemed to indicate that at times he experienced a sense of internal distraction not shared with others. Adam had a full time 1:1 learning support worker and appeared to work best in class when his attention was supported. Successful strategies had included concrete rewards systems such as extra computer time. Adam was described as having a literal understanding of the world and needing clear understandable instructions. It was reported that Adam enjoyed quizzes and being able to find the right answer.

Session structure and material

In the dramatherapy Adam was offered a number of different media: visual images, projective work with fabric and small objects, movement and game structures, original storytelling and enactment. A similar structure for the sessions was used each week, which created a sense of familiarity and trust. The outline of the session structure was:

1. **Welcome** – Adam chose where and at what distance to set the 'talking cushions' and we welcomed each other. Time was offered to share news and issues arising from the week and reflections from the previous session.
2. **Warm-up** – We moved from the 'talking cushions' into the 'playing space'. Usually the work in this space began with simple movements or games. This re-established playful contact each week as well as allowing a space for themes for the session to begin to emerge gently.
3. **The main focus** – Over the period of therapy, Adam explored a number of different themes. I supported his exploration by offering different media for expression, including stories, improvisation, visual images, story cards, fabric, small world objects and clay.
4. **Goodbye** – We moved back to the 'talking cushions' and time was offered for reflection.

In his initial assessment Adam was invited to take part in the Sally–Anne test, a test of Theory of Mind (Wimmer and Perner, 1983). In this test children are assessed individually, seated at a desk opposite the researcher. Two dolls are introduced, Sally and Anne. Sally has a basket in front of her and Anne has a box. A 'naming question' is first carried out. The young person, after being told the names of the dolls, is asked to confirm that they know the names. Sally places a marble in her basket then goes for a walk (disappearing from view). Whilst Sally has gone, Anne plays a trick and takes the marble from Sally's basket and transfers it to her (Anne's) box. Sally then returns. The child is asked the main experimental question, the 'belief question': 'Where will Sally look for her marble?' The correct response is, 'In Sally's basket', because that is where Sally left it, and she is unaware of Anne's trick. The incorrect response is, 'In Anne's box', because Sally does not know this and the child is just telling the experimenter where the marble really is (where they believe the marble is). This would demonstrate an inability to consider what Sally's beliefs are. Two control questions are then asked. The 'reality' question' is, 'Where is the marble really?' This is to make sure the child had paid attention to the transfer of the marble from the basket to the box. The 'memory question' is, 'Where was the marble in the beginning?' This is designed to make sure the child had not forgotten where Sally had left her marble. I also offered the Smarties test (Perner and Wimmer, 1985). In this test the child is shown a Smarties tube and is asked what is inside. The child responds, 'Smarties' or 'Sweets', and is then shown that in fact there are paper clips or pencils inside. The child is then asked to name a friend (X) who has never seen this Smarties tube before. The child is asked: 'If we show this to X, what will X think is in here?' The accuracy of the answer given is then assessed. Adam passed both the Sally Anne test and the Smarties test, suggesting that according to the terms of these tests he showed some ability to understand the perspectives of other; he showed evidence of Theory of Mind. The tests provided simple evidence of Adam's ability to imagine the thought processes of others and to extend his thinking beyond his own internal experience of the world.

At first Adam was unsure about the unfamiliar structure of the sessions and expressed anxiety about it. His first action was to ignore the cushions and to go straight to sit on a chair facing a table as he would in class. We discussed that the sessions could be a space to explore his feelings about transition to secondary school and he reluctantly agreed to try the simple introductory games I offered. As the session developed Adam appeared to relax and he began to explore the activities on offer. He found art materials and looked at the crayons I had brought. After an initial reaction to the fact that the picture on the crayon box did not exactly match the crayons inside and a painstaking rearrangement of them, Adam started to draw.

The wall

The first of Adam's drawings was of a wall. In the same session he made the wall twice, first using the crayons and then again using fabrics. In his second version of the wall, Adam added a gate. This was an important addition as it suggested the possibility of entrance. As a symbol the wall contained and protected, but it also repelled, providing safety. The inclusion of a gate suggested the possibility of a transition from outside to inside. In literal terms the wall might have physically represented Adam's new school, as he had only seen it from the outside, but in metaphor it could also express Adam's wariness about working with his therapist and his desire to resist change and the overwhelming feelings that change may bring.

The bomb

Adam also chose to work with a set of interlocking boxes. He returned to these repeatedly and they appeared to offer him a satisfying play experience. Over time Adam developed his play with the boxes by placing an object into the smallest box and surprising me with it. He displayed enjoyment at showing me the boxes within boxes and witnessing my exaggerated surprise. Adam rewarded me by placing a stone inside the smallest box. I noticed that the stone he chose was one I had previously named as my favourite. His liking for the interlocking boxes seemed to reflect his need for order and containment. The fact that he showed himself able to be playful with the boxes indicated a level of flexibility in his play and an ability to extend beyond rigid or repeated behaviours. His playfulness with the boxes also reflected positively on his ability to cope with change. Whilst Adam enjoyed the predictability of the interlocking boxes he also enjoyed changing their usual pattern.

Early in our work together Adam created the image of a bomb exploding. He created this using different colour clay. He was proud of the image and asked me to keep it safe. I observed the paradox of creating an image of destruction while asking to keep it safe, and wondered if Adam was asking what could be kept safe during this time of change. The image of the bomb was large and Adam accompanied it into action using explosive sounds and movements. Our shared enactment of the exploding bomb felt similar to the earlier surprise play using the interlocking boxes. The fact that this play was more physical and shared felt like a strengthening of

Adam's confidence in our relationship and his ability to play within the safe containment offered by the sessions.

The room of surprises

The room where we worked had a moveable partition that could be used to partially divide the space. Adam explored the possibilities of the partition. He developed this into a game in which he hid but drew attention to where he was, by making sounds or by moving an object to catch my attention. It was my role to respond with surprise. Adam described the objects as moving '*unconsciously*'. Adam was experimenting with our relationship over distance. He was directly eliciting a reaction, a connection with me, but was not ready to allow himself to be seen. The theme of meeting or allowing himself to be seen emerged from this work through the character of *The Silky Stranger*.

Meeting *The Silky Stranger*

The materials offered in dramatherapy included a range of colourful fabrics. Adam chose to take the fabrics into the space with him and to cover himself with them. He then made sounds from underneath the fabric. It became my role to discover the source of the sounds by slowly removing the fabric. Once uncovered, Adam became a living statue, mute, eyes staring ahead. He used his hand to point at things and other simple gestures such as go, yes and no. I offered paper and pens, but these were refused. In the following session Adam indicated that he would like to repeat the action, first by himself, and then with me in role as the stranger. Adam covered me with the materials, then, as I had done, he slowly peeled the fabric away: revealing first an arm, then a shoulder, a leg, a foot and finally the head. The action of uncovering was performed in a careful ritualistic way using slow repeatable exaggerated gestures. Adam was extremely interested in this action. We then changed roles and enacted the sequence again. The quality of the action was careful and quiet and I discovered feelings of shyness. At times during the action I emphasised the character's shyness and Adam responded with gentle reassurances inviting the character to step confidently into the space. In this way the character of *The Silky Stranger* was born.

The character of *The Silky Stanger* and its evolution in the dramatherapy sessions embodied a safe meeting between us in role as *Silky Stranger*s. The co-production (with the therapist) of this imaginative construct enabled successful negotiation of what seemed to Adam to be the profoundly stressful transition to secondary school. Enacted interchangeably, a gradual reveal of layers of silky material became a means through which the young person and the therapist could meet. The challenges of our meeting had the potential to mirror changes elsewhere as well as offering a bridge.

This gradual process of discovery paralleled our actual meeting and in context many other meetings on the pathway to secondary school. Through dramatherapy Adam found a way to slow down the moment of meeting and to make it bearable. He was showing that he needed time to process his experience of change. This could be seen both through his own enactment of becoming *The Silky Stranger* and his desire to watch the enactment performed by me.

In role as *The Silky Stranger*, Adam both showed what *The Silky Stranger* needed and experienced those needs being met. As a witness to the action, he was able to respond to these needs. In this he showed both what was needed and also created an opportunity for the need to be answered. The fact that the stranger was silky was important, not only because it allowed a slow reveal but also because the slow peeling away of the silky fabric and the physical sensation this created made it possible for Adam to process the meeting at a sensory level as well as imaginatively. The fact that the material was transparent allowed an experience of distance and a preparation for the impact of meeting. The creation of *The Silky Stranger* in dramatherapy gave Adam an opportunity to experience meeting in a way that matched his social and emotional and sensory needs at this time of transition.

The title *The Silky Stranger* was adopted during my reflection of our work together. It is probably of significance that Adam did not choose to name the character himself. This may have been because the sequence was largely non-verbal; however, it may also have been because the character had an archetypal quality with a resonance for other meetings rather than just the one enacted in the sessions.

The closing

The intervention was a brief one and we were soon into the ending phase. Adam found the ending very hard. He tried a range of strategies to avoid ending the sessions each week, including pretending to be dead. He described feeling sad and cross. In our final session Adam again enacted *The Silky Stranger* sequence. We looked back at the work Adam had produced in the sessions and he spoke directly about his fear of not making friends at his new school. Adam expressed an interest in the picture of the wall. We placed items of uniform and the school handbook from his new school behind the wall and discussed what was known and unknown. We also returned to the image of the bomb. In my reflections I imagined that the impact of changing schools was like a bomb was exploding in Adam's life. The work of the sessions had explored these changes, not only through words but through metaphor enacted in actions and sound and through visual image.

Through the creation of *The Silky Stranger*, Adam was able to externalise his anxiety about making friends. The removal of the action from the real world into the improvised enactment created enough distance for him to share his vulnerability. In his earlier representation of the mute statue, Adam had shown that he was not ready to express his fears in words. In the here and now of the therapy session Adam had been able to create a relationship with me. He had also rehearsed the possibility of making new relationships and friendships at his next school in a spontaneous, improvised and highly creative way. The fact that he was able to cognitively assimilate this knowledge having experienced the process through dramatherapy was evidenced by his ability in our closing session to articulate his fear about making new relationships.

It is likely that, as a person with ASD in a world that operates in line with neurotypical demands, Adam would continue to experience anxiety about his social relationships. However, it is helpful to look at the creation of *The Silky Stranger* in context. Adam was about to make the transition to secondary school, so there was a particular urgency for him to process this area of his life. It is also useful to look at his work in relation to the referral offered by the school. In the referral Adam was described as highly literal and resistant to change, terms that appeared to be borne out by his initial wariness and desire to fit dramatherapy to his usual classroom experience. So what was it that enabled Adam to respond to dramatherapy in such a creative and spontaneous way?

Dramatherapy and autism: working within the metaphor

If we take as our starting point the voice of those with autism themselves on the subject, it is clear that the observation that there are challenges for those with ASD in metaphoric communication is borne out in lived experience.

> When my mum told me to 'Draw the curtains' because I was reading in my room in the dark, my response, which was the first logical thought that came into my head, was 'But I don't have a pencil!' My mum's reply was 'Are you pulling my leg?', which didn't help the situation at all! (Barton, 2012, p.12)

It is worthwhile at this point to consider the issue of 'double empathy'. It is apparent that non-autistic individuals have just as much difficulty understanding the autistic mind as people with autism have in understanding neurotypicals. So classifying autistic difficulty in 'reading the mind' of the person without autism as a disability, but not the inability of the person without autism to 'read the mind' of those with autism, seems unfair and unreasonable (Hacking, 2009; Milton, 2012). This is known as the 'double empathy' problem (Milton, 2012). Jim Sinclair (1993), a person with autism, uses the metaphor of a foreign language:

> It takes more work to communicate with someone whose native language isn't the same as yours. And autism goes deeper than language and culture; autistic people are 'foreigners' in any society. You're going to have to give up your assumptions about shared meanings. You're going to have to learn to back up to levels more basic than you've probably thought about before, to translate, and to check to make sure your translations are understood. You're going to have to give up the certainty that comes of being on your own familiar territory, of knowing you're in charge, and let your child teach you a little of her language, guide you a little way into his world. (p.6)

Sinclair's challenge is to parents, but it can be equally applied to the role of therapist and society as a whole. In dramatherapy the creation of *The Silky Stranger* allowed the therapist not to ask the young person with autism to empathise with the neurotypical world, but instead provided access for the therapist to enter into the autistic work through a novel metaphor generated by the person with autism. In dramatherapy the therapist was able to place herself in the position of the participant by sharing the role of *The Silky Stranger*. This fits with Stone's (2005) analysis that,

> To establish a separate identity . . . the child must literally get outside himself and apprehend himself from some other perspective. Drama provides a prime vehicle for this. By taking the role of another, the child gains a reflected view of himself as different from but related to that other. (p.149)

The dramatherapist participating in the metaphor alongside the person with ASD has the opportunity to experience the world as it is described by the participant, letting the child teach *'a little of her language'*.

Conclusion

The case study of *The Silky Stranger* illustrates the potential of dramatherapy's 'indirect approach' and 'aesthetic distance' to explore difficult or painful life experiences in children with ASD. The co-creation of his own unique imaginary story enacted through non-verbal means, but in the form of a novel self-generated metaphor, helped Adam navigate a stressful situation successfully. Dramatherapy provided the means, through its core processes of metaphor and a distanced approach, for Adam to explore his internal world. The case of *The Silky Stranger* along with the emerging research into the ability of people on the Autistic Spectrum to use and generate metaphor summarised in this chapter, shows the specific therapeutic potential of dramatherapy for those with ASD.

References

Baron-Cohen, S. (2000) 'Theory of mind and autism: a fifteen year review', in Baron-Cohen, S., Tager-Flusberg, H. and Cohen, D. J. (eds), *Understanding Other Minds: Perspectives from Developmental Cognitive Neuroscience* (2nd edn). New York: Oxford University Press.

Baron-Cohen, S., Leslie, A.M. and Frith, U. (1985) 'Does the autistic child have a "theory of mind"?', *Cognition*, 21: 37–46.

Barton, M. (2012) *It's Raining Cats and Dogs: An Autistic Spectrum Guide to the Confusing World of Idioms, Metaphors and Everyday Expressions*. London: Jessica Kingsley Publishers.

Breuer, J. and Freud, S. (1895/1955) *Studies on Hysteria: Standard Edition, 2*. London: Hogarth Press.

Bruyn, S.T. (1966) *The Humanistic Perspective in Sociology: The Methodology of Participant Observation*. Englewood Cliffs, NJ: Prentice-Hall.

Carveth, D.L. (1984) 'The analyst's metaphors: a deconstructionist perspective', *Psychoanalysis & Contemporary Thought*, 7(4): 491–560.

Freud, S. (1923/1960) *The Ego and the Id* (trans. J. Reviere, ed. J. Strachey). New York: W.W. Norton.

Frith, U. (1991) 'Asperger and his syndrome', in Frith, U. (ed.), *Autism and Asperger Syndrome*. Cambridge: Cambridge University Press.

Gardner, M. (2000) 'The brutality of Dr. Bettelheim', *Skeptical Inquirer*, 24(6): 12–14.

Garner, R. (2005) 'Humor, analogy, and metaphor: H.A.M. it up in teaching', *Radical Pedagogy*, 6: 1–5.

Hacking, I. (2009) 'Autistic autobiography', *Philosophical Transactions of the Royal Society B: Biological Sciences*, 364(1522): 1467–1473.

Happé, F.G.E. (1993) 'Communicative competence and theory of mind in autism: a test of relevance theory', *Cognition,* 48: 101–119.

Happé, F.G.E. (1995) 'Understanding minds and metaphors: insight from the study of figurative language in autism', *Metaphor and Symbolic Activity,* 10: 275–295.

Kasirer, A. and Mashal, N. (2014) 'Verbal creativity in autism: comprehension and generation of metaphoric language in high-functioning autism spectrum disorder and typical development', *Frontiers in Human Neuroscience*, 8: 615, 10.3389/fnhum.2014.00615.

Mashal, N. and Kasirer, A. (2011) 'Thinking maps enhance metaphoric competence in children with autism and learning disabilities', *Research in Developmental Disabilities*, 32(6): 2045–2054.

Milton, D.E. (2012) 'On the ontological status of autism: the "double empathy problem"', *Disability & Society*, 27(6): 883–887.

Nash, H. (1962) 'Freud and metaphor', *Archives of General Psychiatry*, 7(1): 25–29.

Norbury, C.F. (2005) 'The relationship between theory of mind and metaphor: evidence from children with language impairment and autistic spectrum disorder', *British Journal of Developmental Psychology*, 23(3): 383–399.

Perner, J. and Wimmer, H. (1985) '"John thinks that Mary thinks that . . .": attribution of second order beliefs by 5- to 10-year old children', *Journal of Experimental Child Psychology*, 39: 437–471.

Persicke, A., Tarbox, J., Ranick, J. and St Clair, M. (2012) 'Establishing metaphorical reasoning in children with autism', *Research in Autism Spectrum Disorders*, 6(2): 913–920.

Rundblad, G. and Annaz D. (2010) 'The atypical development of metaphor and metonymy comprehension in children with autism', *Autism*, 14: 29–46.

Sinclair, J. (1993) 'Don't mourn for us', *Our Voice*, 1(3): 5–6.

Stone, G.P. (2005) 'The play of little children', in Jenks, C. (ed.), *Childhood: Critical Concepts in Sociology, Volume 2*. Abingdon: Routledge.

Whyte, E.M., Nelson, K.E. and Khan, K.S. (2013) 'Learning of idiomatic language expressions in a group intervention for children with autism', *Autism*, 17(4): 449–464.

Wimmer, H. and Perner, J. (1983) 'Beliefs about beliefs: representation and constraining function of wrong beliefs in young children's understanding of deception', *Cognition*, 13: 103–128.

6

SUPPORTING AGENCY, CHOICE MAKING AND THE EXPRESSION OF 'VOICE' WITH KATE

Dramatherapy in a mainstream primary school setting with a 9-year-old girl diagnosed with ASD and ADHD

Emma Ramsden

Introduction

This chapter focuses on long-term individual dramatherapy sessions, offered as part of an in-house dramatherapy service provided in an inner city mainstream primary school, with 'Kate' – a 9-year-old girl of black British ethnicity. 'Kate' is a pseudonym she has chosen as a means of maintaining her anonymity. Invited to describe herself by way of introduction within this chapter, she replied: '*I'm good at swimming and I enjoy it.*'

The dramatherapy practice in the school is confidential and offered in accordance with the Local Authority (LA) safeguarding policy, the practice ethics as stipulated by the state regulatory body (HCPC, 2015), and adheres to the Code of Practice governing dramatherapists, which advocates that, 'Dramatherapists appreciate the variety of human experience and culture' (BADth, 2015, p.1). An inclusive approach is offered to all children referred to the service without prejudice or discrimination, which promotes welfare through respecting each client's autonomy (Daniels & Jenkins, 2010). This practice framework of ethical beneficence can also be described as fostering *client agency* and enabling the expression of *voice* for each child. Agency is the capacity for personal empowerment and proactive engagement in one's own life (Clarke et al., 2011; Pearson, 2016); and the expression of voice for each child is made possible by the provision of an environment in which they can express, explore and develop their views with adults who are active, effective, and invested in valuing them and the perspectives they offer (Montgomery & Kellett, 2009; Lundy, 2007). Client voice in dramatherapy, therefore, can be described as the client's awareness of their agency and capacity to make choices of self-expression, and to have their communication actively and effectively heard by the therapist, who supports the development of a self-initiated process of change (Langley, 2006).

Key aspects of Kate's therapeutic process over her time in dramatherapy to date are illuminated across three 'analytical snapshots' in this chapter. These aim to provide insights into her engagement with the room itself as a holding container; her choice of story making and role play; and her capacity for reflexivity (which demonstrates the way in which she experiences herself). In order to enable client agency and voice as fully as possible in this chapter any verbatim speech by Kate has been represented using the convention of *bold and italic* text.

The key benefits of providing an in-house dramatherapy service in schools for children with ASD, ADHD and other related conditions, as a vital space away from the highly stimulating and busy school environments both in and out of the classroom, are also discussed in this chapter within the context of current research and practice into psychological services for children in schools.

Kate has a diagnosis of autistic spectrum disorder (ASD) and attention deficit hyperactivity disorder (ADHD), and a statement of educational needs (known since September 2014 as 'Education Health and Care' plan (EHC) (SEND, 2011/2014)). She has attended weekly individual dramatherapy sessions since arriving at the school in September 2012. Her arrival followed a 'managed move', initiated by the LA, after 8 months of home tutoring that had been arranged by them following her permanent exclusion from two primary schools that were unable to contain Kate safely and meet her needs. The account provided by Kate's mother, 'Mrs Haye' (self-selected pseudonym) – gained by way of a semi-structured interview – reveals the long and painful struggle of mother and daughter to identify and understand Kate's difficulties. Mrs Haye describes them both being silenced and unheard throughout pre-school years and up to and including recent times. Following the significant period of time out of school for Kate (while she was being home tutored), Mrs Haye describes having '*to fight* [the local authority] *to reintegrate her back into school*'. She recalls feelings of disempowerment, humiliation and demoralisation in her search to gain support, a medical diagnosis, and the relevant intervention for Kate.

A review of literature

Dramatherapy in mainstream education

Literature shows that dramatherapy and the arts therapies have been offered in school settings from the mid-point of the last century onwards (Karkou, 2010; Jones, 2012). Leigh et al. (2012) suggest that dramatherapy practice in schools in the UK is both under-represented and under-used. Research studies have shown that children with ASD can struggle with the mainstream environment, the school day and the transition from one activity to the next (Hume et al., 2014; Dolphin et al., 2014).

However, the literature pertaining to dramatherapy intervention with children with an ASD diagnosis in schools, highlights work taking place in specialist provisions, and illustrates a range of creative individual and groupwork programmes – prompting the development of social skills, relationships and the maintenance of friendships (Miller, 2005; Tytherleigh & Karkou, 2010). Publications about dramatherapy practice in mainstream UK provision are scarce.

As dramatherapy is not a statutory service within the education system, its funding is often at the discretion of the individual schools in which therapists work. Since Leigh et al.'s 2012 publication exploring dramatherapy in education, the UK continues to experience government austerity measures and cuts to public services; these remain challenging times, in an unstable and difficult financial climate, for the promotion of dramatherapy as a non-statutory provision. Excellent work is taking place in many settings across the UK, but the onus is on individual dramatherapists to negotiate and maintain their funding and contractual arrangements with individual schools.

ASD and ADHD

Chapter 2 in this book has provided a detailed and comprehensive discussion, establishing ASD as a developmental disability and defining its implications for current policy, practice and research within the field of dramatherapy (as well as assessing areas of strength and challenge). We know, therefore, that autistic spectrum disorder refers to a biologically based neurological disability with a wide range of characteristics for individuals diagnosed with the condition, which impacts on social interaction, communication and relationship building (Wilson, 2014; Potter & Whittaker, 2001; Barnaby, 2014; DSM-5, 2013).

ADHD is a condition associated with ASD but not exclusive to it, and refers to difficulties with attention span, impulsivity, and the limited capacity to identify and regulate energy levels. Dramatherapist Ann Dix has noted the challenges faced when forming and maintaining peer relationships. She comments that children with ADHD 'often have difficulty with peer friendships as they find it difficult to negotiate' (Dix, 2012, p. 52).

The findings of research into ASD show that more boys than girls experience the condition, with different studies noting an approximation of ratios (Richman, 2001) such as 'ten males to every female' (Baron-Cohen, 2004, p. 137). Despite this prevalence in males, within the field of practitioner literature concerning children, a healthy number of dramatherapy accounts focusing on girls only – or based on mixed groups with boys and girls – is present (Pimpas, 2013; Lewis & Banerjee, 2013; Chasen, 2011; Tytherleigh & Karkou, 2010).

Dramatherapy and the client

Dramatherapy, like all forms of therapy, aims to enable the potential for self-expression, agency and voice. This aim is realised by working closely with the client (Gersie, 1996) and by adhering to the Code of Practice (BADth, 2015), which outlines key ethical principles such as gaining consent from gatekeepers (parents) and assent (the term used for permission given by children) from the children themselves prior to commencing therapy. Each client is seen as an individual (whether in group or individual therapy, whether a child or adult client) who engages, at their own pace, with choice making within the agreement of a basic contract or working alliance, which includes safety and the consistency of boundaries. This enables the client's agency through their capacity to make choices about issues that they experience, and which affect them (Casemore, 2011; Daniels & Jenkins, 2010). Dramatherapist Carol Bouzoukis (2001, p. 19) describes the therapist's provision as that of a 'non-judgemental, non-threatening and private space, where a child feels free to express and to be who he or she is'. Similarly, Jeremy Carrette (1992, p. 18) notes that 'what best suits the needs of each child will take some time to determine' with regard to dramatherapy and children with autism.

Dramatherapy and play

Play is considered an essential and core process in child development, operating on a range of developmental levels and accommodating an infinite number of imaginative possibilities (Pound, 2006). Writing about the use of play in dramatherapy practice with a girl with autism, Ioannis Pimpas (2013, p. 58) notes: 'Neither play, nor role within dramatherapy are seen as being mere educational tools. They are considered to be a part of an expressive continuum (Jones, 2007) providing the opportunity for self-exploration.' In drama and dramatherapy with children with ASD play has been noted for its capacity to engender optimism in children amongst other qualities and experiences (Chasen, 2011; Jennings, 2011).

The dramatherapy service in school

The part-time dramatherapy service was established in this mainstream inner city primary school in 2001, and offers individual and group dramatherapy to children from nursery entry to secondary transition at 11 years of age (Ramsden, 2011). Children can self-refer or be referred by any member of school staff, or by their parents/carers in the first instance. Once gatekeeper consent has been gained (i.e. parents, carers or legal guardians (Alderson & Morrow, 2011)), assent is sought with the children directly (Ramsden & Jones, 2011; Flewitt, 2005).

The school has undergone a series of changes in management since the inception of the dramatherapy service, which has been housed in different rooms as the school has been remodelled and expanded. The service is currently delivered in a purpose-built, sound-proofed, multi-sensory room – equipped with various specialist items for children with ASD such as sensory and visual play resources (bubble tube, sensory balls, oil lamp, relaxation pod/tent).

The school's SENCo, learning mentor, specialist teacher, and myself as the dramatherapist make up the 'inclusion team'. The SENCo has described the dramatherapy service as being valuable for children with ASD because it can provide vital time away from the classroom. She comments that it is '*a successful intervention in school in enabling those children who have found it difficult expressing their feelings and emotions to move on from their difficulties and participate fully and positively in all areas of school life'*. The learning mentor whose work supports children to access their learning through pastoral methods also values the dramatherapy service, and has described it as *'really important because it goes deeper into the emotions and can help the children to overcome difficulties'*.

Evaluation of children's experiences in dramatherapy

To evaluate client experiences in dramatherapy, and to contribute meaningfully to the school's progress data, a site-specific evaluation method was developed some years ago, and implemented twice termly (six times per academic year) for each child in therapy. The evaluation method profiles the client's own reflections as the central source of evidence in assessing their wellbeing through their dramatherapy experiences.

The evaluation process adds another dimension to the therapeutic process and is different from established stages in dramatherapy, such as reflection at the end of sessions or interim review sessions. Nevertheless, there are potential negative effects when implementing an evaluation/measurement method, requiring the maintenance of client confidentiality and anonymity at all times, in line with ethical standards, and ensuring that a breach of autonomy does not happen. One such area of tension might involve the child giving their assent to the evaluation process in order to please the adult (known as the Hawthorne effect) (Jones, 1992); in this way a child may be unable to be open and honest due to temporary or permanent change of circumstances in life, leading to perceived or actual vulnerability (such as a change of family membership, move to a new area, friendships difficulties or period of illness).

The evaluation is introduced and implemented not as a single event but with the child having the choice to give or withdraw assent in each instance of evaluation as an ongoing process. Their control of choice making enables an equal exchange between dramatherapist and child, in which their competence of being able to make choices is supported (Groundwater-Smith, 2007).

Analytical snapshots

The first of three analytical snapshots focusing on Kate's journey in dramatherapy is offered below. The term 'analytical snapshot' is used here to describe commentary contextualising the client within the setting followed by the presentation of a selection of moments across dramatherapy sessions, which is then followed by a brief analytical commentary to illuminate key areas of process (Ramsden, 2014). This concept is a development from a clinical vignette, where synchronous detailed moments from a particular session are offered and explored in depth (Novy, 2010; Holloway, 1997).

The following analytical snapshot contextualises Kate's arrival in the school and her initial sessions. It demonstrates the way in which the dramatherapy room became a holding and containing space for Kate through her self-devised play structure – a space in which her unique expression of voice began to emerge.

Analytical snapshot A

Mrs Haye has described a long and painful battle with the local authority to *'fight'* for Kate to be placed in a school, following permanent exclusions from two other schools before the age of 6 for unmanageable and aggressive behaviour towards others. Kate was assessed by the NHS communication disorder clinic (CDC) in pre-school years, but the findings were inconclusive. Between the ages of 5 and 7 Kate engaged in 18 months of individual psychotherapy, provided by the borough's child and adolescent mental health service (CAMHS), which was said in a handover meeting between myself and the practitioner to have *'run its natural course'*. In terms of the therapeutic process I understood this to mean that the therapist no longer felt the intervention was meeting Kate's needs, and was not supporting her wellbeing. My sense was that this decision had been based on an adult-led agenda, which might have included factors such as the depth of practitioner skill and possible service constraints. However, if these themes were present they were not discussed during the handover meeting. Kate received a diagnosis of ASD and ADHD in late 2012 – a few months after her arrival in school.

Mrs Haye noted that arriving in school Kate had *'not been around kids for so long* [. . .] *she hasn't got much friends'*. Kate arrived into this large and busy primary school setting aged 6, towards the end of the summer term. Her immediate and enduring presentation was one of high anxiety and physiological stress. The supportive and inclusive deputy head teacher was also Kate's class teacher at that time. She recalls Kate as *'a child who often presented like a wild animal if angered, frightened or upset; who would either scream, wail, hit out, throw tantrums, show open defiance and refuse to be placated, or she would cower and hide behind or under furniture with behaviour that used to remind me of a cornered animal.'* Soon after Kate's arrival, individual dramatherapy sessions were requested by the SENCo and class teacher, initially as a 'crisis management' intervention – the aim being to provide a space for Kate to go to when experiencing overload and stress during the initial weeks and months as a member of the school's community.

> *Each session began with me collecting Kate from her classroom and the two of us walking together to the dramatherapy room, which was a short distance from her classroom. The dramatherapy aim over these months was to develop and negotiate a safe and enabling working alliance with Kate. This emerged as a dialogue of words and actions over time, mostly in response to any unsafe play and communication choices.*

At that time, Kate's dramatherapy sessions were held in a room that was well stocked with play resources but fairly small, with limited storage areas and thus few opportunities to create a neutral space. Kate's arrival for her first session had been planned for how she might react to the situation. (The surroundings were carefully managed to be inviting but not over-stimulating.) For the first couple of months Kate would already be distressed as I arrived to collect her from class; this would often mean she would take her time in making the short journey to the dramatherapy room, stopping to physically expel frustration in a number of ways en route, such as running around the top hall or removing pictures from wall-mounted displays. Once inside the room, sand and other small or medium-sized resources were often thrown across the room during these sessions, with some being broken upon impact with the floor or wall. Kate would offer little or no eye contact during these sessions, and would speak loudly and at times shout instructions at me, such as: '*You stand over there and hold that walking stick!*' She could not tolerate my clarifying any instruction through dialogue. However, despite what may seem like uncontained choices of engagement and communication, Kate's body language, and my sense of her in the room, was that she wanted to be there. Charting her progress over the first few months, it is notable that the throwing of sand and other objects transformed into other play choices. Kate began to identify and return to a group of objects, which she explored and played with in each session. Eventually she spoke of wanting to keep these objects safe, so that they were available for her the following week. Eye contact increased, as did her capacity to listen while I offered some reflections – albeit in short sentences. Kate continued to find intolerable any suggestion from me when responding to her action-based instructions.

This snapshot demonstrates a significant transformation in Kate's presentation over a period of months, brought about by her own working through of the process of familiarising herself with the dramatherapy room and what it might provide or contain for her. In the first evaluation session Kate reflected, '*I love coming here. I don't know why.*' I understood Kate's communication to be in part her unconscious expression of inner states that she could not tolerate or process, and that she may have had limited understanding of.

The next analytical snapshot (B) draws together a series of reflections on Kate's progress after a year of dramatherapy. It explores her choices of story making and role playing as ways of generating experiences in the room and of reflecting on them – and also on her emotions and her experiences of the dynamics of 'power' and control' elsewhere in her life.

Analytical snapshot B

As the months went by and Kate became more confident of her capacity to make choices within sessions, she returned regularly – usually on a weekly basis – to explore the world through story making and role playing. Her play was based on two characters: one who was 'in charge' and the other who was an 'apprentice' or 'student' of some kind. Kate had begun to feel more established in school and was able to stay in the classroom more, although the behaviours noted by her class teacher at the time revealed difficulties with concentration. Also noted was a perceived tendency to exert control over interactions with peers and to determine her own agenda – thought to be consequences of difficulties with communication, social interaction and low self-esteem.

By this time Kate was taking a daily dose of a brand of methylphenidate – a central nervous system stimulant proven in clinical trials to reduce the symptoms of hyperactivity and impulsivity. This prompted notable changes in her presentation within school, as she seemed increasingly able to take on board instructions from adults and to remain in the classroom.

> *Kate often chose to play the character who was 'in charge' in her story making. Sometimes she was the Queen, at other times the Princess with a 'bad way'. These stories involved dressing up in long dresses and wearing crowns. Other characters included the shop owner, or the school teacher. On occasion she was the daughter who wanted to go to the party but who had been sent to her room for 'misbehaving in class'. In role I would be cast by Kate in the opposite role; so if Kate was the powerful Queen, I would be the subservient Princess – and likewise if Kate was the powerful Princess, I would be cast as the silent Queen. I use the word 'silent', as quite often, if the child role was more power-ful than the adult role in the dynamic, my character would be told to 'shut up . . . do what you are told . . . don't give me any "cut-eye".' Within the play world, for many months any suggestion I had in terms of developing my character would be rejected by Kate with all the power and gusto of her 'in charge' character. However, over time, I noted small changes in her capacity to allow some suggestions to be included within the story. This has since developed further, and on occasion – and in role – I may be asked by Kate to suggest the next part within a given story.*

Kate's evaluation reflections at this time illustrate the ways in which she was expe-riencing her dramatherapy sessions – as shown in comments such as: '*I come here to play with toys*'; '*I like making up stories*'; '*I wish I could come here all the time*'. Through her choice of story making she was able to take on powerful and often unkindly roles, and to express her sense of anger, frustration, and the need to control, while being contained within the drama of the story. Kate learned, both through her play choices and through my intervention, how to equip herself with the knowledge of creative process, and the boundary of being 'in role' and 'out of role'. She allowed herself in role to express raw emotions that had possibly overwhelmed her, using the content of the play's story, which she had invented. Similarly, she witnessed the characters she assigned to me as being powerless. Kate was exploring aspects of her inner emotional world – and possibly the interpersonal dynamics and experiences with others – through the safety of her play world.

The final analytical snapshot (C) discusses and reflects on Kate's use of reflexivity – that is, the noting of her own internal process from a position of some distance. It draws upon the dramatherapeutic concept of 'aesthetic dis-tancing' (Landy, 1994), within which it is possible to explore personal distress from the safety of emotional distance.

Analytical snapshot C

The reflections that make up this snapshot are drawn from a session held in recent months. By now more than two years have passed, and Kate is choosing to attend regular weekly dramatherapy sessions. She rarely misses a session, and continues to 'clock watch' in her classroom as the time of her weekly session approaches.

The roles taken in her reality-based situations continue to be the core dyad of one character exercising power over another, the theme that Kate has explored since the start of her dramatherapy sessions. On this occasion the evaluation method was an inclusive part of the session (as it was the first session back after a holiday) and Kate had created a story about a 'bossy and unkind' teacher and a 'frightened' [girl] student. At the end of her storymaking play she began to de-role her character, and was invited to decide whether there was anything to do or say after the costume had been taken off. Kate took off the dress she had put on over the top of her school uniform and said: 'I was the girl today. I was like I was before . . . when I didn't listen . . .' [at this point Kate looks towards me and laughs before continuing] '. . . when I was angry' [laughs again while making direct eye contact]. 'When you were angry?' I reflect, a slight question – or sound of encouragement – in my voice in case her laughter is indicating insecurity about what she is saying and how it will be heard by me. 'Yeah, before – when I came.' Kate's words here came with a sense of a 'full stop', which I took to mean she had ended that part of her reflection. The end of the session arrived, and I noted that day the way in which Kate left the room, which was consistent with the quiet but confident manner I had seen at the end of her sessions for some months now. Having an awareness of time (but not necessarily being able to tell the time), and feeling in charge of this time, enabled Kate to make a choice about the moment she would leave. She did this by moving towards the door, thus making the decision to rejoin the overall environment of the school and leave the dramatherapy world behind for another week.

Here Kate shows her capacity for self-insight as she offers a reflection about a time when she was anxious and scared and did not experience safety. Her laughter demonstrates a level of awareness of what may be regarded as socially 'acceptable' behaviour in the school environment. While her reflection did not explicitly describe how she experienced being in the dramatherapy room during those early months, nevertheless the way in which she calmly reflects on those times could imply that coming to a place where she was able to make choices that were not challenged, and where her presentation of self was accepted, has helped her.

Summary of themes and concluding comments

The snapshots have offered moments drawn together from more than two years of dramatherapy process with Kate. They have demonstrated the way in which a working alliance developed from the therapeutic stance of 'being alongside' her, enabling the establishment of a safe and trusting therapeutic attachment by supporting her capacity to make choices about her means of communication and play. The snapshots have traced Kate's journey from interaction with objects, and limited eye contact, to interaction with sustained eye contact, and on to the continuing development of collaboration through her exploration of interpersonal processes – reflected in the development of her capacity to tolerate others (e.g. to take on board and to invite suggestions).

Kate's great strength now is her capacity to make choices, engaging in the working alliance with respect and kindness to me as her 'play companion' within the dramatherapy process. Kate exudes warmth and offers a gentle affection in her weekly greeting when collected from class. She looks happy for the most part, despite some clear frustrations in the learning environment. She rarely – if ever – reverts to the presentation she displayed during her early months in the school. In my professional view, Kate will need a level of support throughout her school years – and possibly beyond – in order to facilitate the development of her social understanding, and to learn about personal expressions and safety.

Kate's mother has noted that this particular school has been the only constant factor in her education to date. During the interview held in preparation for this chapter, she commented that she feels Kate is happy in school, and that the school supports her well, adding, '*I want her to stay here until secondary school because she is settled.*' Kate herself notes a sense of happiness in dramatherapy: '*I like coming here and playing with things*' and '*I want to keep coming.*' Kate will continue to be offered dramatherapy sessions for the foreseeable future, and possibly until she transfers to secondary provision. Kate has been emotionally well and engaged in the dramatherapy process, has formed some relationships with peers, and is seen as an active member of her class – nevertheless the social gap is widening at this mid-point of her penultimate year in primary school. During dramatherapy sessions I have noted that Kate appears 'stuck' in a developmental play phase notably below her chronological age. As a result she has found it increasingly difficult to relate to her peers in terms of the themes and content of playground chat and play choices. An analysis of the data generated from the evaluation process over time supports this view, with her class teacher noting difficulties in educational attainment targets and a high level of support needed to facilitate collaborative classroom-based peer tasks. SENCo and Educational Psychologist observations of peer interactions have included a lack of interest in the topic of discussion and her choice to play with much younger children in the playground. Referral to a specialist unit within a mainstream school is being explored at this time, and for ethical reasons this is where Kate's story in this chapter will conclude.

This chapter has detailed some of the complexities surrounding Kate's educational history, which highlight worrying concerns within the health and educational systems in terms of the assessment process, liaison with parents, and identifying and developing the correct support and early intervention for children like Kate. These children display difficulties with social communication and peer relationships, and they may present as unmanageable and anxious at the start of their school careers.

In addition, the chapter has shown that a dramatherapist can be an integral part of a school's inclusion team, and that dramatherapy can be a vital intervention in support of a child's psychological wellbeing in mainstream settings, offering a consistent space away from the rest of the school's community. In this space the child is free to make and learn from their own play choices, without any explicit learning agenda being applied.

Acknowledgements

Thank you to Kate for agreeing to her story in school and in dramatherapy appearing in these pages, and for the gift to others that this opportunity provides. Thank you also to Kate's mother, Mrs Haye, who showed bravery in her unrelenting struggle to seek an assessment for Kate. Further, I am grateful for Mrs Haye's candid honesty in the interview conducted to assist in the writing of this chapter, and for her trust in the school's inclusion team and dramatherapy at a time of undue scrutiny by professional services. Finally, I thank the staff and colleagues who supported the development of this chapter.

References

Alderson, P. & Morrow, V. (2011) *The Ethics of Research with Children and Young People: A Practical Handbook*. London: Sage Publications.

BADth: British Association of Dramatherapists (2015) Available from: http://badth.org.uk/ [accessed April 2016].

Barnaby, R. (2014) 'Dramatherapy to support social interactions with peers', in Miller, C. (ed.), *Assessment and Outcomes in the Arts Therapies: A Person-Centred Approach*. London: Jessica Kingsley Publishers.

Baron-Cohen, S. (2004) *The Essential Difference: Men, Women and the Extreme Male Brain*. London: Penguin.

Bouzoukis, C. E. (2001) *Pediatric Dramatherapy: They Couldn't Run so They Learned to Fly*. London: Jessica Kingsley Publishers.

Carrette, J. (1992) 'Autism and dramatherapy', *Dramatherapy: The Journal of the British Association of Dramatherapists*, Vol. 15, No. 1, pp. 17–20.

Casemore, R. (2011) *Person-Centred Counselling in a Nutshell*. London: Sage Publications.

Chasen, L. R. (2011) *Social Skills, Emotional Growth and Drama Therapy: Inspiring Connection on the Autism Spectrum*. Philadelphia, PA: Jessica Kingsley Publishers.

Clarke, G., Boorman, G. & Nind, M. (2011) '"If they don't listen I shout, and when I shout they listen": hearing the voice of girls with behavioural, emotional and social difficulties', *British Educational Research Journal*, Vol. 37, No. 5, pp. 765–780.

Daniels, D. & Jenkins, P. (2010) *Therapy with Children: Children's Rights, Confidentiality and the Law*. London: Sage Publications.

Dix, A. (2012) 'Whizzing and whirring: dramatherapy and ADHD', in Leigh, L., Gersch, I., Dix, A. & Haythorne, D. (eds), *Dramatherapy with Children, Young People and Schools: Enabling Creativity, Sociability, Communication and Learning*. London, Routledge.

Dolphin, M., Byers, A., Goldsmith, A. & Jones, R. E. (eds) (2014) *Psychodynamic Art Therapy Practice with People on the Autistic Spectrum*. London: Routledge.

DSM-5, American Psychiatric Association (2013) *Diagnostic and Statistical Manual of Mental Disorders* (5th edn) (DSM-5). Washington DC: APA.

Flewitt, R. (2005) 'Conducting research with young children: some ethical issues', *Early Child Development and Care*, Vol. 175, No. 6, pp. 553–565.

Gersie, A. (ed.) (1996) *Dramatic Approaches to Brief Therapy*. London: Jessica Kingsley Publishers.

Groundwater-Smith, S. (2007) 'Student voice: essential testimony for intelligent schools', in Campbell, A. & Groundwater-Smith, S. (eds), *An Ethical Approach to Practitioner Research*. Abingdon: Routledge.

HCPC: Health and Care Professions Council (2015) Available from: http://www.hcpc.org/ [accessed April 2016].

Holloway, I. (1997) *Basic Concepts for Qualitative Research*. Oxford: Blackwell Science.

Hume, K., Sreckovic, M., Snyder, K. & Carnahan, C. R. (2014) 'Smooth transitions: helping students with autism spectrum disorder navigate the school day', *Teaching Exceptional Children*, Vol. 47, No. 1, pp. 35–45.

Jennings. S. (2011) *Healthy Attachments and Neuro-Dramatic-Play*. London: Jessica Kingsley Publishers.

Jones, P. (2007) *Drama as Therapy: Theory, Practice and Research* (2nd edn). London: Routledge.

Jones, P. (2012) 'Childhood today and the implications for dramatherapy in schools', in Leigh, L., Gersch, I., Dix, A. & Haythorne, D. (eds), *Dramatherapy with Children, Young People and Schools: Enabling Creativity, Sociability, Communication and Learning*. London: Routledge.

Jones, S. R. G. (1992) 'Was there a Hawthorne effect?', *American Journal of Sociology*, Vol. 98, No. 3, pp. 451–468.

Karkou, V. ed. (2010) *Arts Therapies in Schools: Research and Practice*. London: Jessica Kingsley Publishers.

Landy, R. J. (1994) *Drama Therapy: Concepts, Theories and Practices*. Springfield, IL: Charles C Thomas.

Langley, D. (2006) *An Introduction to Dramatherapy*. Delhi: Sage Publications.

Leigh, L., Gersch, I., Dix, A. & Haythorne, D. (eds) (2012) *Dramatherapy with Children, Young People and Schools: Enabling Creativity, Sociability, Communication and Learning*. London: Routledge.

Lewis, J. & Banerjee, S. (2013) 'An investigation of the therapeutic potential of stories in Dramatherapy with young people with autistic spectrum disorder', *Dramatherapy: The Journal of the British Association of Dramatherapists*, Vol. 35, No. 1, pp. 29–42.

Lundy, L. (2007) '"Voice" is not enough: conceptualising Article 12 of the United Nations Convention on the Rights of the Child', *British Educational Research Journal*, Vol. 33, No. 6, pp. 927–942.

Miller, C. (2005) 'Developing friendship skills with children with pervasive developmental disorders: a case study', *Dramatherapy: The Journal of the British Association of Dramatherapists*, Vol. 27, No. 2, pp. 11–16.

Montgomery, H. & Kellett, M. (eds) (2009) *Children and Young People's Worlds: Developing Frameworks for Integrated Practice*. Bristol: Policy Press.

Novy, C. (2010) 'The Narratives of Change project: dramatherapy and women in conflict with the law', in Jones, P. (ed.), *Drama as Therapy: Clinical Work and Research into Practice, Vol. 2*. London: Routledge.

Pearson, H. (2016) *The Life Project: The Extraordinary Story of Our Ordinary Lives*. London: Penguin.

Pimpas, I. (2013) 'Clinical comment: a psychological perspective to dramatic reality: a path for emotional awareness in autism', *Dramatherapy: The Journal of the British Association of Dramatherapists*, Vol. 35, No. 1, pp. 57–63.

Potter, C. & Whittaker, C. (2001) *Enabling Communication in Children with Autism*. London: Jessica Kingsley Publishers.

Pound, L. (2006) *How Children Learn: From Montessori to Vygotsky – Educational Theories and Approaches Made Easy*. London: MA Education Ltd.

Ramsden, E. (2011) 'Joshua and the expression of make believe violence: dramatherapy in a primary school setting', in Dokter, D., Holloway, P. & Seebohm, H. (eds), *Dramatherapy and Destructiveness*. London: Routledge.

Ramsden, E. (2014) 'A practitioner-researcher inquiry into choice, voice and agency in individual dramatherapy sessions: co-researching with children in a primary school setting' [PhD thesis]. Leeds Beckett University.

Ramsden, E. & Jones, P. (2011) 'Ethics, children, education and therapy: vulnerable or empowered', in Campbell, A. & Broadhead, P. (eds), *Working with Children and Young People: Ethical Debates and Practices Across Disciplines and Continents*. Frankfurt am Main: Peter Lang.

Richman, S. (2001) *Raising a Child with Autism: A Guide to Applied Behaviour Analysis for Parents*. London: Jessica Kingsley Publishers.

SEND (2011/2014) *Special Education Needs and Disability Code of Practice: 0 to 25 Years (July 2014) Valid until 31 March 2015*. Available from: https://www.gov.uk/government/publications/send-code-of-practice-0-to-25 [accessed April 2016].

Tytherleigh, L. & Karkou, V. (2010) 'Dramatherapy, autism and relationship building: a case study', in Karkou, V. (ed.), *Arts Therapies in Schools: Research and Practice*. London: Jessica Kingsley Publishers.

Wilson, R. Z. (2014) *Neuroscience for Counsellors: Practical Applications for Counsellors: Therapists and Mental Health Practitioners*. London: Jessica Kingsley Publishers.

7

BECOMING VISIBLE

Identifying and empowering girls on the autistic spectrum through dramatherapy

Ann Dix

More boys than girls are diagnosed with autistic spectrum disorders (ASD), but recent research has begun to question this gender imbalance, and to suggest that girls with high-functioning autism may be misdiagnosed or simply missed (Gould and Ashton-Smith, 2011). Research indicates that adult women who are later diagnosed as being on the autistic spectrum, were initially diagnosed with learning difficulties, personality disorders, obsessive compulsive disorder or eating disorders and were treated for this, while autistic symptoms were ignored (Rivet and Matson, 2011; Reynolds, 2013). Consequently, many women have spent their lives feeling misunderstood and frustrated, resulting in depression and anxiety.

Autistic spectrum disorder is a term that is applied to a range of behaviours across a wide spectrum. As Stephen Shore (2013) says: 'If you have met one person with autism, you have met one person with autism.' It is wrong to presume that there is one set of common autistic behaviours; however, I believe that signs of autism are being overlooked in girls because they differ from male behaviours, and that by recognising them earlier, support, such as dramatherapy, could be offered to prevent serious mental health issues developing later.

This chapter has developed from a personal and professional curiosity about the representation of girls and women with ASD. I use vignettes of girls who attended dramatherapy groups to illustrate how the therapy enabled them to integrate more fully with their peers. None of the girls was referred specifically for autistic behaviours, but came for various reasons, including anorexia and self-harm. The focus of the groups was to encourage social skills and self-esteem through creative activities, enabling the young people to express their thoughts and emotions through drawing, drama and play.

Permission was sought for this research. The individual girls have been anonymised and any identifying details have been omitted or changed. In some cases, a composite vignette has been created to illustrate a point.

There is growing evidence that dramatherapy is a clinically effective way of working with ASD and that, for young people, 'using dramatic structures to imagine and embody the different parts of themselves can be both a powerful and healing experience' (Wilmer-Barbrook, 2013, p.44).

As dramatherapists, we need to have an understanding of autism in girls. This is not about labelling female behaviour, but understanding the difficulties better. As Ava Ruth Baker says, 'Diagnoses are often thought of as labels but they could also be considered as signposts. Signposts do something more than labels – they help people find their way on a journey' (Baker quoted in Hearst, 2014, p.29).

Working in schools as a dramatherapist, I have met many girls who were struggling in the school environment, but were unable to say why. Usually these girls had no diagnosis, or were presumed to be anxious or isolated. Often, they had some autistic traits, but were able to make eye contact, engage in group activities, and tolerate physical contact, and so were not thought to be on the autistic spectrum. Usually their difficulties were attributed to their gender and they were assumed to be shy or over-sensitive. My hypothesis is that by becoming aware of the signs of ASD in high-functioning girls and diagnosing ASD at an early age, targeted support, including dramatherapy, could be put in place.

People on the autistic spectrum are said to lack 'Theory of Mind' (Premack and Woodruff, 1978; Baron-Cohen et al., 1985) or the ability to interpret one's own and other people's emotional states and empathise. However, many women with ASD suggest that, rather than lacking empathy, they feel others' emotions too intensely to cope with them, and may then withdraw or use self-soothing mechanisms such as rocking or echolalia. Girls and women with high-functioning ASD often speak of having intense feelings of fear and anxiety; in social situations this intense feeling takes an enormous amount of energy, described by Yaull-Smith (2008) as 'social exhaustion', leading to tiredness and angry outbursts when they return home.

The difference in diagnosis of autism in boys and girls

The National Autistic Society website acknowledges there are more boys with ASDs. It quotes Brugha's survey (2009) of households throughout England that found 1.8 per cent of males surveyed had an ASD, compared to 0.2 per cent of females. Wing (1981) found that there were 15 times as many males with high-functioning autism or Asperger's syndrome than females, although when she included people with learning disabilities as well as autism, the ratio of boys to girls fell to 2:1, suggesting that when girls are identified as having ASD it presents in a more profound form, often with other learning difficulties. NAS reports that the ratio of males to females who use NAS schools is approximately 5:1 (male/female) and NAS adult services is approximately 4:1 (male/female).

Recent research has revealed that there is a difference in the way male and female brains develop (Baron-Cohen, 2003; Holtman et al., 2007), suggesting males and females with ASD function differently. This raises questions about how

ASD is diagnosed, and whether there is a gender-bias in tendency towards having ASD – or merely in the diagnostic tools?

The diagnosis of autistic spectrum disorder has increased over the past 20 years, although the reason for this rise remains controversial as research continues to try to find the causes. Explanations have included environmental causes and the discredited link between the MMR vaccine and autism. In the 1990s, the diagnosis of 'autism' was changed to 'autism spectrum disorder' (ASD), which included a broader spectrum of symptoms. Advances in neurological science have given us a greater understanding of how the brain works, while the mapping of the human genome and molecular genetics have produced new theories as to which genes are involved in autism, and how they may affect the development of the brain. Brain imaging has shown that particular areas and circuits may be atypical in structure and function in those diagnosed with ASD (Roth, 2010, p.27). Diagnostic criteria have broadened to encompass a spectrum that links to other pervasive developmental disorders, such as dyspraxia, dyslexia and ADHD. However, this does not explain the difference in numbers of males diagnosed compared with numbers of females.

ASDs are a range of developmental disorders, neurologically based and linked to irregularity in the development of the brain (Frith, 1989; Baron-Cohen et al., 2011). Autism is categorised as a lack or impairment of the social instinct, which is the basis of all autistic spectrum conditions (Gould and Ashton-Smith, 2011). Diagnosis of ASD is based on the triad of impairments: social interaction, social language and communication, and social imagination, identified by Wing and Gould in 1979. However, the history of research into ASD, from Kanner and Asperger in the 1940s to the present day, has largely been based on autistic males, and diagnostic tools, such as interviews, specific tasks and categorisation of behaviours, resulting in quantitative scores for analysis, have been developed according to male phenotypes (Reynolds, 2013; Gould and Ashton-Smith, 2011). It is only since 2000 that research has begun to focus on whether ASDs may affect females differently.

Most biological studies of autism have also focused predominately on males. They have tended to disregard any data falling outside the norm as an aberration, rather than a trait specific to the females in the study, which has led to a predominately male-biased view of autism. Baron-Cohen states that this male bias might reflect the inability of the widely used diagnostic instruments (the Autism Diagnostic Observation Schedule (ADOS) or Autism Diagnostic Interview-Revised (ADI-R)) to detect the subtler ways in which ASD may present in females. Girls diagnosed with autism often have other profound learning difficulties; however, those who may be high functioning frequently miss being assessed or are diagnosed with other conditions.

Females may also go undetected due to a 'non-male-typical' presentation or a greater ability to camouflage their difficulties (Baron-Cohen, 2003; Baron-Cohen et al., 2011). ASD in females could be under-diagnosed because females may be more motivated to conform socially or have better imitation skills that allow them to 'pretend to be normal' (Attwood, 2006; Baron-Cohen et al., 2011; Meng-Chuan et al., 2013).

Genetic hypothesis

It is generally accepted that boys are more susceptible than girls to a range of organic damage, through hereditary disease, acquired infection, or other conditions including autism, ADHD, dyslexia and conduct disorders (Rimland, 1964), and research indicates there might be genetic reasons. One hypothesis is that the gene or genes for autism may be located on the X chromosome inherited from the mother. Girls inherit X chromosomes from both parents, therefore Skuse suggests that the X chromosome, which girls inherit from their fathers, may carry an imprinted gene protecting her from autism (Skuse, 2000). In order for autism to be present in a girl, more genetic mutations are required (Dawson, 2013).

Another hypothesis as to the cause is the effect of foetal testosterone (fT) on the unborn child. In pregnancy, there is a surge in testosterone between 8 and 24 weeks. This is believed to increase the growth of the right hemisphere of the brain, which deals with systemising, patterning and structures, thereby slowing the development of the left hemisphere, which is responsible for empathy, language and communication skills. It has been established that lower levels of fT typically found in females leads to better social and communication skills, eye contact, and use of language (Gerschwind and Galaburda, 1985; Baron-Cohen, 2003). Therefore, the development of language, which is usually stronger in females, may enable girls to interact with each other and learn social interaction by mimicking what they see and hear, so not appearing to be autistic.

The 'Extreme Male Brain' theory developed by Baron-Cohen (2003, p.1) suggests three main brain types. 'The female brain is predominately hard wired for empathy. The male brain is predominately hard-wired for understanding and building systems.' The third type is for individuals in whom systemising and empathising are both equally strong (Baron-Cohen, 2003, p.1). Baron-Cohen argues that these brain types are not dictated by biological sex and that he is categorising sex differences, not stereotyping male and female behaviours. He suggests that autism is possibly a result of an extreme male brain, more geared to organising but unable to understand empathy, and that this may explain why more boys are diagnosed because it 'takes fewer changes in their brains to push boys into the realm of autism than it does for girls' (Baron-Cohen et al., 2011; see also Baron-Cohen, 2003).

How girls differ in their presentation of ASD

The triad of impairment (Wing and Gould, 1979) includes lack of eye contact and dislike of being touched, lack of social interaction and empathy for others, lack of concentration, and disruptive, rigid or repetitive behaviours. These behaviours are more applicable to boys than girls and do not reflect the broad spectrum of autism, nor recognise that girls may respond differently from boys in similar situations (Reynolds, 2013).

Social interaction

Girls on the spectrum may appear to be interacting socially, yet find it difficult to achieve and maintain friendships. They are often on the periphery of a friendship group, because they have learned to copy social skills such as turn taking and responses to others. Reynolds (2013) suggests that girls with ASD either gravitate towards older girls, who may mother them and act as social protection, or choose to play with younger children, who will allow them to dominate and control the play. They may mimic behaviours (Attwood, 2006) but not possess the social understanding of why they are doing so. They may be attuned to the emotions of others, but not understand where the emotion comes from and be unable to read facial expressions, body language or the intention of the other person.

Art psychotherapist Caroline Hearst, herself diagnosed with autism, explains: 'Those with more subtle differences grow up realizing that they are different and that they are unable to achieve some things that come naturally to others – but they generally have no way (even if they are highly intelligent) of understanding or conceptualizing that difference' (Hearst, 2014, p.28).

Vignette 1: Diane

> Diane was playing a game in the dramatherapy group, when one girl began to cry. The girls gathered round, making comforting comments and hugging the crying girl. Diane looked puzzled and watched the others carefully. She stepped forward and said 'Don't cry', touching the girl's arm, briefly, before withdrawing to the edge of the group. Diane continued with the game they were playing, by herself.

By watching and listening, Diane had learned what was appropriate to say, yet could not fully understand why she should say it. She was aware that a caring response was necessary in order to maintain her place in the group, but was not able to empathise with the other child's emotions. Diane could not understand why she did not stop crying straight away, and found it difficult to read the expressions on the faces of the other girls in the group. This made her anxious as she was aware that she did not understand the situation, and returning to the game meant that she could self-soothe by returning to a set of rules she did understand. Girls with ASD may frequently not make eye contact as a form of self-protection because they find it difficult to read facial expressions and may not want to misinterpret situations. When they are young they may follow the more dominant girls in the group; however, when they reach puberty, they may either become more challenging, or withdraw from social interactions.

Social communication

As with boys, there is a lack of understanding of 'small talk' and girls tend to say what they are thinking, but not be able to chatter or understand the nuances of conversation. Speaking their minds may get them into trouble with peers and those in authority as they do not understand the idea of a social hierarchy (Gould and Ashton-Smith, 2011).

Vignette 2: Chloe

Chloe would laugh and play in the dramatherapy group and was able to take turns, but would often want to take control and was perceived as bossy. She watched the others closely to see what they were doing but struggled to join in the group's small talk. She could be quite forthright in her responses and observations about group members and this sometimes caused offence. Chloe appeared to lack empathy with others and did not understand why she upset people.

Social imagination

Girls with ASD are assumed to be unable to use creative play, yet women with ASD are often extremely imaginative, and have become artists or writers, although they may have difficulties with flexible thinking, and prefer rigid routines. They may work in their own idiosyncratic way, as the writer and artist Donna Williams describes: 'I don't think, then paint, I paint then discover the picture, pick it out, bring it to life, then seek to understand what it means to me' (Williams, 2014).

Girls may appear to be using imaginative play, but this can be concentrated, repetitious and lacking in creative freedom. They seldom spontaneously engage in free play, rather choosing to play in a solitary or parallel fashion (Wolfberg, 2009). Boys with ASD often play rigidly with specific toys, which they might put into lines or groups. Girls may also have intense interests, such as animals, dolls and pop stars, or they might collect names and details of their friends in quite obsessive ways, writing them in notebooks and making lists. However, as this is characteristic of many neuro-typical girls, these symptoms often go unnoticed. The key is in the intensity and quality of these interests that become exclusive and all-consuming (Reynolds, 2013).

The increased use of social media provides girls with ASD with a different form of communication, which allows them to be part of a group without having to experience physical proximity or read social cues such as eye contact and body language. There are many internet blogs by women with ASD, with huge followings, where women are able to express some of their worries and frustrations amongst a likeminded community who understand them. Sites such as Facebook provide an opportunity to become part of a peer network, which is more manageable for young women with ASD. However, there are inherent dangers in this, because there may be an obsessive need to be on social media that interferes with face-to-face interaction and the development of social skills. These young women are particularly vulnerable to sexual grooming and inappropriate online relationships because they are often unable to differentiate between genuine friendship and inappropriate behaviours in others, due to impaired theory of mind.

Girls with ASD can have a vivid imaginary world, and frequently write stories or draw and can pretend to be other characters. Janette Purkis described her childhood interests as 'cats and Dr Who' and wrote stories about time travel and space (Purkis, 2006, p.15). Reading fiction is a way girls can escape from the difficulties of social interaction, and many girls with ASD report that they read voraciously, entering into the fantasy world and living out the adventures of their favourite characters, which also can provide a set of guidelines for how they might behave. This preoccupation sometimes goes un-noticed, as girls are 'socially isolated, preoccupied by their imaginary world, but not a disruptive influence in the classroom' (Attwood, 1998, p.152).

Vignette 3: Gemma

Gemma enjoyed watching the TV series Tracey Beaker, *based on the books by Jacqueline Wilson. She had read the books, was able to list the episodes and storylines, and could talk about the characters. She liked Tracey because she was also different and felt like an outsider. She enjoyed the humour and the visual images, including the cartoons, but her descriptions of why events had happened lacked insight and nuance. When Gemma took on the role of Tracey in dramatherapy improvisations she was able to think with the group, what Tracey might do or say. This appeared to increase Gemma's confidence, as she was able to speak as Tracey and not directly as herself. This enabled her to mirror Tracey's interactions with others and allowed her to practise situations with her peers, which reflected situations she might find herself in outside the dramatherapy group. Gemma was able to pause the action and replay it or experiment with different scenarios, allowing her to develop empathy with Tracey and build a rapport with the rest of the group.*

ASD and the teenage years

We can surmise that young girls are more able to hide their disability because of the ways in which they socialise, and the nurturing behaviours of other girls. However, once puberty is reached, difficulties begin to be more pronounced. Whereas boys may continue to mix with other boys with similar interests and their obsessive behaviours are more accepted, girls lose the protective world of primary school. Now they have to mix with many more children, often in crowded corridors, and do not have the same clear routines, which may cause them to feel anxious and overwhelmed.

Puberty brings menstruation and body changes, and there is usually a desire to belong to a group of likeminded peers. This is a time of tribal behaviours, as adolescents seek to separate from their parents, and anyone outside the chosen group may meet with ridicule or rejection. Groups may choose to dress in a certain way, wearing particular brands of clothing, carrying particular bags and phones. To a young woman with ASD, this can be mystifying and she may choose to isolate herself from her peers in order to protect herself from bullying. It is at this time that depression is more likely to develop, as the young woman realises that she does not fit in. Her lack of understanding of the nuances of adolescent chatter may cause her to misunderstand situations, and the desire to control a situation in order to make it manageable may become more difficult. Young women often continue to speak in a childlike manner, and there is a tendency to laugh or giggle in circumstances that may anticipate an expression of embarrassment, pain or sadness (Attwood, 1998). Some young women with ASD may become aggressive and confrontational as they try to cope with these changes.

Vignette 4: Abigail

Abigail sat quietly in the dramatherapy group. She appeared to be absorbed in her own world. Although she did not have a diagnosis of ASD, she had come to the group with severe anxiety. Abigail was intelligent, although she was struggling at school and she found it difficult to make friends. She had a very close relationship with her mother, whom she looked to for support. Abigail would engage with the others in the group when it was a subject she knew about and would talk animatedly about clothes she had bought in a shop popular with teenagers. Her conversation sounded typical for girls of her age, but, when listened to closely, consisted of factual descriptions of shops, items of clothing, colour and price. She was able to list articles for sale and say she liked them, but not how she felt wearing them or why she had bought them. It became evident after a while that the collecting of the clothes was the important thing and that this gave her a window into communication with others in the group. When the conversation moved onto a different topic she would withdraw into herself and return to silence.

Abigail found it difficult to join in dramatherapy improvisations, even when given a specific character; however, her interest in clothes meant that she was drawn to the materials in the room, and would create costumes by wrapping the cloths around herself. She also used dramatic projection by using the fabrics to create scenes for the improvisations. Gradually she felt able to take small roles, often draped in fabrics, which appeared to give her the confidence to be someone else. Abigail's movements became more expansive and she became more engaged in the work.

Difference in behaviours or sexual stereotyping?

Not all girls with ASD share the same traits; however, those that embrace the more stereotypical female interests are more likely to remain undiagnosed, as they appear to be conforming to societal expectations. Many girls with ASD reject traditional female interests, such as fashion and appearance, and as they mature it is more likely that they will rebel against cultural expectations, and want to do things their own way, leading to clashes with parents and schools. Girls with ASD may prefer to have male friends, and feel more comfortable with factual and systemising discussions.

Clearly, socialisation also plays a part. Parents often expect more boisterous behaviour from boys, and girls may find themselves pushed to the edges of the playground while boys play active games in the centre. Boys with ASD usually demand more attention through their behaviour, although this changes in adolescence when it becomes acceptable for boys to gather together in groups to play computer games with little social interaction. Girls, however, often become more disruptive in their teenage years, when they begin to behave in non-stereotypical ways. They may reject gender stereotyping and cultural expectations, refuse to complete tasks, and avoid social activities, while internalising their feelings and anger.

It may be that our perceptions of what constitutes 'female' behaviour blind us to seeing the differences between neuro-typical and autistic behaviours in girls, but socialisation alone cannot explain the differences found between the male and female brain; and as Baron-Cohen argues (2003, p.11), biology also appears to play a significant role.

Research into the creative arts therapies and ASD

Creative arts therapies are important when working with ASD, as they allow the participant to express their inner worlds through activity-based interventions. Sherbourne's developmental movement (2001) offers a model that encourages relationship building and communication skills. Many autistic children are capable of symbolic play, usually with initial training and ongoing assistance: 'although much of the play is ritualistic, it is, nevertheless, play and is their way of declaring themselves' (Mittledorf, 2001, p.257). This is echoed by Shore: 'There is no doubt that parents and professionals who use the arts as specific and intentional tools are likely to achieve significant results in improved empathy, behaviours and language' (Shore, 2013, p.44).

Many people on the autistic spectrum prefer to think visually rather than ver-bally (Baron-Cohen, 2008; Pacheco, 2013). Temple Grandin begins her book *Thinking in Pictures*: 'I THINK IN PICTURES. Words are like a second language to me. I translate both spoken and written words into full colour movies, com-plete with sound, which run like a VCR tape in my head' (Grandin, 2006, p.3). She describes how she uses concrete imagery to explain words and make sense of the world around her. The creation of visual art can offer a powerful non-verbal medium for expression and a way of solving problems, as well as reducing the anxi-ety caused by social situations (Epp, 2008).

The positive effect of Music Therapy on children with ASD has been well documented. It may succeed because music is a system with rules and predictabil-ity (Baron-Cohen, 2008). Moving to a rhythm allows the body to feel different sensations, which may provide a sense of comfort. Kalyva refers to Wimpary's 1995 study of a girl with ASD who reported that music therapy enhanced her interpersonal contact and attention span by combining live music with adult–child interactions. This helped her to plan actions that could be generalised beyond the therapeutic setting (Kalyva, 2011, p.95).

Lanyado (1987) and Bromfield (1989) report that play therapy revealed improve-ments in their clients' language development, social interaction and reduction of stereotypical behaviours, and that these gains were transferred to the world outside the playroom. Weider (2013, p.xii) suggests that play is especially important to children with ASD: it provides an opportunity to develop symbolic capacities as 'they are compromised in their capacity to comprehend and internalise experiences in the form of symbols.'

Karkou and Sanderson (2006, p.197) suggest that, although research studies offer evidence for the efficacy of all arts therapies, dramatherapy might be more suited to clients with ASD, who have some degree of cognitive, physical and emotional skills, because it is potentially more verbal than other art forms.

A dramatherapy project at the University of Kent, in 2014, enabled small groups of children with ASD to enter an enclosed, themed environment with puppets, light, sand and actor/therapists. Results demonstrate that this had a positive effect on all 22 children, particularly in the areas of encouraging empathy and understanding facial expression. The use of small puppets to increase empathy is also described by Jones (2005, p.234).

There are very few dramatherapy case studies written specifically about girls with ASD, particularly those with high-functioning ASD, as most papers reflect the larger proportion of boys. *Dramatherapy Journal* 2013 contains several examples, including Alana, who, despite being described as 'in her own world; egocentric; self-contained and demonstrating no pretence play', becomes able to role play and stay within the metaphor and improvise her response (Lewis and Banerjee, 2013, pp.34–35).

How can dramatherapy help girls with ASD?

Dramatherapy can make an important contribution to this client group (NAS website; Godfrey and Haythorne, 2013), as it develops social skills through a structured framework, which may reduce anxiety through its use of verbal and non-verbal techniques. Dramatherapy is multi-modal and integrates movement, music, art, games, role play and performance to provide ways of making contact with those with ASD (Karkou, 2010). The familiar structure of warm up, exploration and closure can provide the ritual that develops trust and a sense of security (Jennings, 1990; Chesner, 1995), and allows the young person to develop a sense of confidence through a multi-sensory experience. Many girls with ASD become overwhelmed by large groups and situations they feel they are not able to control, so it is also important to provide space for relaxation and an opportunity to have a sense of being alone within the group, considering that too much stimulus can cause a sense of fear and anxiety.

As we have seen, ASD girls often have a strong inner fantasy world and some capacity to be imaginative. The ability of girls with ASD to interact socially, together with their stronger language development, may mean that dramatherapy is an ideal medium to engage and encourage these skills. Dramatherapy can use the individual stories the group brings to sessions, and enable the group to practise social scenes, as well as develop their imaginations through myths and fantasy. Girls with ASD may enjoy structured games, which have rules they can understand, and which provide a focus for concentration and a framework for social interaction within the group; this can help to develop a shared language (Chesner, 1995). This, in turn helps to develop self-confidence and the ability to achieve by themselves.

Vignette 5: Cheryl

> *The dramatherapy group started with a warm-up game. Cheryl (aged 14) was reluctant to stand up and join in. She pulled her jumper tighter around herself and chewed her fingernails. The game involved throwing a beanbag to each other. It was played enthusiastically by the other group members, who took care to include Cheryl at the edge of the room. Gradually, Cheryl began to return the beanbag, laughing when others did not catch it. She began to throw it so that they had to jump up or sideways, and called out their names as she did so. Her own movements became more expansive and her body looked more relaxed. Cheryl had issues with her body image and usually wore layers of large baggy clothes, which hid her shape, so it was surprising when she took off her sweatshirt. In subsequent sessions, Cheryl would ask to play this game, and gradually built up a repertoire of games she enjoyed and which she could engage with others in the group. She was also more able to stand close to other group members without feeling anxious.*

Even when they can engage in playing such games, many autistic young people become overwhelmed by anxiety and are unable to explain their feelings in words. The use of dramatic projection is a valuable tool in helping the young person to 'project their fears or anxieties onto something concrete, so that they can "see" it from a safe distance.' This may allow for unmanageable or inarticulate feelings to become manageable (anonymous vignette in Andersen-Warren, 2013, p.9).

Some girls with ASD show more interest in pretend play activities, although it is unclear whether this is because they are better at imitation of others or have a better capacity to pretend. Many have an elaborate fantasy world with imaginary friends, often based on fictional characters (Purkis, 2006; Knickmeyer et al., 2008; Gould and Ashton-Smith, 2011). They are able to enjoy drama and role play and Ashton-Smith recommends that work with girls should focus on their more subtle presentations and directly teach the skills that typically developing girls learn indirectly. Some may benefit from working in girls-only groups with others who share their difficulties to work together on issues such as practising social scripts and creating social situations in which to rehearse teenage chat. Accessing dramatherapy in school may have a major impact on other areas of school life, particularly in less structured times such as break and lunchtime, because it increases self-confidence and sociability.

Many teenage girls with ASD like to read, so there is the possibility of using dramatic scripts to develop themes, expand their worlds and enlarge a poor vocabulary (Jones, 2014). Role play developed from television or film characters may enable discussions about what a character should do and why they are behaving in a particular way, or decoding of simple body language and recognising facial expressions. This may also be helpful in identifying unacceptable behaviours, as girls with ASD can be particularly vulnerable to abuse and exploitation because they do not recognise the intentions of others.

Many girls on the spectrum want to make social connections, and dramatherapy can help them begin to relate to others by using role to become another person and learn how others feel and behave (O'Leary, 2013). Through dramatherapy, girls may practise how to behave in difficult situations in the safe environment of the therapy group, by rehearsing and replaying social skills until they are integrated into behaviour (Godfrey and Haythorne, 2013). Girls with ASD may have low self-esteem and self-confidence and the dramatherapist can model clear communication and encourage positive relationships with others. Through the use of stories, they can develop more independence and practise strategies that will reduce their vulnerability. The flexibility of dramatherapy and its range of creative methods enables it to respond to each individual child's needs in order to maximise their potential (Carrette, 1992). Dramatherapy works with the individuality of the whole person and allows this exploration to take place in their own time without judgement. For girls with ASD, this allows them to develop who they want to be and enables them to become visible.

Conclusion

It is important not to make assumptions and stereotype all young people with ASD as being the same. Many girls fail to get adequate support or diagnosis, either because they are simply regarded as 'odd' or because we are looking for the wrong signs. They become invisible, and spend their lives feeling frustrated and angry. Cultural expectations of women and assessment tools developed for males with ASD compound the problem, by not seeing that females have different behaviours. Current research is beginning to address this omission, which will lead to better knowledge and support for young girls in schools, CAMHS and in the wider community.

There is no cure for ASD, but hopefully, with more recognition and understanding, the lives of young women can be improved. Dramatherapy is already building up evidence to suggest that it can address difficulties in communication and encourage social understanding. It is sometimes assumed that girls with ASD cannot use imagination and creativity, and will merely repeat the roles without understanding why, yet this is refuted by many women with ASD. Early research is indicating that the use of stories and projective play enables those with ASD to increase their sense of self, while physical movement and relaxation exercises allow girls to work with their body image. This is an area that requires more research, particularly with girls who do not have a formal diagnosis. If girls can be identified early and provided with individual and group work, they can be offered an opportunity to understand that, although they may think and behave in an atypical manner, they are not alone and there is much that they have to offer. By helping to make girls with ASD more visible, we give them an opportunity of a happier and productive life.

References

Andersen-Warren, M. (2013) 'Dramatherapy with children and young people who have autistic spectrum disorders: an examination of dramatherapist's practices', *Dramatherapy*, 35(1), pp.3–19.

Attwood, T. (1998) *Aspergers Syndrome: A Guide for Parents and Professionals*. London: Jessica Kingsley Publishers.

Attwood, T. (2006) *The Complete Guide to Asperger's Syndrome*. London: Jessica Kingsley Publishers.

Baron-Cohen, S. (2003) *The Essential Difference: Men, Women and the Extreme Male Brain*. London: Penguin.

Baron-Cohen, S. (2008) *Autism and Aspergers Syndrome*. Oxford: Oxford University Press.

Baron-Cohen, S., Leslie, A. M. and Frith, U. (1985) 'Does the autistic child have a "theory of mind"?', *Cognition*, 21 (1985), pp.37–46; also available via www.autismtruths.org [accessed April 2016].

Baron-Cohen, S., Lombardo, M. V., Auyeung, B., Ashwin, E., Chakrabarti, B. and Knickmeyer, R. (2011) 'Why are autistic spectrum conditions more prevalent in males?', *Public Library of Science: Biology*, available at http://www.ncbi.nlm.nih.gov/pubmed/21695109 [accessed April 2016].

Bromfield, R. (1989) 'Psychodynamic play therapy with a high functioning autistic child', *Psychoanalytic Psychology*, 6(4), pp.439–453.

Brugha, T. (2009) *Autism Spectrum Disorder in Adults Living in Households Throughout England: Report from the Adult Psychiatric Morbidity Survey 2007*, NHS Information Centre for Health and Social Care, via *Autism: why do more boys than girls develop it?*, available via http://www.autism.org.uk [accessed April 2016].

Carrette, J. (1992) 'Autism and Dramatherapy', *Dramatherapy*, 15(1), pp.17–20.

Chesner, A. (1995) *Dramatherapy for People with Learning Difficulties: A World of Difference*. London: Jessica Kingsley Publishers.

Dawson, G. (2013) At www.autismspeaks.org [accessed May 2015].

Epp, K. M. (2008) 'Outcome-based evaluation of a social skills program using art therapy and group therapy for children on the autism spectrum', *National Association of Social Workers: Children and Schools*, 30(1).

Frith, U. (1989) *Autism: Explaining the Enigma*. Oxford: Basil Blackwell.

Gerschwind, N. and Galaburda, A. M. (1985) 'Cerebral lateralization, biological mechanisms, associations and pathology: I. A hypothesis and a programme for research', *Archive of Neurology*, 42, pp.428–459.

Godfrey, E. and Haythorne, D. (2013) 'Benefits of Dramatherapy for Autism Spectrum Disorder: a qualitative analysis of feedback from parents and teachers of clients attending Roundabout dramatherapy sessions in schools', *Dramatherapy*, 35(1), pp.3–19.

Gould, J. and Ashton-Smith, J. (2011) 'Missed diagnosis or misdiagnosis: girls and women on the autistic spectrum', *Good Autism Practice*, 12(1), pp.34–41.

Grandin, T. (2006) *Thinking in Pictures and Other Reports from My Life with Autism*. London: Bloomsbury.

Hearst, C. (2014) 'Autism in the therapy room', *Therapy Today*, 25(1), pp.26–30, available via www.therapytoday.net/ [accessed February 2014].

Holtman, M., Bolte, S. and Poustka, F. (2007) 'Autism spectrum disorders: sex differences in autistic behaviour domains and coexisting psychopathology', *Developmental Medicine & Child Neurology*, 49, pp.361–366.

Jennings, S. (1990) *Dramatherapy with Families, Groups and Individuals: Waiting in the Wings*. London: Jessica Kingsley Publishers.

Jones, H. (2014) *Talk to Me: Conversation Strategies for Parents of Children on the Autism Spectrum or with Speech and Language Impairments*. London: Jessica Kingsley Publishers.

Jones, P. (2005) *The Arts Therapies: A Revolution in Healthcare*. London: Brunner-Routledge.

Kalyva, E. (2011) *Autism Educational and Therapeutic Approaches*. London: Sage Publications.

Karkou, V. (ed.) (2010) *Arts Therapies in Schools: Research and Practice*. London: Jessica Kingsley Publishers.

Karkou, V. and Sanderson, P. (2006) *Arts Therapies: A Research-Based Map of the Field.* Edinburgh: Elsevier Churchill Livingstone.

Knickmeyer, R. C., Wheelwright, S. and Baron-Cohen, S. B. (2008) 'Sex-typical play: masculinization/defeminization in girls with an autistic spectrum condition', *Journal of Autism and Developmental Disorders*, 38, pp.1028–1035.

Lanyado, M. (1987) 'Asymbolic and symbolic play: developmental perspectives in the treatment of disturbed children', *Journal of Child Psychotherapy*, 13(2), pp.33–44.

Lewis, J. and Banerjee, S. (2013) 'An investigation of the therapeutic potential of stories in Dramatherapy with young people with autistic spectrum disorder', *Dramatherapy*, 35(1), pp.29–42.

Meng Chuan, L., Lombardo, M. V., Suckling, J., Ruigrok, A. N., Bhismadev, C., Ecker, C., Deoni, S. C. L., Craig, M. C., Murphy, D. G. M., Bullmore, E. T., MRC AIMS Consortium and Baron-Cohen, S. (2013) 'Biological sex affects the neurobiology of autism', *Brain: A Journal of Neurobiology*, 136(9), pp.2799–2815, available via www.brain.oxfordjournals.org [accessed September 2014].

Mittledorf, W., Hendricks, S. and Landreth, G. L. (2001) 'Play therapy with autistic children', in Landreth, G. (ed.), *Innovations in Play Therapy: Issues, Process and Special Populations.* London: Taylor & Francis.

O'Leary, K. (2013) 'The effects of drama therapy with Autism Spectrum Disorders', Honors Undergraduate Student Research. Paper 1, available via http://scholarworks.bgsu.edu. honorsprojects [accessed April 2016].

Pacheco, I. (2013) 'The effects of art therapy on the language abilities of autistic children', *Mount St Mary College Journal of Psychology Research Proposals*, 3, available via http://brainwwaves. mamc.edu [accessed April 2016].

Premack, D. and Woodruff, G. (1978) 'Does the chimpanzee have a "theory of mind"?', *Behavioural and Brain Sciences*, 4, pp.515–526.

Purkis, J. (2006) *Finding a Different Kind of Normal: Misadventures with Aspergers Syndrome.* London: Jessica Kingsley Publishers.

Reynolds, K. (2013) 'Is autism different for girls?', *Sen Magazine*, available via https://www. senmagazine.co.uk/articles [accessed April 2016].

Rimland, B. (1964) *Infantile Autism: The Syndrome and Its Implications for a Neural Theory of Behavior.* New York: Appleton-Century-Crofts.

Rivet, T. T. and Matson, J. L. (2011) 'Review of gender differences in core symptomatology', *Research in Autism Spectrum Disorders*, 5(3), pp.957–976.

Roth, I. (2010) *The Autism Spectrum in the 21st Century: Exploring Psychology, Biology and Practice.* London: Jessica Kingsley Publishers.

Sherbourne, V. (2001) *Developmental Movement for Children.* London: Worth Publishing.

Shore, S. (2013) *The Art of Autism: Shifting Perceptions*, available via www.the-art-of-autism. com [accessed April 2016].

Skuse, D.H. (2000) 'Imprinting the X-chromosome, and the male brain: explaining sex differences in the liability to autism', *Pediatric Research*, 47(1), pp.9–16.

Weider, S. (2013) 'Foreword', in Gallo-Lopez, L. and Rubin, L. C. (eds) (2013), *Play-Based Interventions for Children and Adolescents with Autism Spectrum Disorders.* London: Routledge.

Williams, D. (2014) Available at www.donnawilliams.net [accessed April 2016].

Wilmer-Barbrook, C. (2013) 'Adolescence, Asperger's and acting: can dramatherapy improve social and communication skills for young people with Asperger's syndrome?', *Dramatherapy*, 35(1), pp.43–56, http://dx.doi.org/10.1080/02630672.2013.773130

Wing, L. (1981) 'Sex ratios in early childhood autism and related conditions', *Psychiatry Research*, 5, pp.129–137.

Wing, L. and Gould, J. (1979) 'Severe impairments of social interaction and associated abnormalities in children: epidemiology and classification', *Journal of Autism and Developmental Disorders*, 9, pp.11–29.

Wolfberg, P. J. (2009) *Play and Imagination in Children with Autism* (2nd edition). New York: Teachers College Press.

Yaull-Smith, D. (2008) 'Girls on the Spectrum', *NAS Communication Magazine*, National Autistic Society.

Website

The National Autistic Society (NAS). At www,autism.org.uk [accessed April 2016].

8

INTROVERSION, MINDFULNESS AND DRAMATHERAPY

Working with young people with autism

Jeni Treves

Introduction

In this chapter, I explore how a particular style of working as a dramatherapist impacts on young people who have autism and the personality trait of introversion. The voices of the clients are of paramount importance here. Authentic feedback is the focus of this chapter and was obtained from individuals who are currently attending or have attended dramatherapy. Vignettes from sessions are also included. The involvement of the young people as 'partners of research' is integral to the chapter (Grainger, 1999).

What is dramatherapy?

The word drama means 'action'. Therapy means 'change'. The action is what we do and the change is what we are hoping for. The process of using dramatherapy can be healing in and of itself for those taking part. Using the imagination can be key to bringing about change. The dramatherapist is witness, actor, audience, and most importantly the midwife of the participant's process. Jennings suggests that the arts bring into focus that which cannot be spoken. Dramatherapists offer the unspoken a voice. This can lead to insight, awareness, and potential for change. However, there are multiple ways of working in this field. It is important to hold in mind that 'the temptation can be to want one monolithic approach, but I would counsel against this . . . there are many approaches, just as there are many individual needs in clients' (Jones, 2011, p.58).

The tools of dramatherapy

The tools I use have changed over almost thirty years of practice and teaching. At present, the physical props I take into sessions are puppets, objects such as mythical figures, stones, buttons and action figures, story-making cards, and plenty of art materials. There are also the skills carried in my head, the unseen resources, that can be found in a moment should they be needed: fairy tales and myths, role-play ideas, improvisation games, and not least the ability and awareness to intervene when needed and to know when this might be.

My style and practice

After training as a dramatherapist in 1986, I became interested in psychotherapy and graduated as a Hakomi Body Centred Psychotherapist in the early 1990s. These two disciplines appear to have quite different methodologies for the therapist. Dramatherapy is a 'doing', action-based therapy, in which the client and therapist can be active and expressive. Hakomi focuses on the therapist 'being', in other words, witnessing and supporting without the need to 'do' anything other than practise from a place of mindful curiosity.

I am attracted to both disciplines. Each holds the principles of non-judgement and empowerment. Through finding a way to incorporate both approaches, my style of working has become quieter, simpler and, I believe, more empowering for the young people with whom I work.

What does this way of working look like?

As part of my 'doing' role I provide dramatherapy tools, and appropriate verbal or non-verbal interventions. The young people are able to use the materials to explore and respond as they wish to the interventions.

My 'being' role involves quietly listening and watching with full attention and without judgement. This is part of the practice of 'mindfulness', which enables me to be aware of my own process, thoughts, feelings and reactions. It helps me monitor how my own process may influence the session.

It is my belief that, through self-directed exploration, the young person can gain a sense of empowerment. Having this witnessed without judgement affirms their expression, which is a part of them. This can be described as the Person-Centred approach and philosophy (Rogers, 2001).

My preferred style of working is also reflected in how I refer to the people with whom I work. Yalom suggests that, rather than calling people clients, patients or analysands, we use more equal terminology. He says, 'I prefer to think of my patients and myself as "fellow travelers", a term that abolishes distinction between "them", the afflicted, and "us" the "healers"' (Yalom, 2002, p.8). For the purpose of this chapter and in the spirit of Yalom's thoughts, I will use the term 'young people with autism'.

What is mindfulness?

Mindfulness is an ancient practice based in the Buddhist tradition. It is the practice of consciously being in the moment using breathing and meditative techniques, seeing clearly what is happening within oneself, yet not becoming identified with this. It enables the witnessing and managing of one's own process in order to be fully present for the other.

Kurtz suggests that therapists must stay with the experience and wait, 'before following immediately by emotional reaction, discriminative thought, reflection, purposeful action' (Kurtz, 1990, p.27).

Joel Gluck explains how mindfulness and dramatherapy can inter-connect in practice. One is a discipline or approach for our everyday lives, looking inwards, a state of being, a conscious awareness; the other is a method of using creativity and action to express ourselves. Bringing the two together, 'every moment of a drama-therapy session can be an invitation to return to or be in the present moment, with awareness' (Gluck, 2014, p.108).

Introversion

There are many definitions of introversion, and though there has been much research, no one definition fits all introverted people. One trait of introversion is when a person gains energy from within themselves as opposed to from outside themselves. This suggests a state of self-sufficiency and a preference for being alone, without excessive stimulation. In being alone the introvert will feel calmer and less anxious. Being alone does not bring fear; instead, it brings peace. It has been suggested that introverts, 're-charge their batteries by being alone' (Cain, 2012, p.10). Bainbridge suggests that introverts are energised by being alone to enjoy and develop their own thoughts and are drained by being around other people (Bainbridge, 2014).

Autism and introversion

Recent research into autism and introversion suggests that there may be a connection between the two. Some of the traits of each appear to have similar qualities, such as the need for time alone, being over-stimulated by too many people or too much noise, enjoying one's own thoughts and feelings, and perhaps having less of a need to be in relationship than typical extroverted people.

In her research about autism and introversion, Grimes (2010) proposes, 'when introversion and autism are placed on the same continuum, the nature of the relationship of the traits become[s] more apparent, and new possibilities are available for exploration of both autism and introversion.' Grimes creates a model of the different traits of introversion, and concludes that these traits could be placed on the continuum of autistic traits, proposing that there are overlaps with both presentations.

It is also suggested that sensory processing difficulties (Karim, Ali and O'Reilly, 2014) are more common in younger children with ASD and that by the teenage years these difficulties lessen.

Dramatherapy and autism in practice

It is important to briefly acknowledge the immense volume of research on 'Theory of Mind' and 'the Triad of Impairments model'. In brief, Theory of Mind refers to lack of empathy. The Triad of Impairments describes difficulties in social understanding and interaction, impaired communication, and limited flexibility in thinking (Karim, Ali and O'Reilly, 2014). While vital for scientific and medical research, I believe that each human being is unique and that it is important to see beyond the apparent disability. A young person with autism may experience sensory problems, but may also be a 'natural' introvert. It is therefore essential to hold in mind my own personality traits and adapt my style to avoid the possibility of overload and demand on the young person. To illustrate this, I provide a short vignette of some recent work done with a young person with autism.

Vignette 1

A young person with autism and traits of introversion attends dramatherapy sessions on a one-to-one basis. He presents in the school environment as quiet, withdrawn and depressed, as reported by those working with him. He rarely speaks and has good receptive understanding.

He enters the room, and sits down. The room is small and almost empty apart from beanbags, two chairs and a small table. Dramatherapy resources are on display. I notice that his energy seems depleted; he chooses to sit with his body hunched and caving inwards, as though he is carrying a heavy load. I let him know that puppets and materials are available, should he wish to use them. There follows a silence lasting five or six minutes. He is not moving and neither am I. I model his physical position and we wait.

He then leans down and chooses a puppet, a squirrel. He chooses a koala puppet and offers this to me. He places his hand inside the squirrel puppet and begins to move it, then makes a noise. It sounds like crying and I name this. He nods a 'yes' and spends a further six or seven minutes making this sound, which I in turn mirror, back to him. Then comes a change. He leans forward and moves my hand with the koala puppet on it, and tells the koala to hug the squirrel. This carries on and he begins to smile, then chooses to leave the room and finish his session. His shoulders are down, and no longer hunched.

Reflection on Vignette 1

The combination of dramatherapy and mindfulness appeared to work well in this session. There was no demand upon the young person. In choosing what he needed in an atmosphere of non-judgement, he used dramatherapy tools to express himself and have his expression witnessed. He brought some feelings that were observable through his body language and initially he was not able to be in relationship. By the end, this had changed and he had initiated an interaction. It was my experience that this was an empowering session for him.

As a dramatherapist, I endeavour to 'meet' individuals wherever they are, through mindfulness. I wait for the individual to feel ready to express in whatever way is helpful for them. I believe and trust in their wisdom. When working, I 'look out of the other's window' (Yalom, 2010, p.18) and, in so doing, I try to see the world from that person's perspective. From this experience, there is then hope that the young person with autism will feel seen, understood and empowered.

The voices of the young people

I now offer feedback from young people with autism and traits that I identified as introverted. This is a small sample only, and the young people are from differing socio-economic backgrounds. The voices come from a mix of high functioning and low functioning individuals, and as such the expressions and articulations are unique. All the young people are in education: Mark and Drake attend an ASD base within a secondary school, and Joseph used to attend a mainstream secondary school.

Each student was invited to respond to the phrase, 'My experience of dramatherapy'. They took a sheet away and wrote their responses on their own without pressure or intervention. They were reassured that their comments would not affect their ongoing dramatherapy work. The school and the young people's parents and carers gave written permission for these comments to be included. Only pseudonyms were used.

Mark

Mark was referred for dramatherapy due to on-going concern regarding his anxiety levels and self-esteem. He was diagnosed with autism at an early age, and told me that until he was four he did not speak at all. The dramatherapy began when he was in year 8, aged almost thirteen.

Mark is highly articulate and presents as a young person with many thoughts and ideas. He stated from the start that he would like to attend sessions alone.

Much of the time, Mark would draw. This seemed to help him to relax and he expressed discomfort at moving this artwork into dramatic expression. He was a natural artist and began this work in pencil, initially alone. Sometimes he was silent, other times he shared his feelings and thoughts about family life and school life. After four sessions Mark asked me to draw alongside him. I interpreted this as a way for him to feel in relationship. By nature Mark is an introverted young man. In our sessions, he shared his private thoughts and feelings. As he reports below, had he been in a group, he would not have felt comfortable to express himself in this way.

Throughout the therapy, Mark reflected on his lack of confidence and in particular his anxiety. The work came to an end when he expressed that he felt more confident and no longer needed to talk or draw as he wanted to focus on joining mainstream classes that he had not had access to prior to dramatherapy. He successfully attended a number of new classes and pursued his love of music. Mark reported that the dramatherapy offered him a space to be accepted, listened to, and supported to feel okay with being who he was.

Mark's experience of dramatherapy in his own words

Dramatherapy helped me to express my feelings in a set-up that I felt was secure, caring and trustworthy. Any problems I had I could discuss with the therapist, who would be extremely caring and supportive.

What worked best for me was to have the session on a one-to-one basis as opposed to a group. This way I felt more comfortable talking about my problems when there was nobody else there. I preferred to draw and talk at the same time instead of acting, as this was for me the most efficient worry-free way of speaking to the therapist about my thoughts and feelings.

Thanks to the supportive therapist and a style of support that was compatible with my needs, dramatherapy helped me to improve my self esteem, confidence and wellbeing.

Reflection

Mark found the regular space and quiet of the sessions healing. His artwork began in the literal, where he drew guitars in pencil. This moved on to drawing how he felt in challenging situations in school. The final drawings were in vibrant colour and from his imagination. This suggested to me that by the end of the intervention Mark felt more able and free to move away from the literal to the imaginative.

Mark taught me to become quiet. If I offered interventions, he was able to say 'no' and make choices, which was empowering for him. If we place this in the context of how Mark saw his life, a life where he felt choices were constantly being made for him, and his sensitivity to feeling patronised, then we can see that in Mark's saying 'no' to my suggestions he was gaining the confidence to ask for what he needed. His artwork was his outward expression as opposed to more typical tools chosen from the dramatherapy repertoire.

Drake

Drake has a diagnosis of autism and attends an ASD base within a mainstream setting. He was referred to dramatherapy because of high anxiety levels, and he was finding it hard to make friends and manage the transition from primary school to secondary school. He would frequently become angry and frustrated, and was beginning to not want to attend the base.

Drake started his sessions in year 7, at the age of eleven. He was mistrustful and in our first therapy session he asked, 'What do you need from me?' In hindsight, this was a very appropriate comment. It helped inform me of what he might need. I understood from his closed body language and his initial choice to not attend followed by his pertinent question that he felt and thought that I might need something from him. He spoke about his fear of being judged and was not sure if he wanted to attend. Reassurance by staff and myself helped him to decide to try out the work with the proviso that he could choose at any point to stop. At the time of writing Drake had been attending dramatherapy for a year.

The dramatherapy intervention used with Drake was chosen by him after I told him a story in the first session. He decided that he wanted to create his own stories and this remains the main focus of his dramatherapy sessions to this day, although as will be seen he also worked deeply with a traditional fairy tale that he chose over four weeks.

Drake's experience of dramatherapy in his own words

It helps me to calm down when I am angry. Basically I am taking one of my favourite subjects and using it to calm me down. I feel I am not left out in dramatherapy. I feel I am listened to.

I enjoy making stories using my mind. They are about how I want to be when I am older. My autism used to be anger issues. Now I come to dramatherapy that doesn't happen anymore. I don't lose my temper so much.

I don't like my special needs. It makes me sound greedy, wanting more than everyone else is getting. That isn't really fair.

I normally like working by myself. Groups don't really work for me. I trust my therapist. We laugh a lot.

Reflection

Drake uses story as a means of communication. Analysis of the themes in his stories, suggests that they have changed gradually over the year we have worked together. He expresses anxiety and fear through his characters that are often alone and in frightening situations. In the beginning stages of the work, the main characters would find themselves in danger, running from perpetrators and trying to find safety. I checked each week where his ideas had come from, and only twice did he say that they were based on films or games that he had watched. In other words, it seems as though they were emerging from his imagination and unconscious (Kegan, 1946). These stories appeared to contain projected images of his loneliness, mistrust and anxiety.

Puppets and figures were introduced, and with these he was also able to re-enact scenarios that were current for him. He would invite me to play with him using puppets, and often wanted me to be the rescuer or a mother figure. At other times, I would become the 'witness' while he played or told a story alone.

Grainger (1992, p.106) writes about one-to-one therapy, suggesting that 'the dramatherapist in a one to one situation does not always work in role. At times, she may take a more distanced stance, encouraging the client to work on his own.' This role was important for Drake as he worked through difficult feelings through metaphor and symbol. He was aware that I was there, with him, as a witness.

More recently, Drake has become interested in listening to other stories. He chooses the story as I read the titles out to him. I then tell the story. His favourite is 'Hans My Hedgehog' (Grimm and Grimm, 1948). In this tale, a baby is born to a childless couple but the father rejects him because he is half boy, half hedge-hog. Hans grows up sleeping behind the fireplace, and eventually decides to leave home. A journey is taken on a cockerel and Hans is finally accepted for himself by a 'maiden'. A transformation happens, and Hans becomes a man.

Drake reflected on the character of Hans, likening him to a boy with special needs who is much misunderstood. He was able, after the second telling, to 'talk' to Hans. Through a 'hot seating' technique he asked me to become the character of Hans while he became the interviewer. He spoke to the character, saying that really what all people need is love, care and kindness, and that he thought hedge-hogs were 'really cool'. He reflected on the father in the story, criticising him for his rejection of Hans. He followed this by saying that he thought Hans had anger issues and that perhaps people were frightened of him. He said to Hans that he found it useful to try to see things from others' points of view. He reminded Hans that, even though there was a bad king, there was also a good king, who was kind and welcoming. This was a profoundly moving moment for both Drake and myself as we gathered that he was saying this about himself and all his friends with autism. He ended by saying, 'We all need love, care and kindness.'

This feedback reminds me of the importance of fairy tales in the work. Through dramatherapy, Drake was able to gain insight and awareness into his process through hearing, doubling and reflecting on this story. He did this by himself, with no direction from me. The story had a profound meaning for him.

Joseph

Joseph was diagnosed with autism at the age of two and a half. His parents referred him to dramatherapy. He had just transferred from primary school to a large secondary comprehensive. His parents shared that Joseph had found this transition difficult, in part due to some introverted traits as well as his autism. As explained by him during our earlier sessions, there were too many changes, too much noise, and too many people. He clearly needed time on his own to re-invigorate his energy and have his own quiet time. His parents were concerned for his wellbeing. The school was aware of his diagnosis, and he had a Statement of Special Educational Needs.

Joseph was struggling on a number of levels within the school environment. I was asked to offer him weekly dramatherapy sessions. Joseph presented as a polite, articulate young person. He was not keen to attend dramatherapy. He expressed that he saw no point in it, and he seemed self-conscious about needing this type of support. We did access creative methods of work, but only when he felt com-fortable enough with the relationship. It was the manner in which the therapy was delivered that mattered to him. Joseph experienced periods of depression and suicidal ideation. His self-esteem was low. My challenge was to find a way to help him. If there was too much noise, or too many people, or if some of his peers were unkind to him, Joseph would become overwhelmed and unable to calm himself down. It would be fair to say that the secondary school environment was challeng-ing for Joseph.

Joseph, now 22 years old, has a degree in script writing. When I spoke to him about this book, he was keen to share his experiences of dramatherapy in his own words.

Joseph's experience of dramatherapy – a retrospective view

I remember not particularly wanting to start seeing an in-school therapist at first, being under the impression that it would be tedious, dull and a complete waste of my 11-year-old self's time. This is, of course, why I am not in the stock market. I found the experience to be unexpectedly life affirming, helping me to express my feelings in a way I had never done before. For example, using toys to represent certain people in my life at that time. It gave me the ability to be more open and honest with people outside the therapy, knowing how I see them and not being afraid to confront them.

The honesty, more than anything, helped me the most throughout my time with the therapist. It so easily could have turned into an hourly session of false hope and condescending advice. The therapist, however, brought a lot of truth to our sessions together and never once made me feel like I was beneath her; she treated me as an equal, something I was rarely used to especially in the early years of secondary school. She stands today as being the first person to tell me that I had Asperger's syndrome, which in and of itself was a life-changing revelation to me, and if she hadn't been so upfront and earnest about everything we had talked about before then it would have been far more upsetting. After a very brief period of being under the false misapprehension that the therapist had just diagnosed a fatal disease unto me, I felt at peace knowing that I had learned this information through my most trusted ally at the time.

There is honestly little I can say that failed to work as well as dramatherapy. Had it been a much more straightforward therapy with your everyday run-of-the-mill psychiatrist, Sigmund Freud beard and all, then it perhaps would have been a different story. If that were the case I would be more aware that they were just paid handsomely to help deal with my problems, and likely would have seen me as just another pay cheque. I never got that feeling with this therapist, who always seemed genuinely interested in talking with me about anything.

When I first started seeing the drama therapist, I had only just made the transfer to high school and subsequently was finding it more and more difficult to cope with everyday life. And let me tell you, from personal experience, the mixture of new and pressing environments and raging young teen hormones rarely leads to good results.

Even in the first few sessions I was rebelling and made it clear that I did not want to be there. But here's the clincher . . . she listened to me. As a fairly young individual just starting a new and much bigger school alongside other young individuals, I was not a special snowflake and was overlooked by staff members who had far more important things to do in their day. With the knowledge that someone was actually taking my problems into account and not just dismissing it as an everyday occurrence, I felt tamed and even a little proud that I had made a connection to an adult in my time of need. Over the years as I repeatedly came to session after session I went in assured that no matter what I had to say there was someone paying attention. I feel this helped me become a stronger, more independent person. It gave me a sense of pride that I could be willingly the focus point of another person and that I could make that happen by my own merits. There were a few times when I could feel the dramatherapy working. One particular memory was of feeling anxious when my parents went away. I admitted in my session that I was frightened that something bad would happen. I remember colouring in moods felt in my body. Another incident was when I came in to the *session cross from an incident earlier in the day. I sat beside the therapist and did nothing! I sulked and did not say a word. The therapist had this patience with me. She was just there.*

I now have raised self-esteem and am confident with people in my own age group. I am much more open about who I am, happily discussing my Asperger's.

Reflection

Joseph took a long time to trust the process of dramatherapy. He thought it would be a challenging experience, where he might feel patronised. Artwork, objects and visual material helped him to gain insight, but, as he reports, the most valuable part of this extended piece of work was the listening, non-judgement and care. The diagnosis had been made by a paediatrician in his pre-school years. Through healthy and honest discussion with his parents and the school's Special Educational Needs Co-ordinator (SENCo), it was decided that telling Joseph about his condition would be really important for him. It had to be done in a contained environment and it was agreed that I would do this as we had established a trusting relationship.

Joseph's parents also wanted to write their thoughts about the dramatherapy sessions.

Joseph's parent's feedback

Our experience of dramatherapy for our son has been fantastic. Our son was diagnosed with autism at two and a half years old. During Infant School this diagnosis became clearer and he was designated as having Asperger's syndrome. From then onwards he was awarded a Statement of Special Educational Needs. Our son is highly intelligent and had few if any problems coping academically. In consequence he attended mainstream schooling throughout. His difficulties centred on communication – especially as he found it hard to pick up signals from those around him. The amount of hours and funding support he received varied through his school life, but it increased and was most needed during secondary school between the ages of eleven and eighteen.

He was introduced to dramatherapy soon after arriving at this school aged eleven. Sheer size of school, pupil numbers, and unfamiliarity made him frustrated and bewildered. This made him vulnerable to verbal and physical bullying and he found himself highly stressed and this was reflected in his behaviour. He became increasingly anxious and unable to express himself. This became amplified as he became a teenager. We, his parents, were unable to provide appropriate support.

The school agreed to fund regular dramatherapy sessions, which made an instant and big difference. It was a huge help for us to know that he had regular contact with someone he trusted, who was receptive, sensitive and knowledgeable about ASC and how this affected him personally. The therapy was non-judgemental, patient, and the therapist took time to allow Joseph to build trust based on exceptional listening skills. She used a wide range of ways and methods to help him express his feelings initially non-verbally through drama and art, eventually helping him to express more and more confidently in writing and verbally. He knew he could speak to the therapist in confidence, and we in turn respected his right to privacy. Knowing he had someone to turn to other than us has undoubtedly helped to develop and maintain the healthy relationship we enjoy today as his parents.

Reflection

Introversion traits were present throughout Joseph's sessions. He tried role-play but expressed discomfort with this. His need for privacy was great, and it was clear that, for Joseph, time away from the hordes between classes and in lessons reduced his high anxiety. Sensory overload at the beginning of our work presented itself. Joseph found crowding in the corridors particularly difficult, his agitation showing in his body and hands, with increased tics. He would sometimes say that he just needed quiet. I was always impressed with his strength to simply get through a day. He said throughout that it was a relief to attend dramatherapy sessions, to know that someone was there who empathised with him.

He spent a little of his school career mentoring another younger boy who also found school overwhelming and who had recently been diagnosed with autism. He also wrote a play about autism in order to try to convey to his peers how he experienced the world they all shared. Because of this play, which he also directed, friendships were deepened and understanding grew. Joseph was and is a courageous and sensitive young man.

The three young people who have written their feedback have used dramatherapy sessions in different ways. The more comfortable and secure they felt, the more they were able to express themselves The implication of what each has fed back is that the non-judgement and empathy from the therapist seemed to be key to their moving forwards. It was in the 'doing' and 'being' that this was able to happen. All three had traits of introversion shown in different ways. Mark was explicit in his communication about needing quiet, privacy and non-judgement. Drake, who had more energy and was keen to explore his life experiences through drama and puppetry, also expressed that he was more comfortable in a one-to-one setting. He too spoke of enjoying private time. Joseph said he can be sociable, but, again, he finds this stressful and needs alone time. The need for one-to-one sessions, privacy and low demand, was asserted by each through verbal and non-verbal means. These were acknowledged and accepted by the therapist and in so doing each young person expressed that this helped them to feel more confident and empowered.

Conclusion

This exploration evidences, through the words of the participants, that the combination of the 'doing' of dramatherapy, and the 'being with' of mindfulness is effective for young people with autism and introversion. These young people can find their unique voice and in their own time can express and explore what is meaningful and relevant to them. They can gain a sense of themselves and of their own value through being seen and heard, without expectations and without judgement. The commonly expressed theme from the young people taking part referred to the therapist's style of working. It was clearly significant to them that they had the space and time to unfold their thoughts, feelings and expressions *in their own time*. It was important to them that they could say 'no' to joining in with an offered exercise or sit for long periods without speaking.

This level of acceptance is not commonly experienced in everyday life and less so in school. Through story, art, role-play, silence, projected puppetry and quietly being together, some healing happens and we as dramatherapists are merely the midwives of a shared process.

In my experience, dramatherapy can help young people with autism and introversion to feel included. Their different ways of expressing can be seen, heard and accepted, initially by themselves. At the beginning of this chapter is a quote by a 13-year-old who says he wishes autism could be seen as just a combination of personality traits. This is important for us to hear. Each person with autism is so much more than the pathology; each person has his or her own unique personality. We must be careful and remember to use the art form with mindfulness and respect.

I would like to conclude with quotes from two writers with autism, Temple Grandin and Naoki Higashida.

> I think life is a continuum of normal to abnormal. The really social people are not the people who make computers, who make power plants, who make big hotel buildings . . . the social people are too busy socializing. (Grandin, 2011, p.5)

> During my frustrating, miserable, helpless days, I've started imagining what it would be like if everyone was autistic. If autism was regarded simply as a personality type, things would be so much easier and happier for us than they are now. (Higashida, 2013, p.16)

My thanks to all the young people who gave voice to their experiences.

References

Bainbridge, C. (2014) 'Introversion and the gifted child', available via www.giftedkidsabout. com (accessed July 2014).

Cain, S. (2012) *Quiet*. London: Penguin Books.

Gluck, J. (2014) 'Mindfulness and dramatherapy', in Rappaport, L. (ed.), *Mindfulness and the Arts Therapies*. London: Jessica Kingsley Publishers.

Grainger, R. (1992) 'One on one: the role of the dramatherapist working with individuals', in Jennings, S. (ed.), *Dramatherapy Theory and Practice 2*. London: Routledge.

Grandin, T. (2011) *The Way I See It: A Personal Look at Autism and Asperger's*, 2nd edition. Arlington, TX: Future Horizons.

Grimes, J. (2010) 'Introversion and Autism: a conceptual exploration of the placement of introversion on the Autistic Spectrum', available via www.psychologytoday.com (accessed July 2012).

Grimm, J. and Grimm, W. (1948) *Grimm's Fairy Tales*. London: Routledge.

Higashadi, N. (2013) *The Reason I Jump*. London: Sceptre.

Jones, P. (2011) *Drama as Therapy*. Hove, East Sussex: Routledge.

Karim, K., Ali, A. and O'Reilly, M. (2014) *A Practical Guide to Mental Health Problems in Children with Autistic Spectrum Disorder: It's Not Just Their Autism!* London: Jessica Kingsley Publishers.

Kegan, P. (1946) *The Psychology of C. G. Jung*. London: Trench, Trubner & Co.

Kurtz, R. (1990) *Body Centred Psychotherapy: The Hakomi Method*. Denver, CO: Life Rhythms.

Rogers, C. (2001) *A Therapist's View of Psychotherapy: On Becoming a Person*. London: Constable.

Yalom, I. (2002, 2010) *The Gift of Therapy*. London: Piatkus.

9

MOTHER, SON AND THEN SOME

On autism, dramatic reality and relationship

Maria Hodermarska

The Son writes from the role of Mother:

> *Confidence in someone else, it's a funny thing sometimes. Particularly building confidence in a relationship with someone else. It always feels like no matter how many times this happens there is always something that feels tangled up. No matter what happens each time, I am his mother and he is my son and then some.*

Introduction

I am a drama therapist in the US whose 21-year-old son is a college student and activist with interests in art and writing, and a person who functions somewhere on the autism spectrum. This chapter will offer reflections upon how the Son has utilized drama as a form of self-therapy to examine questions about his identity and relationships. Drama therapeutic core processes of 'projection, performance, empathy and distancing, representation/personification, and witnessing' (Jones, 1991, 2011, p. 8) are placed in a dialogue with key diagnostic criteria of autism—Theory of Mind and Self-Efficacy. This chapter is meant to contribute to drama therapy praxis and the emerging body of knowledge in the fields of drama therapy and disability-performance studies (Chasen, 2011a; Corker & Shakespeare, 2002/2006; Jennings, 2011; Sandhal & Auslander, 2008).

For the Son, role-play is his best way through life with autism because it 'empowers in order to make connections' (David, personal communication, September 21, 2014). This chapter explores how the literal and metaphoric performance of the Son's selves has been an essential part of his construction of existential consciousness. From the outside in, through performing the self and others, ultimately reversing roles and performing each other, we examine our relationship anew. Performance is and has always been the Son's vehicle to process experience, to consciously address areas of functional deficit, to reflect upon his being, to structure and coalesce his identity.

On the ethics of heuristic research and study of an intimate other

Building upon a clinical comment written for *Dramatherapy* (Hodermarska, 2013), this chapter is both a theoretical reflection on disability and performance and a form of heuristic, qualitative research into the Son (in his many selves). It should be acknowledged, however, that any attempt to theorize about the Son's being must take into account the relational power dynamics inherent in a caregiver–care receiver relationship.

The first step is the issue of consent, which bioethics philosopher Deborah Barnbaum (2008) addressed in her excellent meta-synthesis, *The Ethics of Autism*. Consent is a tri-partite process that requires 'understanding' of the research, the capacity for abstraction, and an 'appreciation for alternatives', including the consequences of not performing the action (p.189). We tailored our informed consent accordingly: (1) all recognizable risks and benefits have been discussed; (2) Mother and Son conferred about the benefits and risks in the presence of David's father and stepfather (both of whom reviewed this chapter independently and discussed it with David); (3) Mother and Son agreed that this chapter reflects a snapshot in time; (4) the Son has read and approved all material shared here; (5) we agreed not to use the Son's real name but to call him 'David'.

The investigation in this chapter is both ethnographic (the study of other people, their culture, phenomena, lived experience) and autoethnographic (the study of the researcher's lived experience). Qualitative researcher Carolyn Ellis (2007, p.3) in writing about ethical responsibilities in such studies of 'identifiable' and 'intimate others' proposed standards for what she called 'relational ethics' in research. This author has employed Ellis's standards, with particular attention to her recommendations as to how it operates in a *caregiving* situation.

Social constructivism, disability theory, and embodiment

Within the dramatic worldview, we see everything as socially constructed and performed. Even disability, in this post-modern sense, does not exist outside of social construction because it is a pure product of it. We create culture-bound, often medicalized categories of illness/health, ability/disability, into which people are placed based upon sets of criteria.

Drama therapists working clinically and aesthetically embrace psychological theories built upon the constructions of everyday life (regarding language and quintessence and exteriority). Theoretical bases for drama therapy (see Landy, 2008) are strongly influenced by the work in the twentieth century of constructivist sociologists and symbolic interactionists, e.g. Mead (1934), Cooley (1922), and Goffman (1959), theater artists like Growtowski (1998/2002) and Meyerhold (1978), whose dramatic principles were built upon examining embodied and sensorial essential-ism, and the pedagogy and politics of oppression (Friere, 2000; Boal, 1979/2006). These theories ask clinicians to consider deeply just how we represent the body and encounter/relationship. Tobin Siebers (2001) and Judith Butler (1990/2006) cautioned that this constructionism may be an insufficient means of understanding the materiality of bodies and the nuances of encounter between them, particularly where disability is concerned. Disability, Siebers (2001) argued, places bodies and encounters in a liminal space outside of normative social interactions. Social con-structionism for Siebers renders the disabled body and its experience unrecogniz-able as it 'privileges performativity over corporeality, favoring pleasure over pain, describing social success in terms of intellectual achievement, bodily adaptivity, and active political participation' (2001, p. 740).

The way through the deep challenges presented by studying an intimate other who lives with a disability is to encounter those challenges head-on with openness, care, and reverence, and then to find a way to 'play' within and from those challenges.

A definition of autism through lived experience of the son

> To a person living with autism, the world is like a bunch of different pieces of music playing all at the same time. You hear all the parts all at the same time rather than hearing things like an organized melody. And you explain these things in a precise way, because it is easy to get confused.
>
> (David, personal communication, September 24, 2014)

How does autism perform?

Is autism the performance of a disability (the consequence of atypical neuro-cognitive wiring)? Or is autism a performance of ability (an attempt by the person living with the condition at connection, interaction, through the means available)? Or is autism both? And, how does autism perform in relationships? Autism both limits and delim-its the relational drama requiring, at times, endless repetitions to forge safety and comfort and, at other times, the development of new ways of being in and compre-hending relational experience that fall outside of typical interactions. In our family, there is much time spent reviewing experiences where David is anticipating anxiety or fearing abandonment. We also have our own relational touchstones, including hand-over-hand assistance with shaving or slicing, that ground us in embodied rela-tionship (mimicking our earliest merged encounters)—we seem to return to these when Mother and Son feel abstracted and detached from each other.

The term relating, refers both to *responding to* and *telling a story about* something. If we strip away the surface show of autism, such as arm flapping, twirling, rocking, and poor eye contact, and look more deeply towards the broken cord of relating, we might see autism as *the* disturbance of representation and essentially, relationally, non-performative. There is no *mirror* to hold up to *nature*. But for drama therapists, locating all psychological difference within the dramatic worldview is our primary clinical mission, our praxis. As a drama therapist, therefore, the Mother examines autism as a 'clinical' form of self-performance and relationally regards this performance as reflecting something about a shared and co-constructed world.

Autism performs both our individual and communal fear of life's mercurial nature and its *instability* (Johnson, 2009). Autism also performs our fear of the *spontaneity* that is required in order to cope with such unpredictability (Moreno & Moreno, 1969). In the face of autism, we confront our profound anxiety not only with our own stuck-ness, but also with our fears that life may really offer no theatricality, no duality, no drama. Drama is inherently paradoxical and does not exist without two truths functioning in concert and in opposition simultaneously. The stage is the threshold through which the me/not me, real/fictive, both/and are performed (see Duggan & Grainger, 1997).

What, in the most basic sense, is being enacted, activated, demanded, and made conscious in the performance of autism in our family? If we regard autism's social challenges, obsessions, neuro-cognitive quirks, sensory difficulties, and general isolation as performance, what theater are we in? For some families it may be Beckett or the Greeks. For ours, it more closely resembles Monty Python's *Flying Circus*.

David in performance

> Whether I shall turn out to be the hero of my own life, or whether that station will be held by anybody else, these pages must show.
>
> *(Charles Dickens,* David Copperfield, *p. 1)*

What is being performed in autism may be the lack of duality or drama. It is also true that David's disability places him, ever-so-dramatically, between worlds. First, what is most true or consistent about people with higher-functioning autism is that they are as unalike each other as they are alike. David functions 'somewhere on the autism spectrum' but not at an easily defined point on a graph or within a strict set of criteria. Psychologists use the term 'sub-test scatter' to refer to the variability of skills as measured on psychological assessments of people with autism. Somewhere in the random explosion of psychological data of abilities present and absent, you will find David.

Second, David's life is, by his own accounting, '*(a) life in the theater*' (Mamet, 1977). When there is a part to play, he flourishes. When he is struggling to define the role, he is like Mamet's lonely veteran actor, Robert, wandering a bit aimlessly, seeking a role to play for dinner. Does he 'exist' outside of the *theater of* (his) *mind* and being (Whitehead, 2001)? Do any of us?

For David as a toddler, a chair was not something to sit on. It was an object to be examined and understood independent of its function, discovered by painstaking trial and error, not quick inference.

As his existential life of objects without subjects matured, the objects became roles. His interactions with the world became a collection of roles.

Drama therapist Landy (1996), following Artaud (1994), offers us the metaphor of a double life. Like an actor, secret agent, and most especially a clown, David is always conscious of his standing apart, his being just off to the side, odd, different. For someone who lacks certain metacognitive skills (thinking about one's thinking, awareness of how one thinks), David is surprisingly able to *play with* his awareness of this distance and, therefore, with his awareness of his relational challenges.

David is an excellent mimic. His mimetic skills are a happy consequence of the early echolalia and non-generative speech that distinguishes most children with autism. His impressions include, but are not limited to, Julian Barratt and Noel Fielding in their *Mighty Boosh* personas, Mick Jagger, Ray and Dave Davies, and, my favorite, Michael Caine. The characters appear both in directly quoted monologues and, spontaneously, in conversation. When the roles appear extemporaneously, though, they often speak in the third person in a form of reflective narration.

For example, David will readily offer me words of love both in and out of 'role'. From 'David' I get sweet and lilting (if not immature and melodramatic) professions of love: 'Oh Mother, I love you so.' From 'Michael Caine' I typically receive something ironic and decidedly more age appropriate: 'Michael Caine loves his mother more than Mitt Romney or Rudolph Giuliani.'

The reader will note a distinctly Anglophile bent to his cast of characters. David enjoys word-focused humor even though words can confound him. He finds British humor more word-centric and, oddly, more comprehensible than the slapstick of an American *Three Stooges*, for example. When visual processing is impaired, actions without words are perplexing. Action combined with language is easier for him to decode.

Like many people with autism, David lacks easy physicality; language actually frees him from bodily confines. Yet words can also, like the chair of his early explorations, be objects independent of purpose.

David is both an inspired producer of malapropisms and a witty punster, another aspect of his double life. Much like a Constable Dogberry (Shakespeare, 1969) or a Mrs. Malaprop (Sheridan, 1958), he can feel the sting of his 'wordly' otherness; at other times he is oblivious to it. And yet, he unapologetically and charmingly luxuriates in the lexical world of his making.

David participated in a drama therapy group for a year. He has been in therapeutic theater productions at his primary and secondary school. He joined a community teen theater and has performed in musicals with them. But the specific dramas presented here—except for the last one—are theatrical episodes that emerged spontaneously in the danger, heat, and terror of a moment requiring his transformation.

Theory of Mind and Superman

Theory of Mind is the ability to ascribe independent mental states to one's self and others in order to explain or predict behavior (Happé, 2003; Premack & Woodruff, 1978). People with autism tend to have severe challenges with this cognitive function.

Baron-Cohen's (1995) *false belief tests* established that persons with autism struggle to recognize the experiences of others as separate from their own.

The resulting ego-centrism places individuals at the center of the affective world. People with autism can find empathy challenging, which can complicate the basic dramatic action of role-taking and role-playing.

If the ability for distance defines relationship (Duggan & Grainger, 1997) between Self and Other, the functional struggle with Theory of Mind and the desire for physical and emotional proximity can at times actually obviate relationship for David. When he was a toddler, if I held David up to help me turn off the light switch in a room, he would take my hand and, with his hand over mine, guide my hand to turn the switch off. We were relating in an ego-centric way, not in the 'gesture-calls' that Whitehead (2008) attributes to healthy social mirroring. We were merged.

Superman

A persona of real meaning for David was Superman. Shortly after he turned seven, David's father told him that he was moving out. David held his beloved and already well-worn Superman doll close to his chest, facing outward, like a shield, as he listened to his father's announcement. Superman took the hit that day and protected David for a time (see Haen, 2011). But it was only when he was able to achieve *aesthetic distance* (Landy, 2008) from the role that he was able to use it functionally in relationship. Aesthetic distance refers to the range of affect and distance that extends from an abundance of emotion (without thought) to an abundance of cognition (without feeling). Aesthetic distance is the balance of cognition and affect.

After his father's departure, David took to having Superman with him at all times. Wherever he went, Superman would fly ahead and lead the way. Like any child at play, David was able to project his fearlessness outward in order to incorporate the role of the brave one into his mind theater. He would acknowledge that Superman had a different set of skills from his own. But the Superman role could easily become stuck, recursive, and pathologically protective.

By the summer of 2002, when David was eight, the Superman doll was in a state of rapid decay and could not be taken outside. David found an American flag at my mother's home on the Fourth of July. He put on a yellow shirt and a woman's neck scarf for a cape. He ran around the outside of the house with the flag, recreating a final scene between Superman and the villain, Nuclear Man, from the film *Superman IV: The Quest for Peace* (1987). In this role play, he not only activated a Theory of Mind, but he was able to embody the complexities of Role Theory (Landy, 2008), both hero and villain, role and counter-role. Clearly, where David lacks a Theory of Mind he achieves compensations through his *theatre of mind* (Whitehead, 2001).

Empathic mirroring, identity, and the stranger

Face to Face

At 16 years, David and his best friend embarked on a more elaborate film project in which his collaborator took aesthetic elements from the Bergman films *The Seventh*

Seal (1957) and *Persona* (1966) and David and his collaborator explored themselves as people living with disabilities. The film that they called *Face to Face* is an angst-ridden and decidedly non-linear teenage art film. With a Beatles song as the score, a young man trades his identity in the form of a wallet for the identity of another young man in the form of a mask. Wallet and mask are exchanged and each goes his separate way. The blurring of Self and Other, the longing for relatedness, and the obliqueness of relationship are well represented in the brief exchange.

I acted in this film in another scene and played the 'Mother's voice', speaking off camera to her son, who was played by David. The mother's words are clear and intelligible. The son's response was edited to sound like the 'Wa Wa Wa' used to represent the adult voices in Charlie Brown cartoons of my youth. From a general teenage perspective, adults always speak unintelligibly. In this case, the teen speaks unintelligibly and, therefore, the scene becomes a rather sophisticated commentary on the lack of comprehensibility of self that David and his friend sometimes experience.

Mirroring the mirror

> By holding the mirror of drama up to the mirror of social skills building neuron activity, we illuminate previously obscured angles . . . empowering a practical as well as metaphorical peripheral vision of sorts.
>
> *(Chasen, 2011b)*

The neural impairments of autism often limit eye contact and prohibit a process of face-to-face mirroring, as with the traditional actors' exercise. Autism itself originates in the profound disruptions in that visual–empathic axis. It is a mirror dysfunction.

Lee Chasen (2011a) amusingly reminds us of what happens when a person examines their bald spot in a three-sided bathroom mirror. 'When you hold the mirror up to another mirror you gain access to sides of yourself you are not usually able to see' (p.64).

There is no greater example of David's profound ability to mirror the mirror, than can be found in the origins of his 'Michael Caine' persona. In a fascinating hall of mirrors process, David's Michael Caine imitation (his mirror) emerged as his distillation of Steve Coogan and Rob Brydon's own imitations of Michael Caine (their mirrors too) in the film *The Trip* (2010). 'Michael Caine,' therefore, emerged for David from his literally mirroring a mirror.

I have come to recognize that for David social-mirroring (Whitehead, 2008) is a challenge when unmediated by role. David can find himself by taking on a role and then see himself reflected back. He can mirror the mirror.

But of course for David, mirroring is just the first part of the problem; his next, and perhaps greatest challenge, is knowing what to do with that information. Operationalizing, strategizing, and contextualizing become immense cognitive challenges. I believe that this is true for most people with high-functioning autism—putting the role into the scene or action, using it in relationship, is the hurdle.

Is it possible for a person with autism to distance self from self?

David mirrors people he loves with great intensity. Depending upon whom he is with, he becomes *his* version of *them*. It's his form of empathy. He has an uncanny ability to get into or encounter another person's zone of experience, mood, and humor. This is his functional taxonomy of roles (Landy, 1993). One is no less authentic than the simple neuro-typical understanding that we can be different with different people.

For David, this ability is part of his externalized self-ideations, as well as the aforementioned merging (residual from his early life). Both the external self-in-role and the accommodation of the other, serve at times to inhibit potential intra-psychic identity formation.

David's mirroring is unique in that the shared embodied experience feels uni-directional towards the other rather than bi-directional reflecting out and back to the 'I'. It is intended for the other but not as a way to know the self. When neuro-typical people look in a mirror, they are engaged in that transferential process of identifying and projecting. This is ultimately about looking for the 'self'. When David mirrors others, he is looking for *their* self. It is accommodation (adjusting to the information received) without assimilation (taking in new information and testing it against existing schemas) (Piaget, 1969/2000). David can imitate without the ability to generalize from the particular human experience in front of him to all experience. Each experience, each encounter, is another country to be explored without the ability to bring much information from the old world to the new one.

This mirroring/merging has challenged David. His schemas are specific and relationship bound. This behavior engages him joyfully with the world around him, but it also reflects a fundamental singularity. With his parents, siblings, grand-mother, best friend, he has three-dimensional relationships. With the general world, he has something else. It is this discrepancy that also is autism in performance.

Strangers

The day begins with my observation of David at a meeting with his case manager. David's gifts of externality manifest not only in his vocal expressions but also in his extreme fashion consciousness. He is tall, dark, and handsome, with a full face and dark brown eyes. He is thin and only partly shaved, with hair that appears tousled just so. The hair and partial shave are by accident, not on purpose. The hair and shave *appear* cultivated but are the product of his ability for only partial attention to shaving in the mirror and difficult sensorial challenges with running a comb across his head. He almost always wears a hat, cultivated for effect. His 'look'—splendid but usually a bit off in one way or another—is another way that he presents an identity to the world. But this morning he is rustling through a succession of his many residual autistic behaviors: leaving his belongings scattered around the meet-ing room. I watch him smell his hands, obsessively explore the stubble on his chin with his fingertips, stare out a window when someone is talking directly to him. This performance of his autism is an empty caricature that is impaired, stuck, and a-theatrical. This presentation of David's self, while appropriate to the scene, is at the same time a stranger to me. For David it is either a reflection of his anxiety or an attempt to self-soothe.

At dusk on this very same day, we are walking across a bridge over a highway to a guitar lesson. With his guitar strapped to his back, David says that he has consciously not worn a hat that evening: 'It would be too stereotyped to walk into the blues club [where the lessons are held] with a guitar and wearing a hat.' He is truly self-conscious in this moment. He is communicating as 'David'. His concerns are straightforward. How would other people at the club see him? Would he be seen as affected if he arrived in a hat? How could he present himself genuinely? David's autism is not in the least a part of this thought or expression. In this moment, I glimpse an 18-year-old young man who is so frequently a stranger to me, but whose reflection I catch in the mirror from time to time.

Self-efficacy, stuck-ness, and aesthetic distance

> Ability is not a fixed attribute residing in one's behavioral repertoire. Rather it is a generative capability in which cognitive, social, emotional and behavioral skills must be organized and effectively orchestrated to serve numerous purposes.
>
> *(Bandura, 1993, p.118)*

Self-efficacy is defined as confidence or belief in one's own ability to do things and to be effective at doing them. The Son-as-Mother's opening monologue here addresses this as a relational concept.

David once had a girlfriend who was far more interested in exploring physical intimacy than he was. He addressed her repeated advances by asking her, 'Do you want to play cards?', then left her alone on the couch when her repeated answer stated her preference for having her head on his lap.

David's 'stuck-ness' (his autism) and his corresponding challenges with problem solving were evident in his exchange with the young woman. From a drama therapeutic perspective, he was caught in a discrepant crisis between his desire to mirror and his desire for self-assertion. Most notably in this exchange, he lacked confidence in his own ability to assert his needs. David was also aware that most 19-year-olds in a similar situation might give in to the temptations such a scenario presented.

Later that afternoon, David began skipping around the backyard like 'Tinky Winky,' a children's television character, carrying what he called his 'man purse'. Observing David, I had some sense that there was a conscious level of exploration going on about identity and sexuality. David later confirmed that he was thinking that if he didn't want to be intimate with his girlfriend, then maybe he was gay. He wondered at his own fear and was openly able to both regress and return to the safety of child play and to engage with the possibility that his resistance might be due to his as-yet-unexamined sexuality. David's absolute willingness to be open to any explanation for his stuck reaction, along with the joyful bouncing with the 'man purse' that accompanied his thinking, was stunning. He determined that he was simply not ready for that kind of physical intimacy and has, since breaking up with that girlfriend, sought other friendships with young women. It was *embodied encounter* (Johnson, 2009) that revealed an absence of confidence in his ability to assert himself and it was embodied self-encounter through the role-play on the lawn that revealed both potential confidence and emergent problem solving.

For David, everything—even a hard meditation on sexuality—is reason for skipping, for celebration. Once again, David showed himself to be the hero of his own life.

Aesthetic distance

Landy has asked, 'On the scale of emotion and distance, where and how do individuals with autism locate themselves as actors in life's drama?' (R. Landy, personal communication, January 14, 2013). Can we assess the role-taking potential of autism on the scale of emotion and distance used in drama therapy? In observing David here as both ambivalent Romeo and Tinky Winky (Shakespearean romantic hero/children's TV character), drama therapists might consider the relationship between aesthetic distance in theater and therapy as it relates to the cognitive function of Self-Efficacy. In this example, David moved from experiencing himself as an ineffectual actor to an effective and transcendent human one.

Recommendations for future study

If, as suggested at the beginning of this chapter, we drama therapists consider high-functioning autism not just as a disturbance of representation but also as a performance of identity, then the following may be worth considering. The spectrum of autism potentially reflects the range of *aesthetic distance* (Scheff, 1979; Landy, 2008). Drama therapists might consider how aesthetic distance can be used to assess the presence or absence of certain cognitive functions like Theory of Mind, Executive Functioning, and Self-Efficacy. In this inquiry the author has attempted to put these concepts in a conversation that invites the focus of future research in drama therapy.

Role-playing of the kind that David has discovered is possibly a meta-state that can help him progress towards more frequent times when, as in the story of the hat, David is playing David. In entering the next phase of collaboration and our own form of participatory action research, we intend to explore the uses of aesthetic distance to reveal and ask questions about our relationship.

Conclusion

For me, the mother, this living inquiry process is a study in praxis. I feel deeper awareness and insight into my son's being. And, according to David, collaborating with me on this writing has given him awareness and insight into mine.

For David, my son, self is not a solipsism. Everyone is *not* like him. He does not have the profound deficits in Theory of Mind, Executive Functioning, Self-Efficacy, and facility with aesthetic distance that some people living with autism do. David's ability to enter into and play in *dramatic reality* (Pendzik, 2006) results in a transcendent Buddhist-like worldview: he is (potentially) everyone. This dramatic worldview is not theoretical for him. It is simply his way of being (see Baggs, 2007).

There is no denying, however, the profound sense of social isolation that comes with David's autism, which David himself acknowledges. With the constant rolling parade of service providers in his life, he is aware of how all relationships are contingent. In an attempt to tell another story of autism here, the story of the 'autos', the aloneness, must at least be acknowledged. I remind the reader that the origins for the word alone from the Middle English are 'all plus one'. The peopled world of David's *theater of mind* (Whitehead, 2001) stands in at times for the absence of emotionally intimate relationship.

The instinctual performance of his self and selves has permitted David to think through and be present in social interaction, to contemplate and integrate dissociated or challenging personal aspects, and to constellate meaning and establish ego identity. His form of self-performance permits him '[t]o be *and* not to be' (Landy, 2008).

David uses his drama as therapy without a prescription or a doctor or the dramatic structuring or lead of his mother. He found it on his own. It's organic. It brings him out onto the stage and into the world with related, generative meaning. It changes his being.

In Mamet's *A Life in the Theater*, the two actors critique a fellow actor's performance by saying that she has '[n]o fellow-feeling' (Mamet, 1977, p. 8). In some general sense, the same might be said of people with autism. But it does not reflect my son or how his disability performs. Exquisitely loving, loyal, guile-less, with his cast of thousands, my son is beloved by many. He is, indeed, *all* fellow-feeling, and '[a] fellow-feeling makes one wondrous kind' (Garrick, 1850, p.357). I believe that it is David's form of drama as therapy that helps make him so.

Acknowledgments

With gratitude to Jenn Dees, Liz Edwards, Tami Gatta, and Penn Rhodeen for their inspiring thoughts and questions.

References

Artaud, A. (1994) *The Theater and Its Double*, trans. M.C. Richards. New York: Grove.
Baron-Cohen, S. (1995) *Mindblindness: An Essay on Autism and Theory of Mind*. Cambridge, MA: MIT Press.
Baggs, A.M. (2007) *In My Language*. Retrieved from: https://www.youtube.com/watch?v=JnylM1hI2jc (accessed March 2015).
Bandura, A. (1993) 'Perceived self-efficacy in cognitive development and functioning', *Educational Psychologist*, 28(2): 117–149.

Barnbaum, D. (2008) *The Ethics of Autism: Among Them but Not of Them*. Bloomington, IN: Indianapolis University Press.

Bergman, I. (producer) & Bergman, I. (director) (1966) *Persona* (Motion Picture). Sweden: SvenskFilmindustri.

Boal, A. (1979) *Theatre of the Oppressed*. New York: Theatre Communications Group.

Boal, A. (2006) *The Aesthetics of the Oppressed*. New York: Routledge.

Butler, J. (1990/2006) *Gender Trouble*. New York: Routledge.

Chasen, L. (2011a) *Social Skills, Emotional Growth and Drama Therapy: Inspiring Connection on the Autism Spectrum*. Philadelphia, PA: Jessica Kingsley Publishers.

Chasen, L. (2011b) Web blog post for *Social Skills, Emotional Growth and Drama Therapy: Inspiring Connection on the Autism Spectrum*. Retrieved from: http://jessicakingsleypublishers/webblog (accessed March 2015).

Cooley, C. (1922) *Human Nature and the Social Order*. New York: Scribner's.

Corker, M. & Shakespeare, T. (eds.) (2002/2006). *Disability/Postmodernity*. New York: Continuum.

Dickens, C. (2000) *David Copperfield*. New York: Random House.

Duggan, M. & Grainger, R. (1997) *Imagination, Identification and Catharsis in Theater and Therapy*. Philadelphia, PA: Jessica Kingsley Publishers.

Ekelund, A. (producer) & Bergman, I. (director) (1957) *The Seventh Seal* (Motion Picture). Sweden: Svensk Filmindustri.

Ellis, C. (2007) 'Telling secrets, revealing lives: relational ethics in research with intimate others', *Qualitative Inquiry*, 13(1): 3–29.

Friere, P. (2000) *Pedagogy of the Oppressed*, trans. Myra Bergman Ramos. New York: Bloomsbury Press.

Garrick, D. (1850) *Library of English Literature: A Collection*, vol. II. Philadelphia, PA: E.H. Butler & Co.

Goffman, I. (1959) *The Presentation of Self in Everyday Life*. New York: Anchor Books Doubleday.

Growtowski, J. (1998/2002) *Towards a Poor Theater*, trans. Eugenio Barba. New York: Taylor & Francis Group.

Haen, C. (2011) 'The therapeutic use of superheroes in the treatment of boys', in Haen, C. (ed.), *Engaging Boys in Treatment*. New York: Routledge.

Happé, F. (2003) 'Theory of Mind and Self', *Annals of NY Academy of Sciences*, 1001: 134–144.

Hodermarska, M. (2013) 'Autism as performance', *Dramatherapy*, 35(1): 64–76.

Jennings, S. (2011) *Healthy Attachments and Neuro-Dramatic-Play*. London: Jessica Kingsley Publishers.

Johnson, D.R. (2009) 'Developmental transformations: towards the body as presence', in Johnson, D.R. & Emunah, R. (eds.), *Current Approaches in Drama Therapy, 2nd ed.* Springfield, IL: Charles C Thomas Publisher.

Jones, P. (1991/2011) 'Dramatherapy: five core processes', *Dramatherapy* 14(1): 8–15.

Kagen, M. (producer) & Furies, J. (director) (1987) *Superman IV: The Quest for Peace* (Motion Picture). USA: Warner Brothers Home Entertainment.

Landy, R.J. (1993) *Persona and Performance*. New York: Guilford Press.

Landy, R.J (1996) *Essays in Drama Therapy: The Double Life*. London: Jessica Kingsley Publishers.

Landy, R.J. (2008) *The Couch and the Stage: Integrating Words and Action in Psychotherapy*. Lanham, MD: Rowman & Littlefield; also available at https://www.psychologytoday.com/blog/couch-and-stage/201204/be-and-not-be [accessed April 2016].

Mamet, D. (1977) *A Life in the Theater*. New York: Grove Press.

Mead, G. (1934) *Mind, Self and Society*. Chicago, IL: University of Chicago Press.

Meyerhold, V. (1978) *Meyerhold on Theater*, ed. E. Braun. New York: Bloomsbury.

McEldowney, K. (producer) & Renior, J. (director) (1951) *The River* (Motion Picture). France/USA: Oriental International Films.

Moreno, J.L. & Moreno, Z.T. (1969) *Psychodrama*, vol. 1. Beacon, NY: Beacon House.

Pendzik, S. (2006) 'On dramatic reality and its therapeutic function in drama therapy', *The Arts in Psychotherapy*, 33(4): 271–280.

Piaget, J. (1969/2000) *The Psychology of the Child*, trans. Barbel Inhelder. New York: Basic Books, Inc.

Premack, D. & Woodruff, G. (1978) 'Does the chimpanzee have a Theory of Mind?', *Behavioral and Brain Sciences*, 4: 515–526.

Sandhal, C. & Auslander, P. (eds.) (2008) *Bodies in Commotion*. Ann Arbor, MI: University of Michigan Press.

Scheff, T. (1979) *Catharsis in Healing Ritual and Drama*. Oakland, CA: University of California Press.

Shakespeare, W. (1969) *Much Ado About Nothing*, William Shakespeare: The Complete Works. Baltimore, MD: Penguin Books

Sheridan, R. (1958) *The Rivals*. Woodbury, NY: Barron's Educational Series, Inc.

Siebers, T. (2001) 'Disability in theory: from social constructionism to the new realism of the body', *American Literary History*, 13(4): 737–754.

Whitehead, C. (2001) 'Social mirrors and shared experiential worlds', *Journal of Consciousness Studies*, 8(4): 3–36.

Whitehead, C. (2008) 'The neural correlates of work and play', *Journal of Consciousness Studies*, 15(10–11): 93–121.

10

BEING MEN

Men, Asperger's and dramatherapy

Adrian Benbow

This chapter is an investigative study of dramatherapy with men with Asperger's syndrome. Becoming a man is confusing and complicated, with social, personal and intimate hurdles to negotiate. Asperger's may multiply these issues. Three case-studies present examples of the author's dramatherapy work with men with Asperger's and a broader context is given through referencing data collated from questionnaires completed by other dramatherapists working with this client group. This study will provide insight into the specific support dramatherapy can offer.

Introduction

When a care organisation I worked for opened a new home for men with Asperger's, a resident expressed interest in dramatherapy and I arranged to meet him. I had worked with people on the autistic spectrum before, but I was immediately struck not only by this young man's ability, but also by his aspirations of a 'normal' life rarely possible within care environments.

Adolescence and the journey into adulthood have always interested me. This life stage is so rich in conflicts and deeply influential in developing adult confidence and persona (Stevens, 1990). My personal experiences of difference during adolescence prevented me from feeling able to work therapeutically with teenagers for many years. Growing up gay in a non-gay world was difficult, and eventually finding a place to fit in was incredibly powerful. Andersen's ugly duckling struggles to see his own value until he meets others like him, the other swans. I wondered if Asperger's men, growing up in a neurotypical world, perhaps feel similar and that connecting with others with the diagnosis in later life helps them belong and feel good about who they are.

The National Autistic Society (NAS) describes Asperger's as a form of autism where people 'have fewer problems with speaking and are often of average, or above average, intelligence. They do not usually have the accompanying learning disabilities associated with autism, but they may have specific learning difficulties', such as dyslexia, dyspraxia, ADHD and epilepsy (2015). Asperger's often remains undiagnosed as those affected are generally competent in many areas of life though struggle with the triad of impairments: social communication, social interaction and social imagination (Wing and Gould, 1979).

Asperger's may lose its specific name in scientific classification, in favour of the generic 'autistic spectrum disorder', but I believe it will continue as a powerful, proud social label where those affected can experience belonging. The community is coming together. The NAS's contributor-led magazine *Asperger United* ('*AU*') is quoted within the chapter. Numerous social media groups and internet websites indicate developing understanding and a new social charter for people affected. Autobiographies embrace the diagnosis: 'An enormous weight had been lifted and I felt hugely relieved – almost "high"' (Rowe, 2013, p.21).

While Asperger (1944), writing under the Nazi eugenics policy of 'removing' disability, advocated and defended social inclusion for his study clients, today the socially inept but mathematical genius has become a modern archetype (Stevens, 1990). Arts and media have raised interest in Asperger's with the 2014 film *The Imitation Game* about code-breaker Alan Turing, who brings several of this chapter's themes together: Asperger's, gay, punished for his difference in a different time, and suicide victim. There is also Mark Haddon's best-selling novel *The Curious Incident of the Dog in the Night-Time* (2003) and Channel 4 Television's *The Undateables*, in which disabled people look for love.

Understandably not all find the media 'hype' useful: 'a self-aggrandising sub-group of individuals, celebrating and trivialising the condition from which I and so many others have suffered for so long . . . when the curiosity of the audience has been satisfied, attention will be re-directed towards the next freak on the block' (Edward, *AU*, 2014, pp.12–13).

Introducing the themes

Some people with Asperger's live 'normal' independent lives and others progress with effective support and encouragement. Many know the opportunities available and what it is they seek. What can be difficult and challenging is how they identify and connect with the particular world they want to inhabit: fit in socially, pursue preferred careers, find a partner, have relationships and children. Wilmer-Barbrook (2013, p.47) felt adolescents in her dramatherapy study believed 'prospects of further education and future employment were both inconceivable and impossible . . . these deeply held beliefs had seriously affected their self-confidence and self-esteem.'

None of the men included in this study lives independently, though many are working towards this; the potential for conflict or disagreement perhaps parallels an endless adolescent period where guardian and child struggle to balance the dependence–independence axis. Erikson (1951) suggests working through conflicts that typify the stages of psychosocial development help us move on. The conflicts of identity and role confusion (puberty and adolescence) and intimacy and isolation (young adulthood) are the most prevalent in this study.

Asperger observed exaggerated male behaviour patterns in his clients (1944). Baron-Cohen (2010) has researched this idea of gender characteristics, such as systemising (male) and empathising (female), and statistics appear to support the theory of an extreme male profile. This might affect the Asperger's man trying to adapt to a competitive society with other men, where his drives are extremely male, yet his language perhaps overly formal and un-male. Connecting with female qualities might also be harder: 'My attempts to get to know a member of the opposite sex in a special way have all ended in complete failure due to my shyness and lack of social skills, and I'm pretty much resigned to accepting that it's not going to happen for me' (Colin, *AU*, 2014, p.4). Additionally Asperger's men greatly outnumber Asperger's women.

Attwood's (2006a) Foreword to Henault (2006) says: 'The area of sexuality is more than a collection of facts and data. There are issues of self-perception and self-esteem, attitudes and prejudices, past experiences, empathy and intimacy' (p.9). Men with Asperger's often feel isolated, with fewer close friendships where they feel confident to discuss sexual matters; some typical adolescents might even enjoy misleading the naive person with Asperger's (Attwood, 2006b). Accessible pornography provides functional learning, but it ignores the intimacy of relationships. Henault (2006) finds that 'individuals with AS have been open-minded and curious' (p.11) and advocates researching sexual needs to develop effective support. Most of my male Asperger's clients had experienced difficult situations around sexuality, through inappropriate behaviour, or by being taken advantage of.

Informal resources suggest a high proportion of Asperger's men identify as gay, but academic research has not proved this. Hellemans et al. (2007) reported high incidence of bisexuality in their male sample, while Gilmour et al. (2011) found increased incidence of homosexuality amongst women and a high percentage of asexuality in both sexes. Dewinter et al. (2015) discovered that boys with ASD were more tolerant towards homosexuality than the control group. Perhaps men with Asperger's are less affected by social constraints and more open to the spectrum of sexuality and, like the gay community, making new rules.

Whatever the sexual orientation, 'some people with autism just don't have the people skills to develop a relationship' (Colin, *AU*, 2014 p.4). 'Far from being loners, most of us are lonely . . . my place seems to be with other mainstream outsiders, diagnosed/diagnosable or not . . . I have just barely enough social contact to stop me feeling worthless and pointless' (Ruth, *AU*, 2014 pp.14–15).

Mind, the mental health charity, says, 'Being lonely can . . . contribute to mental health problems, such as anxiety and depression' (2015). Hare et al. (2014) compared the thoughts of adults with Asperger's with those of neurotypical adults around real-time everyday experiences and found that people with Asperger's were significantly more anxious. Paquette-Smith et al. (2014) studied the issue of suicide in people with Asperger's and found that 35 per cent of their sample had attempted suicide at least once.

There is a clear case for additional support for men with Asperger's.

Introducing the study

Most literature about dramatherapy and Asperger's focuses on children, although Wilmer-Barbrook (2013) presents dramatherapy research with adolescents and Porter (2014) writes about adults, but not specifically men.

At the core of this study are three case-studies from my practice, which I believe typify my work with men with Asperger's. Names have been changed and identifying details have been removed for confidentiality. Each gave consent for inclusion in the chapter and guardians were informed.

I invited members of the British Association of Dramatherapists working with men with Asperger's to complete questionnaires. The data generated provide a comparison and contrast to my work, which I will use to illustrate and comment on my case-studies. Four dramatherapists (two female, two male) completed questionnaires covering five male clients with Asperger's or a closely aligned diagnosis (pragmatic language disorder was included). The dramatherapists will be referred to as DTA, DTB, etc., to maintain confidentiality for their clients.

Questions covered the dramatherapists' experience and training, work context (setting, funding, duration, evaluation), client background and referral, dramatherapy interventions and therapeutic relationship. Outcomes focused on relationships, self-esteem and confidence, anxiety and well-being.

Introducing the men

Each case-study client has experienced group and one-to-one dramatherapy. Robert was working with a dramatherapist colleague, and was subsequently referred to a men's group I was facilitating. Simon and Paul live in the same residential home for men with Asperger's. Prior to individual dramatherapy, they worked in a group until other members moved on or took up work placements.

Combining the three case-studies with the five questionnaire clients, this study has a sample of eight men aged between twenty and early forties. Five live in residential care, one with family, one in university accommodation, one in a forensic setting. Two have no additional diagnoses, four have mental health issues, one has a learning disability and one has a physical disability. The higher-than-average incidence of mental health issues in people with Asperger's is noted above; DTA reports that a dual diagnosis created a 'complex issue . . . of staff wanting to isolate which part of his behaviour was personality disorder and which part Asperger's'.

Introducing dramatherapy

Two questionnaire clients funded sessions privately; all others were funded by organisations (residential, health, youth services). For questionnaire clients one-to-one sessions outnumber group 4:1. Reasons for referral to dramatherapy included: transition/change, social/self expression skills, anxiety and anger. None of the clients self-referred, but during the assessment process consent to therapy is discussed and sought. When sessions start, the client begins to identify their own goals and the work often focuses directly on these.

Case studies

Robert

Robert is in his early twenties and moved from his family home 4 years ago, to live in supported housing. He shares his home with a man he claims is intellectually inferior, 'a loser' whom he finds deeply annoying. Robert has been attending a weekly dramatherapy session for 3 years, in a closed group, with four service users and two therapists. He was referred to support anger outbursts against his house-mate, and to develop a greater self-understanding. The general group aim is to provide a supportive space to explore personal issues that members wish to bring. No other group member has Asperger's: they have mild/moderate learning difficulties and some have additional mental health issues.

Robert maintains an overtly optimistic approach to life, failing to realise, or choosing to ignore, that his differences might create problems in life. He believes he is handsome and talented, with the world at his feet. In this supportive group, we listen and accept what he says, though we try to encourage him to explore other possibilities through the dramatic media.

Sessions start with percussion instruments to express individual feelings and energies, before tuning into the group by playing together. Sharing news is structured, with turn-taking and themes (something enjoyable, annoying etc.). We often play games with a group task (like keeping a ball in motion) to begin connecting physically. Improvisation exercises warm up the imagination and the main exercise usually involves acting, story-work, role-play or further improvisation. After creative work, we reflect on the session and close with a song.

Robert enjoys acting and creative writing, and is theatrical in his manner. He rarely plays 'ordinary' characters, preferring roles of power, especially villainous ones acted with a dash of melodrama or camp; he often plays the outsider, imbuing a sense of separation from the others.

Robert's head is full of creative stories. Initially he brought to the group a prepared poem or scenario to act out that he resisted moving away from. However, as relationships and trust have developed, he has gradually allowed drama to develop as a shared group experience, being more able to sit with the unknown. The creative negotiation appears to mirror his home situation, and the relationship with his house-mate is explored obliquely.

Robert says that fantasy helps him deal with the 'awfulness' of real life. He values the opportunity to step away, escape difficulties, and find something vibrant and fun. Through creative play and interaction, we can explore fantasy and social issues in a symbolic and refreshing way.

The factual part (structured news) of the session means Robert has been able to share some of the challenges in his life (his thinning hair, a rejected manuscript), knowing that creative work will follow. He has begun dating and has asked some practical questions that he seems comfortable to share in a men's group. Robert has engaged with others and now sees himself as part of the group. Banter appears to represent something of the sense of belonging, enabling social conventions to be explored and social risks to be taken.

Dramatherapy has supported Robert to be more comfortable with his peers in the *group play* and he has developed tolerance of others. His *creative fantasy* has become better balanced, allowing 'not knowing' and 'being in the moment'.

Group play

In a group, the Asperger's client may find it difficult to field the unexpected contributions of peers, to understand their meaning and take on board information outside their own interests. Peer respect and relationship seemed important to support Robert to be happy in a communal home. DTB writes: 'They didn't think they were going to enjoy dramatherapy and they were worried about the noise levels and the behaviour of other clients.' Often inter-personal issues are best confronted within a group, which DTA acknowledged by recommending, 'a group process at a future point; the aim being to develop his experience of listening to others and being with others'.

The weekly structured dramatherapy session provides a safe container for the exploration of issues. In sharing the space with others, Robert found he didn't need to rely on pre-prepared ideas and developed resilience to cope with the unknown, which could support his home life. DTB's client, 'benefited from being in a group that he had no control over . . . he had to learn to tolerate his peers'.

Play forms an important part of sessions. Winnicott (1971) believed the potential space where play and creative activity takes place is the space between the mother and baby, which shifts and changes as the needs of each develop over time. It is in play that the individual can be truly creative, and in this way use the whole personality. This sense of changing space is perhaps emulated by therapist and client, or society and individual, as the Asperger's client processes and re-balances their independence–dependence needs.

The all-consuming energy of play allows Robert to let go of his usual patterns, to do new things and see people differently. Play can be the simplicity of a simple ball game, shaking his hands to expel the surge of excited energy, or the more sophisticated banter (often described as beyond the reach of Asperger's people) that bonds him to the other group members, through competitive conversation, controversy and innuendo.

Play is apparent in improvised drama where participants come together in conflict as their chosen characters. Robert's enjoyment of high-status eccentric roles was possibly the initial reason he kept attending. Landy's Role Theory (1993) suggests that exploring other roles might help find more balance in life, and provide a channel to challenge some beliefs. Exploring being powerful when elsewhere perhaps Robert felt powerless was useful, although getting him to access new, unknown perspectives to help him empathise more, has had limited success so far.

Creative fantasy

Robert told me with excitement about a macabre fantasy screenplay he had written about a cat with nine lives. I explained that 'nine lives' was an expression about feline good luck, not a reality. Robert questioned this vehemently, then his body visibly slumped. I had burst his fantasy bubble.

Attwood (2006b) suggests that people with Asperger's can create a fantasy life with imaginary friends and social success to compensate for feelings of isolation and limited understanding. Many use fantasy as an enjoyable, mental escape: it is only problematic when it becomes delusional. Robert separates from his fantasy by acknowledging and reflecting on it.

DTA's client expressed 'enjoyment and at times laughter in the doing of the creative work . . . being inside the fairy-story and being able to repeat again and again the experience as the central focus'. Fantasy worlds hold others too: 'Sometimes the pressure of life can get a little bit too much . . . and for me, watching an episode of *Doctor Who?* is the perfect escapism' (Laura, *AU*, 2015, p.6).

Paul

Paul is 40 and has Asperger's and a mild learning disability. He attended group dramatherapy before starting one-to-one work. When funding changes threatened the sessions, the enthusiasm for story-making that he had conveyed to his family in regular telephone calls, led them to support him financially to continue dramatherapy. Initially referred simply because it was a service offered to residents, work around assertion, confidence within a group and developing imagination were quickly identified as personal aims for Paul.

Initially Paul appeared to struggle with taking initiative and needed prompting for every task: removing his coat, sitting down, session exercises. Assertion seemed difficult and contributing to group conversations appeared stressful. There was much laughter and Paul joined in, but it was not always clear if he understood the humour, and he rarely made jokes himself.

He seemed to value the session structure. The opening ritual, warm-up exercises and other practical sections seemed to help him access the more creative and 'unknown' parts. Turn-taking meant he could relax and anticipate the focus on him and the contained space to talk. Sharing weekly news gives value to activities and interests and Paul began to speak for longer on broader topics, such as describing the latest movie plots, or his golf techniques.

The group warm-up included choosing a piece of music for everyone to dance to, supporting movement expression and freedom to play. One group member cut diagonally across the dance space with energy and enthusiasm, while another made convoluted body shapes as if exploring physical potential. At first Paul stood motionless, but over the weeks, watching and learning from the others, he began to sway, then lift his feet and deliberately move other body parts. His balance issues were explored through dancing and also he developed confidence and connection to the others.

Paul worked with creative stories in the group, but his imagination really began to develop when we started one-to-one sessions. Assisted by images, words or costumes, we journeyed together in drama, from science fiction to ancient folklore. He was fascinated by stories of kings and knights and began to leap into improvised drama armed with just a character and trust that a story would follow. Riding horses became a recurring theme and staff reported that he had begun visiting a local stable and was gradually getting closer to riding the horses. The symbolic characters supported him to develop real relationships with horses.

Paul is now more able to work in abstract ways. A box of postcard images prompts the initial response of making a physical shape or mime with his body, leading to exploring thoughts, and personal experiences through acting or talking. For example, he responded to a photo of an aeroplane by standing up and lifting an imaginary suitcase; he waved and said, 'Bye! I'm off on holiday!', and began an improvisation.

In the sessions, he has shared childhood memories that I understand he appears to avoid sharing elsewhere, often mentioning his strong sense of privacy. Perhaps being more open about his past has also enabled him to share more aspirations and opinions too.

For Paul, the dramatherapy *session as a container* is important and has enabled him to access *symbolic imagination and creative risks*.

Session as a container

People with Asperger's often focus on patterns and rituals, to avoid social challenges. Paul's confidence grew as the familiar structure seemed to provide safety to explore and take risks, within and outside the session. 'These structures can be very helpful to people with fragile egos . . . the process of opening and closure, containing within them an experience which brings people close to unconscious material, becomes a model for strengthening the ego's necessary defences' (Syz, 1996, pp.152–153).

Paul learnt new skills through watching and copying his peers, and, contained within the session, felt safe enough to try out new things in front of them. Their responses gave affirmation to what he was doing. Jones (2007) develops this concept of peer audience within the group as 'active witnessing'. DTB describes a rolling improvisation game called 'Park Bench', where the client was initially anxious when peers played rogue characters and seemed confused by laughter. Through repetition, he became comfortable watching and eventually playing a character: 'he developed his ability to be observed, initiate and respond to conversations as well as make eye contact'. Accepting the audience's laughter as 'normal' was significant, as although he could not always control the environment, the exercise made it easier to manage and he could stop it at any time.

DTC noticed that, as her client's confidence grew, the work changed: 'more role-play, defining methods of intervention, less relaxation or mindfulness techniques'. As in the case study of Paul, developing enthusiasm for action, rather than connecting passively, facilitates translating the issues from the mind into the physical creative space. Jones says: 'By physically participating in a dramatic activity the body and mind are engaged in discovery. Issues are encountered and realised through physical embodiment' (1996, p.113)

Symbolic imagination and creative risks

Paul beginning to trust his imagination with an improvised story is significant and brave. Picking up the suitcase and saying the accompanying words both clarified his idea and invited me into the drama, initiating a story outside his personal experience. 'Whatever the unconscious may be, it is a natural phenomenon producing symbols that prove to be meaningful' (Jung, 1964, p.102). Paul produced useful symbols spontaneously as 'the language of metaphor or symbol frees the exploration' (Jones, 1996, p.235).

Paul's exploration of symbolic imagination contrasts with the questionnaire responses, which indicated client preference for direct/factual work in one-to-one dramatherapy. However, symbolic work appeared more common in group dramatherapy, perhaps as the medium to connect several people's material.

Simon

Simon was in his thirties when he started dramatherapy, working for 4 years in a group followed by 4 years in one-to-one therapy. General aims around motivation and expressing anger appropriately were highlighted.

Simon has an imposing stature coupled with a trait of staring at people. He was annoyed that his parents were so present in his life and seemed constantly engaged with an almost adolescent battle with authority. It was hard to watch his younger brother having a job, a wife and a young family – everything that Simon appeared to want but was out of reach. Being stuck seemed central to Simon's life: his ongoing mental health issues, his peers moving on, and his being temporarily incapacitated in a road accident. He was difficult to motivate, his sleep patterns were erratic, and cigarette breaks punctuated everything.

Simon loved cracking jokes and laughing loud and hard, using humour to connect with others. While he could tease, he was also sensitive, appearing to respect and support his peers in the fight against authority.

He was playful with music, singing along and devising dance routines to engage with the others. When we worked one to one years later, we rarely danced, but when we did, he reminisced about the old routines and the peers who had moved on. As the work and trust developed, he discussed his feelings more and explored sensitive issues.

In the group the men created scenarios involving kings, judges, doctors and policemen, engaging with powerful figures beyond their actual experiences. Through dramatic play Simon seemed to free himself from parents and carers to become optimistic about an independent life. In one-to-one sessions, role-plays supported him to practice 'real life', for example job interviews and work placements.

Mental health medication and low motivation meant that Simon often appeared tired. I brought the story of 'Rip van Winkle' to work with in the session. He sleeps for 20 years and escapes his miserable life, awaking to find freedom and independence. It impacted Simon deeply.

'Angus and Charlotte' was an improvisation Simon created and revisited frequently. It was the story of young lovers, from their initial meeting and early romance, to proposal, wedding, and birth of their child. These imaginary lives seemed to support him to make sense of his own aspirations, and through role-playing them he briefly stepped into the life he said he wanted. Angus was a salesman for Aston Martin (Simon's passion) played by Simon and he put me in the role of Charlotte. Through their ongoing lives Simon thought more deeply about his yearnings and rehearsed relationships with others. When dramatherapy was finishing and we worked towards the ending, he returned to 'Angus and Charlotte' and decided they should divorce and go their separate ways. This mirrored our own pending separation, and indicates the special role of the therapeutic relationship.

Simon responded particularly to *role-play* and trust in the *one-to-one relationship*.

Role-play

Simon's connection to real-life scenarios parallels the study clients, and role-play was the dramatherapeutic intervention most commonly used, though defining it is not straightforward.

Landy (1993) suggests that personality comprises a system of roles and that playing different roles in drama enables us to re-balance and work through personal problems. Role-play is a widely used tool for teaching interpersonal skills; Mesibov (1984) researched the positive social effects for people with ASD. Nelson (2010) has published a practical work-book on role-playing scenarios to support people with ASD. Role-play is 'experimenting with social skills and conversations, to find ways to deal with situations he finds difficult' (DTD) or to 'expand on what he talks about and open up other ways of thinking about situations' (DTC).

Williams suggests that people with high-functioning autism are encouraged throughout life to copy others and perform to appear normal; therefore, in drama, 'being able to consider their characters as "performances", the person may come to feel more in control of when they put on characters and not feel so out of control in the hands of other people's expectations to be someone other than themselves' (1996, p.300).

Porter (2014) acknowledges, 'The character acts as a conduit for the client to engage with areas of ability and function that can then be assimilated into their own sense of self' (p.89). For Simon 'Angus and Charlotte' became a safe rehearsal space, stirring strong aspirations and ongoing hopes of a relationship.

All the study respondents claimed difficulties in 'the present' was the greatest focus for the men, often devising role-play from the weekly news, or more specifically 'all that is going wrong in the "here and now" of daily living' (DTA). Role-play, however, can be challenging when there is, 'almost no insight into how he may affect or impact the dynamics within any inter-personal situations' (DTA). DTD's client 'likes to role-play what he would like to happen, which is not necessarily for his benefit'. Several clients achieved what had been practised, like travelling independently or interacting in a shop, suggesting role-play had increased their confidence and assertion.

DTC says role-play 'has developed [his] capacity to notice when he might be being experienced as intrusive', and various roles have helped prevent over-identification. 'He tended to identify and stick with one group. Now, he is more able to think that he can have different groups of friends who reflect back to him different aspects of himself.'

One-to-one relationship

Healthy attachments (Bowlby, 1979) are difficult for men with Asperger's: 'relationships are something I really struggle with. I either go nowhere near people or I get unhealthily attached' (Alex, *AU*, 2014 p.10). The nurturing and non-judgemental therapeutic relationship for some connects with archetypal roles, while for others it is new and unknown. 'It was holding and containing for him that I remembered his ongoing life issues and his stories of past, present and future' and 'calling out a "hello" was quite a fragile thing to do within a group of peers . . . a good example of where he showed a sense of attachment' (DTA).

Colin (*AU*) wants to 'find someone with whom I could talk things through regularly . . . talking sometimes reduces my stress levels considerably and enables me to make progress' (2014, p.4). Regular time with an independent person trained to listen is important. DTD notes, '[e]njoying the interest the therapist has in him' and '[r]espect for each other as human beings', which perhaps replicates the supportive friendships that Asperger's men find hard to maintain. Talking enabled Simon to unburden and reflect on important things, like managing anger and sexuality. The process of talking and expressing needs, models effective communication in other relationships too.

The male dramatherapists believed their gender was significant in compensating for absent or ineffectual role-models – talking with a man, about issues facing men. While Angus was probably Simon, I could not really be Charlotte, and had I been female I don't think he would have been so confident interacting.

The humorous exchange between Simon and me indicated an equal relationship. DTD described 'banter': 'sparring and humour, edginess and sarcasm which often challenged and annoyed the client, but allowed for the complexity of adult relationship as opposed to parent–child which was often present'.

The female therapists also thought gender was influential. For DTA, it 'enabled the work to develop because it was an opportunity to be in the company of a female'. While for DTC there was an erotic transference, but once it was discussed, 'working with a member of the opposite sex and talking about relationships has been valuable and has given him a sense of it being manageable'. One male drama-therapist mentioned erotic transference in considering the therapist's gender.

Outcomes of dramatherapy

Improved relationships

All clients show evidence of developing relationships, one to one with the drama-therapist and also with peers. Rowe says, 'the mental effort and sensory challenges I experience are just about manageable with one person. Two is pushing it. Any more is just overload' (2013, p.142). Therefore Robert and DTB's client both made great strides in managing their groups and DTB concludes, 'He is now working in a café, serving customers and making sandwiches. This . . . demonstrates the progress he has made.'

Increased self-esteem and confidence

Self-esteem and confidence is present in the creative achievements of Robert, Paul and Simon. DTC spoke of confidence in socialising more. Coping with emotions and expressing them better was also attributed to increased self-esteem. One therapist noted the reduction in potentially psychosomatic illness, which is sometimes associated with Asperger's.

Reduced anxiety

Paul's ability to initiate more could indicate reduced anxiety. The dramatherapists suggested improved tolerance of the environment, or greater control over life demonstrated reduced anxiety: 'whilst he likes to try and plan his day he doesn't experience the same levels of stress . . . he can't control his environment . . . but he can survive this without any trauma occurring' (DTB). DTD interpreted diminished anxiety as 'socially unacceptable behaviours have reduced'.

Increased well-being

Increased well-being seemed evident in a stronger sense of self-direction. Additional comments included maturity, responsibility, improved emotional lability and reflecting in a more balance way. 'Ongoing mental health is well supported by sessions and has improved . . . . He gets bored, but is stimulated by the sessions, because it is the intelligent, intellectual element that stimulates his needs' (DTD). DTB thinks: 'this client now has a purpose and direction in his life. He feels part of society and he contributes to it.'

Conclusion

This chapter has documented dramatherapy work with men with Asperger's and has highlighted particular client-relevant issues. Three case-studies have presented some dramatherapy practice and outcomes, which have been contextualised by data from questionnaires, and references from the worlds of dramatherapy and psychology.

The dramatherapy techniques that seemed particularly relevant to these clients, were improvisation (Boal, 1992), story-making (Gersie and King, 1990) and role/role-play (Landy, 1993). These appear to have supported clients to identify which life experiences they would like to explore, rehearse and reflect upon. The therapy enables developing confidence and self-esteem, while supporting the potential disappointment and frustration between aspiration and reality.

The Asperger's community is currently re-defining itself for a modern world. In a final parallel with the gay community, perhaps there are lessons to be learnt. Many gay men have enjoyed newfound freedom, but now, addressing emotional needs and psychological resilience seem emerging priorities. I believe accessible therapeutic support will continue to be necessary as men with Asperger's embark on their own meaningful journeys.

I hope this chapter has conveyed something of my commitment to this work, and my sense of the three wonderful men who agreed to allow their stories to be shared in this way. It has been impossible to document all the fascinating thoughts and interesting ideas from dramatherapists who completed questionnaires. Hopefully more people will write about dramatherapy with men with Asperger's in the future.

References

Asperger United: Relationships edition (2014), p.77.
Asperger United: Fandom edition (2015), p.81.
Asperger, H. (1944), translated and annotated Frith, U. (1991) 'Autistic psychopathy in childhood', in Frith, U. (ed.), *Autism and Asperger Syndrome.* Cambridge: Cambridge University Press, pp.37–92.
Attwood, A. (2006a) 'Foreword', in Henault, I. (2006) *Asperger's Syndrome and Sexuality: From Adolescence through Adulthood.* London: Jessica Kingsley Publishers.
Attwood, A. (2006b) *The Complete Guide to Asperger's Syndrome.* London: Jessica Kingsley Publishers.
Baron-Cohen, S. (2010) 'Empathizing, systemizing, and the extreme male brain theory of autism', available at: http://www.publicpriorart.org/xml/20/1/1/4962/6102/20.1.1.49 62.6102.xml [accessed April 2015].

Boal, A. (1992) *Games for Actors and Non-Actors*. London: Routledge.

Bowlby, J. (1979) *The Making and Breaking of Affectional Bonds*. London: Tavistock Publications Ltd.

Dewinter, J., Vermeiren, R., Vanwesenbeeck, I., Lobbestael, J. and Van Nieuwenhuizen, C. (2015) 'Sexuality in adolescent boys with Autism Spectrum Disorder: self-reported behaviours and attitudes', *Journal of Autism and Developmental Disorders*, 45(3), pp.731–741.

Erikson, E. (1951) *Childhood and Society*. London: Imago Publishing Company.

Gersie, A. and King, N.R. (1990) *Storymaking in Education and Therapy*. London: Jessica Kingsley Publishers.

Gilmour, L, Schalomon, M. and Smith, V. (2011) 'Sexuality in a community based sample of adults with autism spectrum disorder', *Research in Autism Spectrum Disorders*, 6(1), pp.313–318.

Haddon, M. (2003) *The Curious Incident of the Dog in the Night-Time*. London: Jonathan Cape.

Hare, D.J., Wood, C., Wastell, S. and Skirrow, P. (2014) 'Anxiety in Asperger's syndrome: assessment in real time', *Autism*, available at: http://aut.sagepub.com/content/early/201 4/05/07/1362361314531340.abstract [accessed April 2015].

Hellemans, H., Colson, K., Verbraeken, C., Vermeiren, R. and Deboutte, D. (2007) 'Sexual behavior in high-functioning male adolescents and young adults with Autism Spectrum Disorder', *Journal of Autism and Developmental Disorders*, 37(2), pp.260–269.

Henault, I. (2006) *Asperger's Syndrome and Sexuality: From Adolescence through Adulthood*. London: Jessica Kingsley Publishers.

Jones, P. (1996) *Drama as Therapy: Theatre as Living*. London: Routledge.

Jones, P. (2007) *Drama as Therapy Volume 1: Theory, Practice and Research Second edition*. London: Routledge.

Jung, C.G. (1964). *Man and His Symbols*. Aldus Books. Reprinted 1990, London: Arkana, Penguin Group.

Landy, R. (1993) *Persona and Performance: The Meaning of Role in Drama, Therapy, and Everyday Life*. London: Jessica Kingsley Publishers.

Mesibov, G.B. (1984) 'Social skills training with verbal autistic adolescents and adults: a program model', *Journal of Autism and Developmental Disorders*, 14(4), pp.395–404.

Nelson, A. (2010) *Foundation Role Plays for Autism: Role Plays for Working with Individuals with Autism Spectrum Disorders, Parents, Peers, Teachers, and Other Professionals*. London: Jessica Kingsley Publishers.

Paquette-Smith, M., Weiss, J. and Lunsky. Y. (2014) 'History of suicide attempts in adults with Asperger syndrome', *Crisis: The Journal of Crisis Intervention and Suicide Prevention*, 35(4), pp.273–277.

Porter, R.J. (2014) 'Making sense: dramatherapy with adults with Asperger's Syndrome', *Dramatherapy*, 36(2–3), pp.81–93.

Rowe, A. (2013) *The Girl with the Curly Hair: Asperger's and Me*. London: Lonely Mind Books.

Stevens, A. (1990) *On Jung*. London: Routledge.

Syz, J. (1996). 'Working with symbol in the mental health centre', in Pearson, J. (ed.), *Discovering the Self through Drama and Movement: The Sesame Approach*. London: Jessica Kingsley Publishers, pp.149–156.

Williams, D. (1996) *Autism: An Inside-Out Approach*. London: Jessica Kingsley Publishers.

Wilmer-Barbrook, C. (2013) 'Adolescence, Asperger's and acting: can dramatherapy improve social and communication skills for young people with Asperger's Syndrome?' *Dramatherapy*, 35(1), pp.41–56.

Wing, L. and Gould, J. (1979) 'Severe impairments of social interaction and associated abnormalities in children: epidemiology and classification', *Journal of Autism and Developmental Disorders*, 9(1), pp.11–29.

Winnicott, D.W. (1971) *Playing and Reality*. London: Tavistock Publications.

Websites

National Autistic Society (2015) Available from http://www.autism.org.uk (accessed April 2015).

Mind (2015) Available from http://www.mind.org.uk (accessed April 2015).

Film and television

The Imitation Game (2014) Film. Directed by Morten Tyldum. [DVD] UK: Studiocanal.

The Undateables (2012–15) Television. Available from http://www.channel4.com/programmes/the-undateables/on-demand (accessed July 2015).

11

'REMEMBER ME'

Dramatherapy with adults who have autism and complex needs and are non-verbal

Adrian Benbow and Jane Jackson

Introduction

Not so long ago, people with severe autism, profound learning disabilities and complex needs were predominantly cared for in large residential hospitals, on communal wards. We believe that in those environments disabled children grew up to be neglected adults, damaged further by years of insufficient stimuli, some losing the ability to walk, or developing repetitive movements, gestures and behaviours as a means of creating stimulation for themselves.

The authors of this chapter both joined a dramatherapy team in one such residential hospital as newly qualified dramatherapists and were greatly impacted by the histories of their clients.

Over the past twenty years these hospitals have all closed and the residents have moved into the community. Though their lives are very different now, many live with the memories of the past.

There is little literature that is specifically about dramatherapy with adults who have autism and complex needs and are non-verbal. Lindkvist, founder of the Sesame Institute, describes work with this client group, developing 'Movement with Touch' (1981 and 1998), which is documented by Jones (1996) and Pearson (1996). Sesame has further in-house material (Lindkvist, 1997; Graybow, 2008).

Jones's (1996) case-study details story-making techniques, and some of the dramatherapy literature on people with learning disabilities includes references to autism, complex needs and being non-verbal (Booker, 2011; Chesner, 1995; James, 1996a, 1996b). It is our aim in this chapter to add to the evidence of the efficacy of dramatherapy with these clients.

It was difficult to find a useful description for complex needs from the UK, although the term is in common usage. An Australian report by the Department of Human Services (2003) describes complex needs as including one or more of the following – mental illness, learning disability, acquired brain injury, physical disability, behavioural difficulties, social isolation, family dysfunction, alcohol or other substance abuse. The National Autistic Society (NAS) adds other conditions that may be diagnosed alongside autism, such as attention deficit hyperactivity disorder, dyspraxia or dyslexia (2015).

A recent Department of Health (DoH) strategy document (2014, p.36) states that people with autism are more likely to experience mental health problems, but that 'poor mental health is not an inevitable consequence of having autism' and gives guidelines on communication, risk assessment, and adapted treatments and therapeutic environments (DoH, 2015). An NAS report found that in England one third of adults with autism 'say they have experienced severe mental health problems because of a lack of support' (Rosenblatt, 2008, p.5). This echoes our experiences of working with long-term hospital residents.

The term non-verbal refers to people with no or few words. If words are limited, then there is a lack of spontaneous language; words may be copied from others without understanding meaning, known as 'echolalic speech' (Baron-Cohen, 2008, p.18). Sometimes language is understood but not used – 'receptive language' (Karim et al., 2014, p.26). A person without words may still use 'vocalised sounds to communicate' (Chesner, 1995, p.17). But vocalisations may be 'self-stimulation rather than overt communications' (Booker, 2011, p.16).

Our challenge was to find a way to put the unspoken into words, to develop academic investigation in an area where little literature exists; to evaluate drama-therapeutic techniques in cases where the client could not tell us how they were feeling. We wanted to share this work and compare our professional stories and experiences with others. We remember those people from our early days, continue to work with this client group, and support others through clinical supervision and placement management. Jackson (2011) has also researched in the field of self-harm in adults with learning disability.

Being without spoken language and living with additional complex needs means those people's experiences are not easily able to be told first hand. Therefore, it is up to those who support them to speak on their behalf, to share their stories. As dramatherapists, we adopt varied media to discover exciting ways to reach out to people, so that new forms of language without words are given value (James, 1996a, 1996b). Through the process of attunement (Kossak, 2009) we notice and respond to the clues that our clients give us through their body movements, gestures, breath and vocalisations, leading to the potential for a developing therapeutic relationship of secure attachment (Bowlby, 1988). We use the developmental stages of embodiment, projection and role (Jennings, 1998). Working with clients, we focus and respond to our own transference (Rogers, 1990) and countertransference (Heimann, 1950). We attempt to reflect their experiences verbally and non-verbally, begin to understand their world, and offer therapeutic interventions. The work can creatively introduce alternative forms of communication for our clients, who may feel stuck through lack of language, their autism, their complex needs and the difficulty of being understood by others.

As practitioner/researchers, 'one of the things we must do to counteract the effects inherent in the fact that our views are . . . invariably and intrinsically biased – is make proper acknowledgment of this' (Grainger, 1999, p.124). To counteract our bias, we developed a questionnaire to investigate dramatherapy with this client group. Eleven dramatherapists completed questionnaires, with data on twelve clients. Our methodology was underpinned by Smith and Osborn (2008, p.53) where 'the participants are trying to make sense of their world; the researcher is trying to make sense of the participants trying to make sense of their world'. We also use illustrations from the authors' own practice through vignettes from four case-studies, for which consent was obtained. Names have been changed, with no identifying features given.

The researched data is therefore presented in two forms:

1. Results and commentary on questionnaires, which provides a context of dramatherapy work in the field.
2. Detailed vignettes and analysis derived from the authors' own case material, interspersed with direct quotes from the questionnaires.

Questionnaire results

1. Respondents and their backgrounds

Eleven dramatherapists completed questionnaires; nine were female, and two male. The age range was 31 to 52 years (average 43). Most were white European; one identified as mixed race.

Five dramatherapists trained at the Royal Central School of Speech and Drama (Sesame) (as did Benbow), four at the University of Roehampton (as did Jackson), and two at the University of Hertfordshire. Generally, however, they described using several methods of orientation, including person/client centred (eight), psychodynamic (four), ritual theatre model (three), the Sesame approach (three) and Jungian (two; see Jung, 2000).

Years since qualification ranged from 2 to 22 (average 11). The location for practice was southern UK, except one in the Netherlands. Dramatherapists worked between 9 months and 20 years (average 7 years) at the client organisations referred to in the questionnaires.

Direct quotes from the questionnaires are used to illustrate the findings, and to maintain confidentiality dramatherapists are each referred to with the prefix DT and a letter, for example 'DTA', 'DTB'. Several commented on their enthusiasm to contribute to this under-represented topic.

Comment

The gender, age and ethnicity of the dramatherapists were as we expected, compared with the British Association of Dramatherapists membership data

(BADth, 2007). The 'Movement with Touch' focus of the Sesame Method is suited to this client group; therefore, we expected more respondents from this training, but it was not the overall majority. The variety of methods and influences named reveals the eclectic, fluid and practice-sharing nature of our experience of working as dramatherapists in the UK. Although we predicted work with this client group to be long term, we were surprised to see that both years since qualifying and years at the host organisation were high.

2. Settings and referrals

Over half of the sessions took place in day centres, with two each in NHS services and care homes, and one in a college. Day centres most frequently funded dramatherapy from their own budgets; the rest were funded by the NHS, personal budgets, colleges, homes or charitable grants.

Individual sessions outnumbered groups (2:1). One group used a model where each client was supported one to one by a dramatherapist. One group was open/drop-in. All sessions were weekly.

Dramatherapy referrals came from support staff, specialist community teams or previous therapists. The main reasons for referral were to encourage creative expression and develop relationship. Communication, trust and well-being, family dynamics, change and loss, behavioural difficulties, self-harm, and abuse also featured.

Comment

One-to-one dramatherapy costs more per client than group work. However, the responses indicate that funders for this client group understand the need for individual work and prioritise it.

3. Clients

Work with twelve clients was included in the questionnaires – eight men and four women. The youngest was 19, and the oldest were in their sixties, with the ages distributed evenly. The majority lived in residential care homes and some lived with family. Three had a twin sibling and two of these siblings also had autism.

Most frequently the dramatherapists identified their clients as having a learning disability, and/or behaviour that is challenging or self-harming. Mental ill health issues, repetitive patterns, social isolation, emotional dysregulation, abuse, neglect, and physical disability were also mentioned. All clients were ambulant.

The use of repetitive movements was referred to throughout the client descriptions. Dramatherapist N (DTN) wrote: 'she is continually engaged in a repertoire of repetitive behaviours every waking moment of her life'. Other presenting features seemed varied – touch, eye-contact and voice volume were mentioned frequently, but there was no particular trend noticed. The clients' relationship with their senses was significant. DTH wrote, '[the] client is not comfortable in his own body, often experiencing physical pain and feelings of being overwhelmed by a variety of sensory factors'.

The non-verbal aspect of clients and the limited use of words were both described in a detailed range of terms. Four had no words, one was 'a selective mute'; two used vocalisations, and two repeated language. Levels of language comprehension were varied and unclear. Some clients used Makaton or PECS (Picture Exchange Communication System).

Of the twelve clients, six were continuing in dramatherapy. Two ended because of funding, one was a time-limited provision, two dramatherapists left their posts, and one client was ready to end the work. There was disparity over the length of intervention: six had accessed dramatherapy for under a year, three for between 1 and 5 years, and the longest were 5, 12 and 16 years. All the dramatherapists advocated long-term work with this client group.

Comment

Although there are nine males with autism to every female with autism in England (NHS, 2009), our findings (2:1) are less differentiated. In this small sample, potential evidence supported studies into the theory of genetic factors influencing autism (Freitag, 2007). Against expectations, all the clients (questionnaires and case-studies) were ambulant.

Case studies

The authors' views and dramatherapy practice will be represented through vignettes from four case-study clients. Written consent was obtained for each client from their guardian.

Margaret

Margaret is in her sixties and has a moderate learning disability and autism. She lives in a small care home with two women of similar age and ability. All of them previously lived in large institutions. Margaret understands language very well but does not speak; she communicates through gesture, vocal sounds, smiles and occasional eye-contact. She was referred to dramatherapy to reduce her anxiety when expressing her feelings, and to develop relationships. She received one-to-one dramatherapy for four years.

Hannah

Hannah developed autism and severe epilepsy after childhood meningitis. She is now in her forties and lives in a home for people with a range of learning disabilities. She is a strong-minded woman able to make choices. Her occasional words seem like childhood memories, spontaneously naming people, animals and food. She appears to communicate through gestures, strong eye-contact and clear facial expressions. She leads people by pointing or taking them by the hand, and says 'no' using a hand gesture. She communicates anger with body poses, and rage is sometimes expressed by harming others. It is thought she has some understanding of the life she could have had. She was invited to be part of an ongoing dramatherapy session with some housemates, to explore creative expression, emotional support and relationship building, but her attendance was sporadic. Therefore one-to-one dramatherapy at her home had the additional aim of increasing attendance at the group.

Dean

Dean is in his forties and lives in a home with several men with varied learning disabilities and some behaviours that are challenging. Other people have autism, but Dean is the only non-verbal resident. The original referral to dramatherapy identified that he isolates himself from others by staying in his room. Dean has received weekly one-to-one dramatherapy for six years. He expresses himself through movement; he is active and extremely physically fit. Dean seems to create a separate world by using repetitive jumping, patting rhythms on his body, tracing lines on his head and creating visual stimuli with his hands. He appears to use his voice to add intensity and occasionally his energy can build to levels where self-harm occurs. Sometimes his energy is low and he spends time in bed.

Daniel

Daniel was in his early twenties. The severity of his autism had led to self-harm, which left him blinded in one eye and partially sighted in the other. He wore a sports helmet during periods of destructive energy and would often go unprompted to put it on when these feelings were building up. He had his own specially adapted house and two-to-one support. He was driven by sensory stimulation and wanted to touch and smell everything, to feel for vibrations and textures and to experience movement. Dramatherapy sessions ended after six years of one-to-one work. Sadly, Daniel died unexpectedly a year later.

Remembering the client work

The following section explores the client work. Headings have been taken from the questionnaire, and the methodology of Smith and Osborn (2008) used to review the most common phenomena, illustrating these with quotes from the dramatherapists and commenting on each section with vignettes from our own case-studies. Information is collated under the headings of *therapeutic relationship* and *dramatherapy interventions*.

Therapeutic relationship

We believe that the therapeutic relationship (Clarkson, 2003) is at the centre of dramatherapy work with this client group. Adapting to the particular needs of the client and developing a sense of truly being with them is a central aim for the dramatherapist.

'The sessions had an outline structure which allowed a high degree of flexibility to meet the client's needs on that day . . . the client was invited to engage as much or as little as he wanted, with no expectations on how he should respond' (DTB).

Vignette 1

The session boundaries of a regular uninterrupted space at the same time each week can become flexible to increase inclusion. Daniel's need for sensation made staying in the room difficult, so sessions took place when the building was quiet, so it could all be part of the session space. One room was our base and we tried to start and end there. Daniel liked spinning on an office chair, and became lost in this sensory stimulation. I began to mark each revolution by tapping the chair. Gradually he allowed me to interact more by stopping the spin and changing its direction. Daniel also found a partially enclosed corridor with little stimuli, which he began to visit each week. He would stop and drop to the floor here, as if sheltered from stimulation, and I could be there with him. Once he moved closer and rested his head on me for a few seconds before standing up and moving on. This connection grew in repetition and duration over time.

Vignette 2

Although Hannah's choices were respected by staff, on occasions her refusal was challenged (around medication, personal care etc.), often leading to her behaviour becoming challenging. In dramatherapy it was important that every choice was hers and she would be accepted on her terms. By acknowledging everything that she brought, she perhaps gained a sense that I was comfortable with her every aspect, and therefore could support her wholly. This meant I would be with what she needed to be with, and hopefully empower her by accepting and exploring 'no'.

DTD states, 'my role as a witness to, and container of, the client's expression is fundamental to the progression of his/her therapeutic process . . . by allowing that potential space to exist and thrive, both client and therapist can discover a mutual, interactive language.'

From this place of a developing therapeutic relationship, different interventions are offered by dramatherapists to engage the client.

Dramatherapy interventions

Dramatherapy interventions are plentiful, and are methods of conversation that enable the dramatherapist to listen, attune to, and enter into the client's world.

Interventions are person centred, and may be suggested with various aims in mind. Offering creative possibilities in our work is exactly that – an invitation to proceed in a certain way. A client may consent or reject, so close attention needs to be paid to the client's own ways of communicating this.

Sensory materials and story were at the top of a list of thirty creative stimuli used by the dramatherapists. However, when asked about the top interventions preferred by these clients, the results were different. The top intervention favoured by the clients was touch, second was movement, recorded music was third, holding was fourth, followed by objects, voice, mirroring, song and percussion.

Touch and holding

Touch was the top intervention preferred by clients in this study. Porter (2014, p.33) states that 'touch is shown to be a necessary tool to calm, reassure, hold, contain and make contact with clients . . . with the therapist "*reaching out*" not only to the body but to the depths of the psyche.'

DTP explains that, working one to one in a group, they were 'close enough to each other so that the dramatherapists could offer body contact, body holding and gentle massage . . . in a very intuitive, client led manner.' The intention of this process was to achieve a sense of 'being seen and acknowledged' whilst 'trying to verbalise for the client feelings, sounds and thoughts.'

DTA's client was 'sometimes unaware if his touch was too strong . . . connecting physically was partly about enabling him to have a sense of his own strength and energy, and also feel that of another. This could potentially enable him to monitor for himself his own physical boundaries.'

Touch was used with all of the case-study clients and became an important part of the therapeutic relationship.

Movement

Jennings (1992, p.15) states that 'the human body is the primary means of learning'. Supporting a client to develop a stronger and healthier relationship with their body helps them to build a greater sense of self. 'A client may come to experience physical communication as an area of ability and success rather than disability and failure' (Chesner, 1995, p.47).

Dramatherapists use the body through sculpts and movement to generate meaning and language that does not rely on words. It is an essential tool for communication and expression, and therefore of particular use for people who are non-verbal.

DTA 'developed the client's movements through offering extension or changes of position, so he could witness his own patterns and potential variations. I encouraged him to notice his peer's movements, and to try them, fostering an appreciation of difference (without focusing too much on repetitive patterns). We explored Sherborne's relationship play (1990) – caring, supporting, shared, and "against".'

Vignette 3

> *Dean notices that I use my body to be in his world, to connect with and witness his rhythms and energy, from vigorous movements to quiet time, from elation to despair. Eye-contact increases when we are moving together. The emotions appear more joyful. By regulating tempo and use of space in my movements, I try to energise him when his motivation seems low, or calm him when energy seems overwhelming.*

Mirroring

DTB states that 'mirroring and attuning were part of every session . . . to facilitate a connection . . . and give indications of what might usefully be explored.'

Vignette 4

> *Mirroring our clients' movements and expressions can deepen their sense of self. Margaret selected music each week and we listened together. I joined in mirroring her rocking movements and hand gestures. This felt as if emotional content was being expressed through her body, and by mirroring this, I was listening to and being with it. She could see that strong feelings could be expressed and contained without fear of being overwhelmed. A sense of play developed and through this, eye-contact and familiarity grew.*

Chasen (2011) noticed how children with autism were fixated with their reflection in a mirror, pulling faces and captivated by their own movements. This led to the realisation that they had difficulty in perceiving a sense of self.

Vignette 5

> *Dean chose sometimes to work in his room, which has a large mirror, and often watches his reflection. Working alongside him, sharing with his movements and making eye-contact through the mirror seemed to provide a place of a safety from which he could witness himself relating to me.*

Music, voice, song and percussion

Musical interventions cover many areas, and can be passive or active, literal or imaginative. There can be cultural familiarity or the challenge of something new.

DTA describes the use of song. 'Initially, my client would only sing solos, stopping if we joined in. Over time, he became accepting of singing with others, becoming less fixed in his isolating patterns, and more engaging socially.' This client also developed his voice as 'a method of expressing frustrations without resorting to self-harm'. This is reinforced by Jackson (2011, p.102), who states that through 'mirroring and amplifying a client's vocals . . . feelings were not built up internally but released outwards'.

Percussion was used in a variety of ways. Sometimes a drum might be used 'so that the client could express through the rhythm, how he was feeling that day . . . and other percussion was used for play, to illustrate a particular emotion, or to add sound effects to a story' (DTA).

Vignette 6

> *Daniel pressed his face onto an electric keyboard to experience the sensory vibrations. I began playing the other keys and bringing in the sense of melody; gradually he began striking individual keys himself, and made his own tunes. When the keyboard broke, he transferred this developing musical skill to playing the glockenspiel, suggesting the music was now more important than the vibrations. He had developed a new method of creative expression.*

Objects and sensory material

Several dramatherapists facilitated the projective play method of offering objects (figures, small world miniatures, ribbons, shells, pebbles). Some people with autism find eye-contact challenging, so focusing on objects enables a more comfortable method of working together. DTG describes a 'tray of small objects' from which 'we will both pick one, explore on our own, then use them to interact. This interaction will be based on his ideas as much as possible. Then we will tell the story of this using the objects.' DTH's client always requested 'toy figures', which were used with sensory items to create a 'sensory landscape' to journey into.

Vignette 7

> *Objects were used to engage Daniel, and seemed his way of marking territory. As he journeyed through the building, he picked things up, carried them and dropped them somewhere else. My familiar object box placed in the dramatherapy room gave him something to return to and helped establish the room as a base. I carried objects too and they became a way to mirror Daniel and establish connections.*

DTA offered objects as 'a way for the client to release frustrations – to squeeze or throw', and puppets came to have additional significance. 'Using the dog puppet, the client made it "bite" his hand, and during this, he stopped biting his own hand – the puppet was doing it for him, which was a safe alternative to his own self-harm.'

Story

No one described the use of story in any detail. Story can be used as a container for the work, to give dramatic distance from client material, and to enable deeper exploration of emotions or roles. However, 'due to client difficulty in processing language, I used story rarely, unless I had accompanying props to illustrate and use' (DTA). None of the case-study clients responded particularly to story.

Evaluation and outcomes

In evaluating the sessions for this client group there needs to be attunement with the individual and a strong sense of their communication; anything that is recorded could be seen as subjective or biased. Some dramatherapists used recognised evaluation tools, devised their own, or used informal resources within the workplace procedures.

Using 'Goal Attainment Scoring' (Turner-Stokes, 2009) DTA saw 'the client achieving higher for these goals, so less self-harm, more peer contact, and initiative through choice and use of objects'.

DTH uses the 'Guernsey Community Participation and Leisure Assessment' (Baker, 2000) showing more frequent client participation, and the 'Checklist of Challenging Behaviour' (Harris et al., 1994) 'revealed that the frequency of . . . challenging behaviours . . . had markedly reduced' (DTH).

The authors and the dramatherapists saw the role of staff feedback as important in measuring change, through discussing factors such as behaviour or peer relationships. Dramatherapists need to be transparent and informative about the work, whilst maintaining confidentiality, and agree that 'feedback from staff about the client's mood/behaviours/external influences between sessions has been helpful in identifying the possible impact of or on the dramatherapy' (DTD).

Client reviews enable written reports to be presented to the multi-disciplinary team. DTB writes, the reports 'have evidenced . . . changes in his behaviour and the way he interacts with others during and outside the sessions . . . and the benefits of continuing dramatherapy. They have educated staff in the emotional needs of the client and given them a new perspective of being with him.'

The dramatherapists were asked specifically if any changes were noted in terms of *developing relationship*, *self-esteem and confidence*, *anxiety*, and *positive mental health*.

Developing relationship

All the dramatherapists felt that relationship building was a successful part of the work. DTG writes: 'the client's ability to be in relationship with me has improved. He uses more eye-contact and has been able to take a less receptive role and initiate more.' DTB writes: 'the client demonstrated an increased ownership of the sessions . . . we had developed a shared language.'

Those working in groups speak of a developing awareness between clients through turn-taking, passing objects, reaching out to make physical connections. 'People made easier contact with each other via the media of drama, because they shared the same group experiences, pleasurable moments and moments of relaxation and laughter' (DTJ).

Clients in care settings often relate to staff and peers differently. Relationships based on functional care needs (bathing, dressing, escorting) can be transactional and inflexible. Many dramatherapists noted their client relationships were different from other staff/client interactions, and provided input, as DTH states: 'the client's relationship with staff improved as I was able to provide a different narrative to the "monster" narrative they were fixed on.'

Vignette 8

Although Dean continues to have few focused relationships and activities, he is spending more time in the communal parts of the house, and increasingly sits with other residents in the living room. He continues to relate well in dramatherapy.

Self-esteem and confidence

Self-esteem and confidence were identified as central aims and positive outcomes were shared. 'The focused attention the client receives through one-to-one work has an instant visible positive effect. He is energised by it and more able/confident . . . this interaction has a more meaningful quality to it' (DTG). DTN saw a fragmented client develop 'to the point that now she seems to have a sense of herself as a mature woman and of this being seen, appreciated and valued'. Many saw that the familiarity within the sessions led to the client being able to make more decisions and choices.

Vignette 9

Hannah chooses to join the group more frequently, and offers contributions which we incorporate into our activities. Her autism means she will continue to choose how much she connects, but by being flexible there is an ongoing space to support her.

Transferring confidence to the outside world is complicated. DTA states: 'within sessions, my client seems increasingly confident, making choices, expressing himself. However, outside sessions he continues to struggle in making decisions on everyday things and needs reassurance that these are acceptable.'

Dramatherapists spoke of advocating for the client, because 'to be heard and understood is integral to the service user's developing confidence and self-esteem' (DTD). However, DTB notes, of the client's growing autonomy, 'sadly, this was seen in a negative light outside of the sessions, largely, I suspect as staff preferred a more passive response'.

Anxiety

Where present, anxiety seemed to reduce through varied dramatherapeutic interventions. DTA cites the session structure as a useful tool, whilst DTM finds, 'some of the sensory objects have helped contain clients and hold them in anxious times'. DTP advocates touch: 'feelings were met and often supported . . . by acknowledging them, placing hands on his chest, head, back, you could notice calming down in the breathing, and relaxation of muscles.' In sessions, DTE's clients 'appear more relaxed in their bodies, breathing and body language'. Self-harm and distancing behaviours reduced: 'once she settled into the session, she removed from her mouth the neck-scarf she constantly chewed' (DTS).

Vignette 10

> Daniel spent less time exploring the building, and more time in the main room, allowing more connection between us. His self-harm reduced and he didn't need to wear his helmet as often.

Positive mental health

All dramatherapists noticed an improvement in positive mental health, with dramatherapy providing the client with a greater sense of self and developing stability; self-harm reduces and calmness and relaxation are more accessible. DTM writes, 'the sessions promote independence and autonomy', which 'improves their mental health as the client is met where they are and life is explored through ways that they can participate'. DTD's client 'has developed resources such as her range of expressive verbal and non-verbal communication; and her ability to self-soothe appropriately, thereby tolerating heightened emotion to a greater degree'. Other changes noticed included being able to take risks, being happier, and accessing forgotten aspects of self.

Vignette 11

> For Margaret it seemed important that I was a man. The home manager thought dramatherapy sessions were probably the only time in Margaret's life that a man had paid her any attention. She noticed that Margaret would be smiling and excited when anticipating the session, and felt that the therapeutic relationship really impacted on her wellbeing.

Long-term work

Even when funding and organisational policy did not permit, the dramatherapists were unanimous about the need for long-term work with this client group, as difficulty in developing trust is a significant part of autism, often impacted by communal living in a care home.

DTE highlights the 'common attitudes to people with complex needs when the clients would have been growing up and the psychological effects this may have had', where generally functional needs were catered for, but not necessarily emotional growth and development. DTP writes, 'the work needs to be long-term because often the body and mental trauma of these clients is somehow trapped . . . they have experienced abandonment, rejection, disappointment many times . . . and they need to be reassured that you are really there to listen and to meet them fully. A short intervention with this client group cannot ever meet their rhythm.' DTM adds: 'it is only when they are feeling safe and secure that their true responses to interventions show.'

Due to the nature of autism and the associated complex needs, 'it may only be by repeating . . . over many weeks that the client will engage with both the intervention and the dramatherapist in a meaningful way . . . this in turn will take time to "practice" so that the client can internalise the experience and the benefits of therapy' (DTG).

For many of these clients, their long-term prognosis and living environment is unlikely to change. DTB sums this up: 'the client seems to value this private dramatherapy space and understand that it is a place where he can express himself . . . . Having his feelings witnessed and acknowledged is very different to his experience in other settings . . . it is important for him to be . . . empowered in this way – to be with someone who bridges in to his world.' Perhaps an ongoing dramatherapy space can support the client with the difficulties faced every day, and make the rest of the week more manageable.

Conclusion

This chapter demonstrates that adults with autism and complex needs and who are non-verbal have benefited from dramatherapy in a number of areas. The stories of our clients have been remembered and illustrate our findings. We have shown positive results in developing relationship, self-esteem and confidence, anxiety, and positive mental health. The value of long-term work and the importance of regular contact and discussion with others who support the client are vital in sharing knowledge and expertise, so that true systemic work can take place that puts the client at the heart of all of our work.

This continues to be an under-examined area of inquiry, and there is a compelling need for more research to be carried out by dramatherapists and others in this field.

Acknowledgements

With grateful thanks to the eleven dramatherapists who shared their working experiences with us, giving their clients a wider voice, ensuring that they will be remembered.

References

Baker, P. A. (2000) 'Measurement of community participation and use of leisure by service users with intellectual disabilities: the Guernsey community participation and leisure assessment (GCPLA)', *Journal of Applied Research in Intellectual Disabilities*, 13, pp.169–195.

Baron-Cohen, S. (2008) *Autism and Asperger Syndrome: The Facts*. Oxford: Oxford University Press.

Booker, M. (2011) *Developmental Drama: Dramatherapy Approaches for People with Profound or Severe Multiple Disabilities, Including Sensory Impairment*. London: Jessica Kingsley Publishers.

Bowlby, J. (1988) *A Secure Base: Clinical Applications of Attachment Theory*. London: Routledge.

British Association of Dramatherapists (BADth) (2007) *Analysis of Dramatherapy Equal Opportunities Survey*. Available at: https://badth.org.uk/sites/default/files/imported/downloads/information/Equal%20Opportunities%20Analysis%2015.4.08.pdf (accessed: 29 March 2015).

Chasen, L. R. (2011) *Social Skills, Emotional Growth and Drama Therapy: Inspiring Connection on the Autism Spectrum*. London: Jessica Kingsley Publishers.

Chesner, A. (1995) *Dramatherapy for People with Learning Disabilities: A World of Difference*. London: Jessica Kingsley Publishers.

Clarkson, P. (2003) *The Therapeutic Relationship 2nd edn*. London: Whurr Publishers.

Department of Health (2015) *Mental Health Act 1983: Code of Practice*, pp.206–219. Available at: https://www.gov.uk/government/uploads/system/uploads/attachment_data/file/396918/Code_of_Practice.pdf (accessed: 14 March 2015).

Department of Health: Social Care, Local Government and Care Partnership Directorate (2014) *Think Autism: Fulfilling and Rewarding Lives, the Strategy for Adults with Autism in England: An Update*. Available at: https://www.gov.uk/government/uploads/system/uploads/attachment_data/file/299866/Autism_Strategy.pdf (accessed: 21 October 2014).

Department of Human Services (2003) *Responding to People with Multiple and Complex Needs Project: Client Profile Data and Case Studies Report*. Melbourne, Australia: Government of Victoria.

Freitag, C. M. (2007) 'The genetics of autistic disorders and its clinical relevance: a review of the literature', *Molecular Psychiatry*, 12, pp.2–22 [online]. Available at: http://www.nature.com/mp/journal/v12/n1/full/4001896a.html (accessed: 7 December 2014).

Grainger, R. (1999) *Researching the Arts Therapies: A Dramatherapist's Perspective*. London: Jessica Kingsley Publishers.

Graybow, A. (2008) 'Little boy lost: finding a road to reparation', *Sesame Journal*, Spring (7), pp.24–28.

Harris, P., Humphreys, J. and Thomson, G. (1994) 'A checklist of challenging behaviour: the developments of a survey instrument', *Mental Handicap Research*, 7(2), pp.118–133.

Heimann, P. (1950) 'On countertransference', *The International Journal of Psychoanalysis*, 31, pp.81–84.

Jackson, J. (2011) 'Self-harm in clients with learning disabilities: dramatherapists' perceptions and methodologies', in Dokter, D., Holloway, P. and Seebohm, H. (eds), *Dramatherapy and Destructiveness: Creating the Evidence Base, Playing with Thanatos*. London: Routledge, pp.95–107.

James, J. (1996a) 'Dramatherapy with people with learning disabilities', in Mitchell, S. (ed.), *Dramatherapy Clinical Studies*. London: Jessica Kingsley Publishers, pp.15–32.

James, J. (1996b) 'Poetry in motion: drama and movement therapy with people with learning disabilities', in Pearson, J. (ed.), *Discovering the Self through Drama and Movement: The Sesame Approach*. London: Jessica Kingsley Publishers, pp.209–221.

Jennings, S. (1992) *Dramatherapy with Families, Groups and Individuals: Waiting in the Wings*. London: Jessica Kingsley Publishers.

Jennings, S. (1998) *Introduction to Dramatherapy: Theatre and Healing: Ariadne's Ball of Thread*. London: Jessica Kingsley Publishers.

Jones, P. (1996) *Drama as Therapy: Theatre as Living*. London: Routledge.

Jung, C. G. (2000) *Collected Works of C. G. Jung*, eds Adler, G., Fordham, M., Read, H. and McGuire, W. Princeton, NJ: Princeton University Press.

Karim, K., Ali, A. and O'Reilly, M. (2014) *A Practical Guide to Mental Health Problems in Children with Autistic Spectrum Disorder: It's Not Just Their Autism!* London: Jessica Kingsley Publishers.

Kossak, M. S. (2009) 'Therapeutic attunement: a transpersonal view of expressive arts therapy', *The Arts in Psychotherapy*, 36, pp.13–18.

Lindkvist, M. R. (1981) 'Movement and drama with autistic children', in Courtney, R. and Schatner, G. (eds), *Drama in Therapy, Volume 1: Children*. New York: Drama Book Specialists, pp.95–110.

Lindkvist, M. (1997) *And Please Don't Let the Boiler Burst*. London: Sesame Institute.

Lindkvist, M. (1998) *Bring White Beads When You Call on the Healer*. New Orleans, LA: Rivendell House.

National Autistic Society (2015) Available at: http://www.autism.org.uk/about-autism/related-conditions.aspx (accessed: 14 March 2015).

NHS: The Information Centre for Health and Social Care (2009) *Autism Spectrum Disorders in Adults Living in Households throughout England*. Available at: http://www.hscic.gov.uk/catalogue/PUB01131/aut-sp-dis-adu-liv-ho-a-p-m-sur-eng-2007-rep.pdf (accessed: 29 March 2015).

Pearson, J. (1996) 'Marian Lindkvist and Movement with Touch', in Pearson, J. (ed.), *Discovering the Self through Drama and Movement: The Sesame Approach*. London: Jessica Kingsley Publishers, pp.52–71.

Porter, R. (2014) 'Movement with touch and sound in the Sesame approach: bringing the bones to the flesh', *Dramatherapy*, 36(1), pp.27–42.

Rogers, C. (1990) 'The therapeutic relationship', in Kirschenbaum, H. and Land Henderson, V. (eds), *The Carl Rogers Reader*. London: Constable, pp. 63–152.

Rosenblatt, M. (2008) *I Exist: The Message from Adults with Autism in England*. Available at: http://www.autism.org.uk/~/media/nas/documents/get-involved/campaign%20for%20change/i%20exist/nas0038iexistreportengland%20coverpages.ashx (accessed: 21 October 2014).

Sherborne, V. (1990) *Developmental Movement for Children*. Cambridge: Cambridge University Press.

Smith, J. A. and Osborn, M. (2008) 'Interpretative phenomenological analysis', in Smith, J. A. (ed.), *Qualitative Psychology: A Practical Guide to Research Methods 2nd edn*. London: Sage Publications, pp.53–80.

Turner-Stokes L. (2009) 'Goal Attainment Scaling (GAS) in rehabilitation: a practical guide', *Clinical Rehabilitation*, 23(4), pp.362–370.

12

ASSESSING THE IMPACT OF DRAMATHERAPY ON THE EARLY SOCIAL BEHAVIOUR OF YOUNG CHILDREN ON THE AUTISTIC SPECTRUM

Roya Dooman

Introduction

This chapter assesses the impact of a dramatherapy intervention on the early social behaviours of young children aged 5–7 with Autistic Spectrum Conditions. I will use the term Autistic Spectrum Conditions (ASC), as this is the preferred terminology used by parents and the local Autism Outreach Service.

This is an important area of study, as the Diagnostic and Statistical Manual IV highlights 'impaired social interaction' and 'communication' as a precursor to diagnosis (Morrison, 2006, p.512). In using DSM-IV, not 5, I am relating it to the scale that forms part of the assessment.

Dramatherapists have been addressing social communication difficulties in autistic children for many years and assessing changes in social communication since Jones's adaptation of the Parten Scale (Jones, 2007, p.316). However, the delayed development of two particular behaviours seen in young children with Autistic Spectrum Conditions, *responsiveness* and *initiation*, has not been specifically measured before and after dramatherapy intervention since no appropriate measurement tool has been available.

The study described in this chapter uses a new observable assessment tool from Gillis, Callahan and Romanczykv, *The Behavioural Assessment of Social Communication of Young Children* (2011), to measure and collate outcomes, along with rating scales completed by teachers and parents. The study focuses on two separate groups of children in a primary school setting working in collaboration with an Autism Outreach Service.

I will demonstrate that dramatherapy is an effective intervention in ameliorating difficulties in social interaction with young children with ASC. This area is one of the undisputed difficulties cited in DSM-IV as a 'markedly deficient regulation in social interaction through multiple non-verbal behaviours', along with an absence in social or emotional reciprocity (Morrison, 2006, p.512).

I will examine these early behaviours, and how signs of early interactive communication are delayed or seen as deficit. I will argue that sensory processing difficulties account for many of the problems in forming relationships. Delayed processing and hyper and hypo sensitivities all cause retreat from social contact (Bogdashina, 2005; Williams, 1996, 1999). Early intervention around social communication difficulties is crucial, in order to alleviate their significant impact upon relationships in later life (Jordan and Jones, 1999; Williams, 1996; Gillis et al., 2011; Beights, 2010).

Context: the autistic perspective

'The more I became aware of the world around me the more I became afraid. Other people were my enemies, and reaching out to me was their weapon, with only a few exceptions' (1999, p.13). Williams, as an autistic adult, writes that the risk of isolation caused by the stress of hyper social sensitivities or exposure anxiety can lead to severe mental health problems in later life.

Bogdashina states that, if a child's sensory problems and delayed processing start when he is very young, the result is a 'self-imposed sensory deprivation' (2005, p.89). Children whose overload of sensory stimuli can be so uncomfortable and even painful, find themselves withdrawing from social contact. This often results in poor communication skills and deficits in social interaction. As Williams (1999) and Higashida (2013) both illustrate, an individual's ability to form meaningful relationships is threatened, with the consequences of peer rejection and low self-esteem. 'The truth is, we'd love to be with other people. But because things never ever go right, we end up getting used to being alone, without even noticing this is happening. Whenever I overhear someone remark how much I prefer being on my own, it makes me feel desperately lonely' (Higashida, 2013, p.48).

For many children, isolation caused by social communication difficulties may also mean low academic attainment, depression and anxiety (Gillis et al., 2011). Williams suggests that constant attempts to correct children's social communication problems will interfere with their ability to interact and communicate (1996, p.201). Teaching through direct copying of the social behaviour of others can become more stressful and anxiety provoking for the child. As an autistic adult she believes that it is developmentally more constructive to decrease the sensory overload, allowing the child more time to process sensory information gradually before having to respond to another's communication (1996, p.128).

Context: dramatherapy and autism

Dramatherapists have written about minimising the amount of sensory information when focusing on children's 'personal creativity' (Landy, 1996) and their 'creative satisfaction' (Jones, 2007). Dramatherapy can provide rewarding new social experiences, whilst making the rules underlying social behaviour explicit. Chasen believes that dramatherapy can offer a 'multi layered and interactive approach to social skills . . . empowering a deeper level of social learning' (2014, p.124).

Dramatherapists have intervened in the area of social communication for many years and, using qualitative data, have been evaluating its effectiveness (Jones, 1996; Andersen-Warren, 2013; Godfrey and Haythorne, 2013). Scott-Danter's (2006) evaluation of a dramatherapy programme focusing on social interaction, showed positive outcomes for communication and participation, demonstrating that role-play increased spontaneity and co-operation.

Greene (2012) evaluated the effectiveness of a dramatherapy group for children with social communication difficulties, finding an improvement in empathy and problematic behaviour. Wilmer-Barbrook (2013) evaluated the impact of dramatherapy upon the social and communication skills of a young group of adolescents with Asperger's syndrome, concluding that there was significant overall improvement.

According to Andersen-Warren (2013), there are tools for measuring outcomes across dramatherapy practice with people with autism, yet none specifically to observe and measure the impact on early social behaviours of responsiveness and initiating behaviours. I believe, like Sherratt and Peter (2002), that these behaviours are the building blocks of early communication, as they develop enduring qualities in social communication that will affect future relationships.

Introducing the study

Searching for an evaluative tool

For this study, I sought an evaluative tool outside the therapy room that was not dependent on third party reporting, could provide a direct interactive measure of social behaviour, and could be used pre and post a dramatherapy intervention. Research carried out in the USA at Binghamton University New York, '*The Behavioral Assessment of Social Communication of Young Children*' (Gillis et al., 2011), has provided a method to observe and measure changes in the responsiveness and ability to initiate in young children with ASC. Through my communications with the authors of the BASYC, I learnt that it was being used as a repeated measure, in further interventions in the USA.

I felt that this BASYC test corresponded developmentally to the age group 5–7 and to dramatherapy methods. Its play-based observation, through unobtrusive semi-structured interview, is designed as a naturalistic play encounter for children. Given our time limitations in a school setting, the scoring and coding were simpler than other tests, such as the Early Social Communication Scales (see Beights, 2010, p. 11).

(i) The group referrals

We set up two different groups in a mainstream primary school where dramatherapy was part of the Inclusion Service. The children were aged between 5 and 7 years and were identified by the Head of Inclusion as having a diagnosis of autism; all were able to communicate verbally and were seen as 'high functioning'. Because, as Greene notes, there can be a difficulty for identifying dramatherapy as the 'sole contributor to change' (2012, p.203), we requested that the children were not involved in other interventions.

There were four children in the first group and three in the second. The groups ran consecutively for 14 sessions that lasted an hour, including transition time from classroom to therapy and back.

(ii) Permission and ethical considerations

The parents of the children involved were invited to meet individually with the dramatherapist, who introduced the project as a small-scale study, during which the children would be invited to participate in a play test, both before and after the intervention. This would be recorded and parents were invited to view the BASYC video tests of their own child with the dramatherapist at the end of the study.

(iii) The Behavioural Assessment of Social Communication in Young Children

The process involved positioning a teaching assistant with a camera in the room where an adult from the Autism Outreach team was seated at a table with two chairs and a selection of different toys in a transparent box placed between her and the child. The number and types of toy are specified by the BASYC test (Gillis et al., 2011) and this was replicated as closely as possible, including toys that light up and appear immediately attractive, and others that involve pretend play. There are a set of 20 questions for the adult to ask the child during the semi-structured interview. The only role for the dramatherapist was to escort the child from class and back again.

After all the tests, the three adults corroborated the results from the score sheets against the videoed material.

(iv) Choosing a rating scale for pre- and post-therapy assessment

The McConnell and Ryser pro-ed rating scale was chosen, as it is designed to be used alongside intervention strategies by educators and parents to rate children according to the DSM-IV criteria for Autism (2007, p.2). It is also used for assessment by the local Autistic school where the Outreach service was based.

The brevity of the questionnaire meant that it was less time consuming for parents and teachers, who are more likely to complete shorter questionnaires (Greene, 2012).

(v) The McConnell and Ryser rating scale

In the nine subcategories, we asked parents and teachers to answer only the 27 questions concerning Social Interactions and Communication. The category of Repetitive/Stereotyped Patterns was excluded, as it was not pertinent to the study. According to Ryser, excluding an entire subsection rather than some items from a subscale should not have an impact on the results (personal correspondence with the author, 1 April 2015).

The scale requires the parent or teacher to rate the child's behaviours from 0 to 3 as 'Never/rarely', 'Sometimes', 'Frequently' and 'Consistently', giving a maximum total score of 9 in each subcategory. The higher score indicates the severity of Autistic type behaviours as set out in the DSM-IV. Using both this rating scale and the BASYC would help assess any changes in the early social behaviours of the children produced by the dramatherapy.

TABLE 12.1 Abbreviated version of behaviours assessed in the McConnell and Ryser rating scale

Social Interactions
Nonverbal behaviours
Avoids using eye contact Does not use facial expressions Avoids physical contact
Peer relationships
Unresponsive to presence of peers Not initiating relationships Not building friendships
Sharing enjoyment and interests
Not showing accomplishments Not showing an interest in everyday events Not sharing enjoyment in an activity or an object
Social reciprocity
Unwilling to hug, kiss, shake hands Unwilling to take turns Prefers to be alone
Communication
Expressive language
Not speaking spontaneously to others Not using gestures, signs Not communicating his/her needs
Conversation
Not initiating Not using greetings Does not ask questions

(continued)

TABLE 12.1 *(continued)*

Communication
Stereotyped language
Echolalic Perseverate Uses phrases from TV/radio
Make believe play
Not engaging in developmentally appropriate make believe play Not joining in with others Aloof from their peers
Receptive language
Not pointing to body parts Unresponsive when spoken to Unresponsive to requests

Introduction to Dramatherapy methods used

The play–drama continuum

The aim of the dramatherapy groups was to engage both body and mind in developmental stages along the play–drama continuum (Jones, 2007; Sherratt and Peter, 2002). According to Jennings (1995) this continuum is a developmental paradigm of progression, through embodied play, to projective play, then to role. Developmentally, the child begins from a pre-linguistic, pre-symbolic, sensory-dominated world, communicating solely through the body. Relationship with others is purely physical (Jones, 2007).

Sensory motor relational play

Lindkvist (1974) recognised the autistic child's need for sensory-dominated experience placing movement and sound at the forefront of the relationship. The dramatherapy sessions incorporated sensory motor and relational play with physical objects, during which the child might develop relationships with others (Sherratt and Peter, 2002; Jennings, 1995; Jones, 2007). The physical rituals of drumming, singing and movement engage the child physically whilst giving the child opportunities to experience early responding and initiating behaviours with others.

Dramatic play

Building a dramatic landscape for the story, the therapist facilitates the child's entrance into a constructed theatre of social relationships, with an opportunity to expand their everyday roles (Jones, 2007). Children find a role that appeals to their senses, projecting ideas onto that character's function or task in the story. Chasen (2014) suggests a child's engagement with visual and auditory sensory stimuli creates an attraction to playing certain roles.

Children are encouraged to negotiate both in and out of role and the therapist aids the child to respond consciously to the initiations and cues from others (Wolfberg, 1999).

I believe that role-playing is the motivating passion that draws children into deeper levels of engagement within the drama and with each other, finding pleasure in the drama of human relationships.

Transitions and rituals are the stepping stones of dramatherapy

Feeling nervous about what might happen, the autistic child often finds it difficult to enter a new space. Distracting sound, harsh lighting and tactile hyper-sensitivities may cause further anxiety. There are difficult thresholds to cross on entering the space.

Chasen (2014, p.86) demonstrates that rituals of welcome, warm up, de-role and goodbye help define the 'physicality of transition' and the rhythm of the group, to support 'safe encounters' between children.

The opening ritual

An opening ritual in dramatherapy should create a sense of familiarity and order (Jennings, 1995), decreasing social anxiety and sense of threat (Williams, 1999). Focusing on the group ritual, I invite the children to sit on 'stepping stone' mats to mark the transitional steps into the group and out again, enabling the children to view one another as separate. Here they can become more conscious of how they connect to each other.

The warm up

The warm up helps children connect with each other and the creative material, and to process sensory information at their own pace. As the child initiates his drumming rhythm in the circle, he can hear and see the others' responses and hence can initiate again, creating the building blocks for further communication.

At each 'stepping stone' stage, more of the senses are integrated into the play. When preparing for the enactment of a story, the therapist may encourage sensory motor responses, such as growling, high-pitched voices and stamping feet. Smail's concept of 'Bridging In' to the drama (2013, p.62) involves the children literally stepping into the 'dramatic space' as they sing and dance across the 'stepping stones'.

The enactment and embodying the role

Acting a character, taking on the role of other, invites the child to experience another way of being from a different perspective other than their own (Landy, 1996). This is important for the autistic child who becomes 'stuck' in one role.

In the role of 'other' the child can experience behaving differently, thus offering a new experience of themselves responding to others. It is through this connection between thought and emotion, whilst playing a character who is 'responsive and interactive, that the child begins to understand the relationship between self and other' (Chasen, 2014, pp.105–106).

De-roling

When saying goodbye to their characters, the children shake out the feelings associated with their roles as they sing farewell to the scene. The group are invited back onto their 'stepping stone' mats for Relaxation as part of the de-roling process.

Relaxation

When preparing to leave the session, the children focus on colour and movement outside themselves. I use coloured lights, as in Mitchell's 'candle ritual' (1994).

Concentrating on senses outside themselves separates the child from the story and their complex feelings, and prepares them to reflect on their roles and their interactions with others.

Recording before saying goodbye

The children are helped to record their emotional experiences of the session, choosing different 'feeling faces' on visual, tactile recording sheets. The children may share some of their meaningful encounters from their own journey before saying goodbye to the group.

Case vignettes

The following vignettes, based on the therapist's observations, demonstrate how the dramatherapy sessions impacted upon the early social behaviour of the young autistic children in the group, and show how children with different sensory needs were able to become more responsive in their social interaction. Names have been changed to protect confidentiality and permission was given by parents and school to use all case material.

Vignette 1: the start of Leo's journey, from avoidance to laughter

Leo's tactile hypersensitivities and visual perception difficulties led him to avoid relationships other than with his safe adults.

Leo entered the room warily, tilting his head at an angle to view the room sideways through his thick rimmed glasses, looking for reassurance from the therapist. Leo had seen the other children run noisily into the room, throwing themselves down on the floor. His hunched shoulders and head held down, showed that he did not want the other children to touch him or push into his space (and he would let out a high pitch 'no!'). He sat back on his mat slightly away from the others, where he had a good field of vision.

In the first session Leo refused to join in, using my body as a block between himself and the group. In the second session he edged slightly forwards, but he could not physically engage with the others. However, he was watching their responses – especially to the puppet 'Cheeky Monkey'.

By the third session Leo was asking when the puppet would appear. He now wanted to hold it. He brought his stepping stone mat nearer to the other group members so he could take his turn with the puppet.

In later sessions, Leo became attracted to the sound of another child, in Kevin's giggling, and used the puppet to tickle Kevin. Laughter led to Leo's engagement in the session – and he was initiating it.

By playfully engaging Leo's sensory challenges, dramatherapy enabled him to shift towards fuller interaction.

Discussion of vignette 1

Finding the shared 'attentional spotlight' through the dramatic space

Chasen (2014) notes that sensory stimulus, when applied in setting the scene, increases ASD children's ability to engage. Sensory information creates dramatic atmosphere.

Bogdashina quotes Posner's use of the 'attentional spotlight', which correlates with the theatre director's use of 'dramatic spotlights' that illuminate action on the stage (2005, p.90). The dramatherapist enters into this sensory space with the child by starting a 'dramatic' dialogue about what the child finds there, developing her motivation to participate in the dramatic interaction. Watching the children's physical reactions to this new dramatic landscape, the dramatherapist starts to see the story from their perspective.

Children are invited to embody parts of the landscape, rolling, hiding, sliding and projecting their own ideas onto it, often holding on to an object that makes a link between their sensory experience and the scene.

Processing time and director's cue

Creating processing time, within the drama, allows the 'tuning out' or 'shutting down' that autistic adults describe as impeding communications: 'the ability to simultaneously process self and other' (Williams, 1996, p.130).

The use of stage directions, through 'the director's cue', can help the child from becoming overwhelmed by her own feelings or sensory overload. The dramatherapist, like the theatre director, may 'freeze', using the word 'pause', to 'spot light' a particular moment in the scene (Chasen, 2014, p.214).

When the dramatherapist shifts the attention of the group, the individual child can have 'thinking time' to create aesthetic distance, in which to respond to the action and make a connection between their own thoughts and feelings about another's.

Vignette 2: Marco and Joe – communicating through role

At the beginning of the sessions, Marco appeared dazed and disconnected, responding in a compliant, but non-focused, manner when waiting for his turn with the drum. However, when he was invited to move into the dramatic scene, he threw his whole body on the floor, wrapping himself in whatever material was there, to be 'in the forest' or 'in the sea'. Marco was encouraged to amplify the sounds that came from the movements, as he rolled or crawled across the floor.

In session 6 the other children joined him rolling in the sea. Suddenly, Marco called out, 'I'm a shark!', and he swam frantically, calling to Joe, 'I'm coming to get you.' Marco, as the Shark, looked powerful and strong. Joe, dressed as a pirate in a bright silk scarf, was sitting on a table, as a boat. 'Got you!' the Shark roared, grabbing his leg.

'No you haven't,' cried the Pirate; 'I don't want you to.' Joe jumped off the boat and skipped out of 'the sea' to the other side of the room. He picked up some plastic food from the props table.

'Pause,' I called out; 'let's spotlight the Pirate.' I held up my hand as if it were the light. 'Wow, what a good thing that the pirate told the shark that he didn't want to be eaten. I wonder, what does the pirate want to do now?'

Joe looked down at the plastic food he was holding up to his mouth, turned to his fellow pirate and said, 'Let's go to the island to have a picnic.' The two pirates took as much food as they could over to a large piece of coloured cloth and sat down. Joe had managed both to process his feelings and maintain his role in the story.

'Spotlight Shark,' I turned to Marco. 'I'm hungry!' roared the Shark, swimming towards the pirates' new island. 'You can come and have a picnic,' shouted Joe. 'You have pizza, I'll have cake.' Marco struggled to make sense of Joe's offer, as he was still caught up in his own physical sensation of swimming.

To give Marco some processing time, I made another Director's cue, asking all the boys: 'I wonder what the Shark does to show that he wants to join the picnic?' The pirates added their ideas, and when I called, 'Action', Marco chose to climb onto the island and he ate the picnic with the pirates. He then dived into 'the sea' again, where he could reconnect with himself 'rolling in the waves'.

Discussion of vignette 2

Making connections and processing time

Marco and Joe could communicate with each other through role in the play space, and, by the use of the dramatic spotlight, bring intentional focus to the interaction, making it purposeful for both of them. Marco was able to act, but not to process Joe's feelings simultaneously. Joe's processing needed time, and he moved away from the shark so as not feel overwhelmed by Marco's larger movements.

The dramatherapist can assist the child to move into the scene, by developing 'the potential body', to explore the range and quality of their physical communication (Jones, 2007, p.229). The children enter the story by holding onto a prop, by adding a movement or a new voice to begin the journey into a shared dramatic space. The element of 'playfulness', referred to by Jones (2007, p.165), facilitates a non-judgemental atmosphere where the fear of 'getting things wrong', so often experienced by these children, is greatly reduced.

Modelling playfulness, facilitating connections

The role of the dramatherapist in engaging the client in a drama, involves being both a director and an actor. Holloway and Seebohm liken the versatility of the dramatherapist to Boal's 'Joker' or 'difficultator' in forum theatre (2011, p.11).

The playfulness of the therapist's own role-playing facilitates the child's connections with the other. The dramatherapist may take a role in the drama to challenge or support the children's own chosen roles. This intervention can change the pace and tempo of the drama and allow time for the children to exercise their sense of social behaviour, while staying in role, thus *practising* how to deal with the very difficulties that autistic children have in initiating communication with their peers, (Bogdashina, 2005, p.209).

Using the assessment tools

The perspective of the therapist and the voice of the child can both be heard in these vignettes. The perspective of parents and teachers was gained by applying the McConnell and Ryser rating scales and the separate BASYC observation test to provide a different view of the child.

I will discuss the results of the BASYC followed by the results of the Ratings scale used by parents and teacher, and then attempt triangulating the results. Gillis et al. (2011) state that they expect the scores on the BASYC to increase, if, after taking part in an intervention, there is an improvement in social behaviour of children with autism. Analysis of the results, from the two graphs below, shows a positive impact on the children's responsiveness and their initiating behaviours.

Discussion of responsiveness scores

In the pre-test, the responsiveness scores for our group of children were already high, possibly due to previous interventions they had received at school, as well as their actual ability. The pre-test responsivity score averaged 79 per cent and their post-scores increased to an average of 91 per cent, a difference of 12 per cent.

This lower-than-expected gain could be attributed to the higher score pre-test and therefore leaves little room for improvement on this particular scale.

Although the children scored high on their responsiveness pre-test, in the videos they appeared as 'meekly compliant', to use Williams' description of herself as a child (1996). Most merely nodded or said 'yes' to the interviewer. In one instance, when the interviewer offered a 'boring toy', such as a tissue, to play with, the child just accepted it. However, when offered the same object in the post-test, he smiled directly at the interviewer and shook his head to the side.

Post-testing, all the responsiveness rates were over 84 per cent positive and, when viewing the tapes, the three adults noted 5 out of 7 children appeared more physically engaged, with more eye contact and moving physically closer around the table towards the interviewer.

Discussion of initiation scores

In contrast to the responsiveness scores, the children's initiation scores were much lower on the pre-test, averaging 23 per cent, and the post-test results averaged 53 per cent, making a difference of 30 per cent.

The initiation graph shows that for Tim, Joe and Leo there were significant improvements in these behaviours but with more fluctuation in the results. For example, Leo showed an improvement of 61 per cent and Tim 50 per cent and yet Gail's results remained static. Marco, despite initiating the shark attack during the session, did not show any initiating behaviours during either pre- or post-tests. Marco's apparent socially anxiety during both tests, may have been due to his need

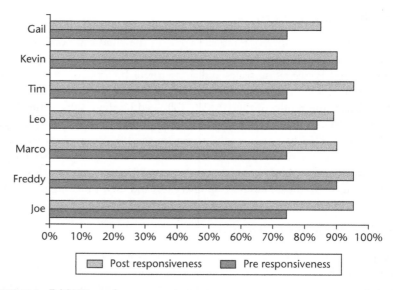

FIGURE 12.1 BASYC results – responsiveness

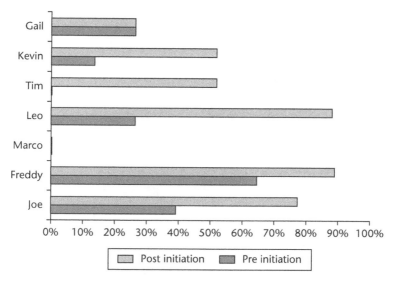

FIGURE 12.2   BASYC results – initiation

for sensory motor play and perhaps the test was undermined by being held sitting at a table.

Two of the children used humour with the interviewer to initiate play. 'Look, I've sat on it!' said Leo, using the toy pizza. 'I've poured the tea on my head!' said Tim, demonstrating pretend play with the plastic tea cup to the interviewer. During our sessions Tim had used humour to involve the other children and invited them to participate with him (note Chasen's use of comedy as a tool for broadening perspective and reinforcing social skills: 2014, p.130).

Comparing responsiveness and initiation scores

The graph results show that the dramatherapy had a big impact on 5 children's initiating behaviours. The children's responsiveness graph results showed more consistency in incremental value in both the pre-test and post-test scores, than did their initiations graph. This is possibly due to the fact that in the test there are 20 questions requiring a response behaviour, as opposed to only 7 requiring an initiating behaviour. With fewer questions, the data may appear less reliable. The responsiveness questions might suggest that, although difference pre- and post-intervention is not so dramatic, it is still significant.

Analysing results from the McConnell and Ryser ratings scale

Both parents and teachers completed the questionnaires and the results were collated using Microsoft Excel. Improvement percentages were then calculated and

TABLE 12.2 Comparing improvement percentages on rating scales between parents and teachers post dramatherapy intervention

Child	Non verbal behaviours		Peer relationships		Sharing enjoyment and interests		Social reciprocity		Expressive language		Conversation		Stereotyped language		Make believe play		Receptive language	
	Parent	Teacher	Parent	Teacher	Parent	Teacher	Parent	Teacher	Parent	Teacher	Parent	Teacher	Parent	Teacher	Parent	Teacher	Parent	Teacher
GAIL	25%	8%	25%	33%	42%	42%	33%	42%	67%	33%	58%	42%	50%	17%	42%	42%	17%	17%
KEVIN	17%	17%	17%	25%	25%	17%	8%	8%	25%	17%	33%	33%	25%	25%	25%	33%	17%	25%
LEO	0%	42%	17%	42%	33%	0%	0%	25%	0%	33%	0%	0%	8%	8%	25%	42%	0%	33%
TIM	8%	17%	8%	25%	0%	25%	17%	25%	8%	17%	17%	33%	0%	0%	33%	17%	25%	0%
FREDDY	25%	25%	42%	50%	25%	25%	33%	42%	17%	25%	8%	42%	33%	25%	17%	42%	17%	25%
MARCO	25%	33%	17%	25%	0%	42%	25%	42%	17%	42%	8%	42%	0%	0%	0%	17%	33%	42%
JOE	17%	33%	25%	42%	33%	58%	17%	42%	42%	42%	25%	25%	25%	0%	17%	33%	8%	17%
AVERAGE	17%	25%	22%	35%	23%	30%	19%	32%	25%	30%	21%	31%	20%	11%	23%	32%	17%	23%

placed on a graph. Changes in pre- and post-scores were calculated as a percentage difference. Where there was no change in behaviour, 0 per cent is seen on the scale.

There is a high variability on the rating scales in parent/teacher responses, which is to be expected when the parent or teacher has more, or less, attunement with a child's particular difficulties. Leo's parent did not perceive the same communication difficulties at home as the teacher saw in school. Leo was an only child, able to have a lot of 1:1 attention at home, and in the pre-test Leo's mother gave him top percentage scores in four areas of communication and social abilities. However, the teacher could see Leo's difficulties in group situations in both classroom and playground.

Gail's parents' pre-ratings scores were low, however, reflecting difficulties at home that they had described to the therapist: 'She just screams so much with her sister, or is silent, it's very hard.' The parent's post-rating scores demonstrated high improvement percentages in her social interactions and communication ratings. The teacher also commented that Gail 'now is included with her peers at playtime' and 'she is generally much more responsive in class, although still needs a lot of adult support'.

Highest improvement percentages

The parents' improvement ratings were highest in the area of expressive language. This is an interesting result, as 'expressive language' in this scale includes the child's ability to 'get their needs met', which the teachers also scored as an overall improvement of 30 per cent.

The teacher's improvement percentages were higher overall than the parent's, which may be down to the fact that the dramatherapy sessions took place in school during teaching time, so perhaps the teachers felt more involved in the process. Wilmer-Barbrook in her study also noted a smaller percentage increase from parents over teachers and suggests that it may be harder to monitor 'the change and development in a family setting, compared to an educational one' (2013, p.52).

Make-believe play and peer relationships

Teachers' ratings were highest on the criteria of Make-believe play, possibly as they had more context for this in school. Jordan and Jones point out that parents often report that their child has limited social opportunities outside of the family (1999, p.45). However, in the early years of school there are frequent opportunities to observe both free play and structured play in both classroom and playground (Wolfberg, 1999, p.51). The importance of pretend play in child development is well documented: 'The transition from simple to advanced pretend signifies a major turning point in the play development in children with Autism' (Wolfberg, 1999, p. 37).

The teachers' improvement ratings score over all the categories averaged at 28 per cent and the parents at 21 per cent, giving an overall change result of 24 per cent from both the parents' and teachers' scores. The categories that consistently saw the highest improvement from both the parents and teachers were Make-believe play and peer relationships. The latter connects directly to the child's ability to initiate and build relationships. For instance, Leo's parent's commented that '[h]e now can attend birthday parties and join in, whereas he hated them before'. Freddy's teacher noted, 'He's now playing with other children at playtime joining in their games, whereas before he kept returning to the classroom'.

A summary of results

Results from the BASYC tests demonstrate that everyone improved in their responsiveness scores and most on their initiation scores. Results from the McConnell and Ryser rating scales are more limited, because of their high variability, except in the area of make-believe play, which suggests that it plays a positive role in developing early social communication.

Critique of the tests

Triangulating results

The two tests are very different: the BASYC is the more quantitative, whilst the high variability on the McConnell and Ryser scale requires a more qualitative analysis. This makes comparison difficult.

The results of the BASYC showed that all the children improved in their responsiveness and that their initiations towards the interviewer increased and were significantly high. The McConnell and Ryser rating scale asked relevant and pertinent questions of the study; however, producing a negative score made it difficult to use as a tool of assessment. This highlights the need for a specific ratings scale for social interaction and communication that can be used more easily as an assessment tool, if we are to produce evidence across all the groups we work with. I do not believe such a tool currently exists.

Variables

One of the variables affecting the BASYC testing was the difference in how the transition into the test was handled. The interviewer commented that one child had arrived for his post-test in a distressed state and needed time to readjust, but the test situation did not allow for his time to be extended. As Jordan and Jones point out (1999, p.55), transitions are a particular difficulty for children with Autism. As this variable is hard to accommodate in the results, I would therefore recommend that a 5-minute transition period be built into the test for all the children with ASCs.

Coding quality of interaction

The current scoring of the BASYC on the occurrence or non-occurrence of a particular behaviour does not examine all the particular qualities involved: for example, the amount of gesturing or physical movement, pitch of voice, or amount of words. From my observations, a coding of these types of expression would show further evidence of the impact of dramatherapy on social behaviours. Most of the children appeared more 'self-assured' and 'confident' in interviews post-dramatherapy, but, unfortunately, these qualities cannot as yet be quantified by the BASYC (Beights, 2010).

The fact that we were only testing for two specific behaviours covered by BASYC, responsiveness and initiation, might seem reductive, but, given the assessment tools available, this questionable choice was necessary if we were to demonstrate the efficacy of dramatherapy beyond its own defined world.

Further study

After this small-scale study, I would recommend more dramatherapists to incorporate BASYC into their work, collecting more data with larger numbers of children, in order to build an evidence-base for dramatherapy. It would be valuable to explore the impact of dramatherapy, particularly in the initiating behaviours, on other children with different degrees of autism, for instant non-verbal, or from an older age group. It would be interesting to see the results of interventions longer than 14 weeks, although this, of course, would have funding implications in the present climate of cutbacks and pressure on professionals to offer short-term interventions.

Conclusion

The results of the BASYC tests provide quantifiable evidence that dramatherapy has an impact on the early social behaviours of young children on the autistic spectrum, while the McConnell and Ryser rating scales provide us with an indication that Make-believe play has an impact upon the responding and initiating behaviours in young children with ASCs.

When evaluating an intervention, all qualitative perspectives should be taken into account, including that of the children, their therapist and other facilitators. Details from individual reflective sheets have only been touched upon here, but all add to the qualitative assessments made by the therapist and child together during the sessions.

The whole study demonstrates dramatherapy's positive impact upon the early social behaviours of young children with autistic spectrum conditions. Moreover, it can offer a safe and non-intrusive intervention to improving social communication skills, by lessening, through the play–drama continuum, the pressure of sensory processing that the children experience day to day.

Acknowledgements

I wish to thank the children who shared their imaginative worlds with me.

I also thank my academic supervisor Dr Ditty Dokter for her clear direction, and the editors of this book for their unswerving support and positive criticism.

References

Andersen-Warren, M. (2013) 'Dramatherapy with children and young people who have autistic spectrum disorders: an examination of dramatherapists' practices', *Dramatherapy*, 35(1), pp.3–19.

Beights, R. (2010) *Validation of the Behavioral Assessment of Social Interaction in Young Children (BASYC) as a Measure of Early Social Behavior in Children with Autism Spectrum Disorders.* Thesis. GS ETD, Auburn University, Alabama: http://etd.auburn.edu/etd (accessed 12 April 2016).

Bogdashina, O. (2005) *Communication Issues in Autism and Asperger Syndrome.* London and Philadelphia, PA: Jessica Kingsley Publishers.

Chasen, L (2014) *Engaging Mirror Neurons to Inspire Connection and Social Emotional Development in Children and Teens on the Autistic Spectrum.* London and Philadelphia, PA: Jessica Kingsley Publishers.

Gillis, J., Callahan, E. and Romanczykv, R. (2011) 'Assessment of social behavior in children with autism: the development of the behavioral assessment of social interactions in young children', *Research in Autism Spectrum Disorders*, 5, pp.351–360.

Godfrey, E. and Haythorne, D. (2013) 'Benefits of dramatherapy for Autism Spectrum Disorder: a qualitative analysis of feedback from parents and teachers of clients attending Roundabout dramatherapy sessions in schools', *Dramatherapy*, 35(1), pp.20–28.

Greene, J. (2012) 'An educational psychology service evaluation of a dramatherapy intervention for children with additional needs in primary school', in Leigh, L., Gersch, I., Dix, A. and Haythorne, D. (eds), *Dramatherapy with Children, Young People and Schools.* London: Routledge.

Higashida, N. (2013) *The Reason I Jump.* London: Sceptre, Hodder & Stoughton.

Holloway, P. and Seebohm, H. (2011) 'When worlds collide: culture, dialogue and identity in multi-professional settings', *Dramatherapy*, 33(1), pp.4–15.

Jennings, S. (1995) 'Dramatherapy for survival: some thoughts on transitions and choices for children and adolescents', in Jennings, S. (ed.), *Dramatherapy with Children and Adolescents.* London: Routledge.

Jones, P. (1996) *Drama as Therapy: Theatre as Living.* London: Routledge.

Jones, P. (2007) *Drama as Therapy: Theory Practice and Research*, 2nd edn. London: Routledge.

Jordan, R. and Jones, G. (1999) *Meeting the Needs of Children with Autistic Spectrum Disorders.* London: David Fulton

Landy, R. (1996) *Essays in Drama Therapy: The Double Life.* London: Jessica Kingsley Publishers.

Lindkvist, M. (1974) *Movement & Drama with Autistic Children.* Abridged report, clinical research project. London: Sesame Institute.

McConnell, K. and Ryser, G. R. (2007) *Practical Ideas That Really Work for Students with Autistic Spectrum Disorders*, 2nd edn. Austin, TX: Pro-ed.

Mitchell, S. (1994) 'The theatre of self-expression: a "therapeutic theatre" model of dramatherapy', in Jennings, S. (ed.), *The Handbook of Dramatherapy.* London: Routledge.

Morrison, J. M. D. (2006) *DSMIV Made Easy: The Clinician's Guide to Diagnosis.* New York: Guilford Press.

Scott-Danter, H. (2006) *Arts Creativity and Mental Health Initiative Reports from Four Arts Therapies Trial Services.* London: Mental Health Foundation.

Sherratt, D. and Peter, M. (2002) *Developing Play and Drama in Children with Autistic Spectrum Disorders.* London: David Fulton.

Smail, M. (2013) 'Entering and leaving the place of myth', in Pearson, J., Smail, M. and Watts, P. (eds), *Dramatherapy with Myth and Fairytale.* London: Jessica Kingsley Publishers.

Williams, D. (1999) *Nobody Nowhere.* London: Jessica Kingsley Publishers.

Williams, D. (1996) *Autism: An Inside-Out Approach.* London: Jessica Kingsley Publishers.

Wilmer-Barbrook, C. (2013) 'Adolescence, Asperger's and acting: can dramatherapy improve social and communication skills for young people with Asperger's syndrome?', *Dramatherapy*, 35(1), pp.43–56.

Wolfberg, P. J. (1999) *Play & Imagination in Children with Autism.* New York: Teachers College Press.

13

AN EXPLORATION OF THE IMPACT OF DRAMATHERAPY ON THE WHOLE SYSTEM SUPPORTING CHILDREN AND YOUNG PEOPLE ON THE AUTISTIC SPECTRUM

Emma Godfrey and Deborah Haythorne

Introduction

This chapter builds on a study of written feedback post dramatherapy intervention for children and young people with Autistic Spectrum Disorder (ASD) provided by parent/carers and teachers (Godfrey and Haythorne, 2013). The study revealed five key themes, with no negative comments being recorded. This offered encouraging support for dramatherapy sessions in schools as delivered by Roundabout, a charity (Godfrey and Haythorne, 2013). However, the feedback was brief and the written format meant that comments could not be explored in detail. As a result, this chapter reports on an interview study, which was conducted with relevant stake holders to facilitate a deeper understanding of the impact of dramatherapy on children, families and schools.

The main diagnostic criteria for ASD include a triad of impairments in reciprocal social interaction, language and communication, and repetitive and stereotypic interests and behaviours (Goodman and Scott, 2012). People on the autistic spectrum have been described by Frith (1989) as having 'literal minds', meaning specific deficits in emotional intelligence, theory of mind and the use of metaphor. People with autism have difficulties in recognising and processing both their own and other people's emotions and mental states (Hill, Berthoz and Frith, 2004; Silani et al., 2008). As a result, their behaviour can be seen as inappropriate or immature, and considerable difficulties are encountered with peers. Children and young people with ASD are therefore at risk of anxiety and depression as they mature and become more aware of their social impairments and limited life opportunities. Studies have shown a relationship between these deficits in social skills and social anxiety, suggesting that an intervention targeting social skills could be appropriate for this group (Bellini, 2004).

Dramatherapy is particularly suitable for this client group (National Autistic Society, 2012) because it develops social skills and supports the expression of feelings using structured work that helps reduce anxiety. The dramatherapist can model clear expressive communication, as well as facilitate developing relationships with others, by giving participants opportunities to rehearse and replay social skills until they are learned and integrated into behaviour. Carrette (1992) has suggested that the very flexibility of dramatherapy and its spectrum of creative–expressive methods enables therapists to respond appropriately to each child's needs, with the aim of maximising their potential. Such potential will vary depending on participants' abilities and special needs, but the content of sessions can range from non-verbal movement and sensory awareness work to role play within sophisticated storytelling and performance (Lindkvist, 1997; Crimmens, 2006; Lewis and Banerjee, 2013; Wilmer-Barbrook, 2013).

Recent research suggests that social skills training can help children and adolescents with Asperger's syndrome and high-functioning autism. Lerner et al. (2011) used a 'socio-dramatic affective–relational intervention', a type of drama-based social interaction intervention, to improve social skills. They found clients demonstrated encouraging improvements in assertion and their ability to detect emotions in adult voices, and subsequently parents reported fewer social problems. The study included 17 participants aged 11–17 years and employed a manualised intervention. However, the intervention was conducted over two weeks in an American summer camp setting without using either dramatherapy or trained dramatherapists, so the findings may not necessarily apply to other contexts or practitioners. Indeed, Corbett et al. (2014) suggest more research into longer-term school-based interventions is needed.

Tytherleigh and Karkou (2010) report on a small study, based on six weeks of dramatherapy with children focusing on relationship building through Embodiment activities, Projective techniques, Group interactions and Role-playing. They suggest further research is needed into the effectiveness of dramatherapy within special education. Dooman, in Chapter 12 of this book, measures social communication in a group of children between the ages of 5 and 7 years attending weekly dramatherapy sessions, using 'The Behavioural Assessment of Social Communication of Young Children' pre and post the play-based observation test (2010). Feed-back from parents, carers and teachers was also assessed through questionnaires focusing on the children's social interactions and communication skills using the McConnell and Ryser (2007) pro-ed rating scale. The results are generally very encouraging, showing positive improvements in children attending this group.

A more extensive piece of research has been carried out by dramatherapist Lee Chasen (2011), investigating positive communication and social interaction through his Process Reflective Enactment programme, using games, role play, stories and improvisations. He suggests all children are capable of learning social skills through play and that a dramatherapy-based approach 'to social skills and emotional growth in autistic children enacts processes that mirror critical functions within developmental systems, prompting psychodynamic awareness and insight, and perhaps more significantly for this particular population, integrates processes that support competence with the manual shifting of gears between perception of and pragmatic response to self and other' (pp.69–70).

Wilmer-Barbrook (2013) reports on a group of 8 young people aged 16–24 years with Asperger's syndrome attending a 36-week dramatherapy group in a specialist education and therapy service. She chooses to focus on four main categories for evaluation, producing quantitative outcomes through questionnaires completed by the clients, their tutors and their parents/carers. The areas she assesses are: self-confidence and self-esteem; communication skills; social skills and ability to co-operate; and ability to express emotions – all of these fall broadly under the heading of 'social and communication skills'. Her results show that there was an overall 'improvement' across all categories of 24 per cent, suggesting that, through attending weekly dramatherapy session over an academic year, 'Friendships are forged, relationships grow and life experiences are shared in a safe, containing environment' (p.55). However, the study shows little consideration for the impact of other variables in the young people's lives that might have confounded the results. In addition, caution is needed when interpreting these results, as reference is made to some issues around relationships between clients and their families and difficulties in eliciting feed-back from families when the sessions are carried out at the specialist education and therapy service.

It is clear that issues associated with ASD create difficulties in forging strong and supportive relationships (Miller, 2005; Sherratt and Peter, 2002). The anxieties the condition often generates can make familiar situations challenging, and make new situations an ordeal (Grandin and Scariano, 2005; Grandin, 2006; Williams, 1996, 1998a, 1998b); thus many children and young people with ASD struggle to develop relationships and need specialist teaching and support if they are to progress or thrive at school (Potter and Whittaker, 2001; Balten et al., 2006). Research to date shows that dramatherapy offers a therapeutic approach that can begin to address some of these difficult issues (Lindkvist, 1997; Jones, 1984; Wilmer-Barbrook, 2013).

Roundabout dramatherapy

Roundabout is a dramatherapy charity comprising a large team of professional Health and Care Professions Council (HCPC) registered dramatherapists working in over fifty weekly projects with a range of service users of all ages. Roundabout has developed a specialism in working with people with ASD in a wide variety of settings and believes that dramatherapy is particularly effective for people with ASD, irrespective of age, ability and background. Over the last two years (2012–2014) Roundabout has run 15 different weekly projects with people with ASD. These have taken place in a variety of specialist provisions including primary schools and secondary schools, specialist day centres, and residential homes.

Engagement with dramatherapy in Roundabout's projects takes many forms, for example two therapists to one child/adult or one therapist to a group. In a group setting, the preference is for working with small groups of up to three or four clients, where both individual and group aims can be addressed. Referrals for the service are made by the service users themselves or by teachers, key-workers,

tutors, social workers, and parents or carers. The dramatherapist will assess suitabil-
ity for therapy by meeting potential service users and offering a number of assessment sessions. Following this, the service user may be offered a further short or
longer course of dramatherapy. Therapists may set up meetings with parents/carers
and teachers to offer feed-back and will carry out a series of evaluation processes
before and after the sessions.

Evaluation

The evaluation of Roundabout dramatherapy projects takes a number of forms
depending on what is accessible to the service users. Some evaluation methods are
self-reporting pre- and post-therapy evaluation methods, such as Psychlops Kids
(www.psychlops.org.uk/kids) and 'Hopes and Wishes'. Other methods of evaluation are used by the therapists or parent/carer, such as Strengths and Difficulties
Questionnaire (Goodman 2001; Goodman and Goodman, 2009), Behavioural
Summarised Evaluation (Barthelemy et al., 1990), and Therapy Outcomes.
Roundabout invites written feed-back from the teachers, key workers, parents and
carers of each individual who attends dramatherapy. Consent to attend therapy is
given in writing by parents/carers prior to sessions starting and by service users
before they attend and again during the work. Confidentiality is explained in an
accessible way, including the statement, 'See it here, hear it here, leave it here', and
information is shared on a need-to-know basis.

Aims for dramatherapy sessions

Roundabout's projects use dramatherapy to generate a number of benefits for all
service users. Dramatherapy aims for each individual are identified through the
referral form and the assessment process. These individual aims fall within the
framework of the main aims, which are to help service users with ASD to take full
advantage of the educational, cultural and social opportunities available to them.
The dramatherapy intervention thus focuses on achieving the following outcomes:

→   increased confidence and self-esteem
→   improved sense of self and how to relate to others
→   increased opportunities to develop creativity and imaginative thinking
→   improved co-operation and turn-taking
→   greater social and communication skills
→   improved skills to work effectively alone and with others
→   improved mental wellbeing.

The basic structure of a session remains the same every week in order to increase
confidence and reduce anxiety related to change. However, within the basic structure the main theme for each week will change in response to feed-back from
the group in the sessions and the issues that arise over the course of the project.

The dramatherapists work with both verbal and non-verbal forms of communication, introducing structured ways of saying hello and goodbye, songs, ball and drama games, storytelling, imaginary play, movement work, and relaxation. The sessions offer clearly defined boundaries and structures that help build trust and familiarity in the sessions and with each other (Chesner, 1995; Tytherleigh and Karkou, 2010). In this therapeutic environment, people with ASD are able to explore expressing and communicating their needs, feelings and interests.

Interviews with stakeholders: young people, parents/cares and teachers

One of the Roundabout dramatherapists interviewed 12 people for this study, either at home or at their schools. The interviewees included: 5 parents/carers, 5 school staff members and 2 young people, who were interviewed with their mothers. One young person was interviewed alongside his mum and his grandma, and the other young person was interviewed with his mum. The other three parents were mothers of boys who had finished attending dramatherapy. The school staff were all from primary schools and comprised: one teacher and one deputy head teacher, attached to a specialist unit in a mainstream primary school; two teaching assistants, attached to a specialist unit for children with autism; and one Emotional Literacy Support Assistant.

Interviews were semi-structured with a topic guide, and included open questions about the perceived effect of dramatherapy, as well as exploring themes identified in the earlier study of written feedback (Godfrey and Haythorne, 2013). Participants were encouraged to talk openly about areas they felt important and relevant. They were asked to be as comprehensive and honest as possible in their responses, and to provide examples to enable a clear understanding of their thoughts and feelings. Permission to audio-record the interviews was sought and given by each participant prior to the interviews for publication purposes and they were assured that their responses would be anonymous and confidential.

Interviews were recorded and then transcribed verbatim, and a thematic analysis was undertaken. This approach involves identifying, analysing and reporting patterns (themes) within the data. It organises and describes the data set in rich detail (Braun and Clarke, 2006). The transcripts were read carefully to create an initial code list. Each transcript was read line by line and any concepts fitting these codes were categorised accordingly. If any new concepts arose from the transcripts, they were added to the initial code list. The next stage involved organising the codes into themes. The data were then interpreted by identifying re-occurring themes, and similarities and differences were highlighted. The final stage involved data verification by rechecking both the transcripts and codes so the researcher could verify or modify their previous hypotheses (Sarantakos, 2012). Following this process, the *codes* were reviewed by another researcher to ensure interpretive validity, and finally the *themes* were reviewed by a participant to ensure respondent validity.

The results included seven key themes, as detailed below:

- Feelings: a safe place to explore emotions.
- Anxiety: a noticeable reduction in anxiety through coming to the sessions, facilitated by the repeated structure of sessions.
- Social skills: gaining better social skills and behaving more appropriately, with role play providing a short cut to learning and practising these skills.
- Confidence: increasing confidence and sense of self-worth secured by praise from dramatherapists and one-to-one attention.
- Classroom: changed behaviour in class particularly towards school work in terms of improved attitude and motivation.
- Families: supporting the whole system.
- Peers: being included and making friends.

Thematic analysis

Each of the seven themes will now be explored in more detail and illustrated with relevant quotes from the participants.

1. Feelings: a safe place to explore emotions

This theme explains how the dramatherapy group provided a safe place where clients felt accepted, which facilitated the exploration of difficult experiences and emotions without judgement. Many people on the autistic spectrum really struggle with and become confused by expressing and understanding feelings (Attwood, 2008), so it is really interesting that parents and teachers reported that the dramatherapy sessions offered an outlet and safe place for exploration. Parents and teachers also reported a change of attitude towards school on the days when dramatherapy was provided.

> *I think that it sort of gave him an outlet . . . kind of be a bit more physical and act out some of his sort of quirky imagination. Erm, so I think that would have made, that made him happy, happier at school coz he kind of had a, like an outlet if you like, somewhere to go and, um, not have to sort of hold it all together. He could sort of go and, um, just be himself and you know, not have to worry so much about how loud he was talking or you know. . . .* (Mother, participant 5)

> *I'll start at the beginning. Well at the beginning he really was the most unhappy at school and then we noticed once he started Dramatherapy on Friday morning, Friday was the one day he didn't mind getting up and getting ready for school and it became very obvious it was because it was Dramatherapy day.* (Grandmother, participant 3)

> *. . . and they love it! And they will wait all week and it will be like the pinnacle that, of their week and, and you can almost see afterwards that they've been, you know, walking back to class, you can almost see sometimes like the weight that's gone off their shoulders, because they've had that opportunity and that space and that time,*

just to get things off their chest. And as I say, whether that's just by talking to you, or through the context of whatever story they've chosen, but you, you literally sometimes, it is almost they're just three feet taller, because they, that weight that's been, you know, kind of pushing down on them for the last week has gone. And it just lasts a few days and then they just need another little slot. (Teacher, participant 9)

2. Anxiety: a noticeable reduction in anxiety through coming to the sessions, facilitated by the repeated structure of sessions

This theme relates to how the dramatherapy session content and structure works for children and young people with ASD, reducing anxiety and building confidence. Teachers and carers spoke about how children were often overwhelmed by their anxiety and how this was lessened by coming to dramatherapy sessions, where they had the opportunity to actively work through these fears.

Yeah, because it's not just about the learning and the education, if it's not addressing their inner anxieties . . . the learning isn't going to happen . . . because they're dealing with all the other stuff, they're overwhelmed. (Teacher, participant 4)

I do remember that when we spoke to you . . . and you would say, oh he's talking about the police and making these stories about the police and he's this and that and the other and we could see these were all things that had been bothering him. And yet he was able to make stories out of it and make it lighthearted and fun and we noticed, didn't we, he was working through those anxieties and which made it easier to learn if he was less anxious. (Grandmother, participant 3)

I think for some of our children there's an awful lot going on, at home, there's an awful lot going on in their lives so that their heads are just full the whole time of all of their angst and their worries and I think Dramatherapy allows them to offload. (Teacher, participant 9)

3. Social skills: gaining better social skills and behaving more appropriately, with role play providing a short cut to learning and practising these skills

This theme reflects the importance of imitation and role play, which can offer the opportunity to rehearse real life situations (Attwood, 2008), with dramatherapy sessions often employing imitation, mirroring and role play to encounter and re-enact real life in a rehearsal space (Chasen, 2011). Participants commented that children were able to practise expressing and learning to control emotions in the session and then this enabled better communication and behaviour outside the session.

. . . we've noticed, although he still does get angry, it's not manifesting in, in violent outbursts so much as he's, you know, sort of getting more articulate . . . and he said that he thought when he was younger, it helped him because that's when he wasn't

talking as much and I think he, he felt that . . . it sort of helped him to express himself when he couldn't verbally express himself. (Mother, participant 8)

. . . and he still acts things out when he's troubled, doesn't he? Like when he had that seizure in the summer when he kept doing it and I think that's his way of communicating that he's bothered about it. (Mother, participant 2)

. . . it gives them the opportunity to play out their scenarios that are going on in their head that might not be socially acceptable outside of the room. Erm, that wouldn't, would be you know, in, not a better term, but, frowned upon . . . it gives them the opportunity to play that out, that they, they need to play out, because they need to sort of get over that in their head before they can carry on with their, like their normal day or their, you know, their, the structure of the rest of the day. They need to do that, but sometimes in the real world, so to speak, um, they're not able to do that. They're not able to express themselves the way they need to express themselves. (Learning support assistant, participant 10)

4. Confidence: increasing confidence and sense of self-worth secured by praise from dramatherapists and one-to-one attention

This theme demonstrates how the dramatherapy group supports service users to develop confidence and self-esteem through practising social situations and in storymaking and drama enactments. It is also clear from our findings that the personal contact with a skilled, empathic practitioner was highly valued, as Chasen (2011) notes: 'The dramatherapist's own engaging and animated personality is an inseparable component of neurological development and learning' (p.259).

. . . Dramatherapy was the one therapy that he would look forward to, each week. And, it used to be on a Friday and it would be 'Friday, it's Deb on a Friday!' And, it was a chance for him to be creative, not be told to be quiet, because I think he had a very vivid imagination . . . if his brain sort of went off at a tangent, he was told, alright, ok, shh shh shh. You know, er, don't. . . be disruptive. Not, you know, probably like that but um, but at least dramatherapy gave him the freedom and the space to express himself and to also, um, deal with his anxieties I think. (Mother, participant 1)

. . . .I wasn't afraid to try, like I just, you know, like, never bothered wanting to try anything . . . I don't know, I just really never tried anything but you know, I thought, since this seemed fun I thought, yeah I'll try it. (Young Person, participant 6)

. . . so he used to, like when he get told off, like he always saying, I'm a bad boy, no one, no one likes me or no one welcomes me but through the dramatherapy and he got really confident and he knows he can do this and he really likes this so it's kind of showing like his strength. (Mother, participant 7)

5. Classroom: changed behaviour in class particularly towards school work in terms of improved attitude and motivation

This theme illustrates how dramatherapy can encourage the use of better strategies for pupils with ASD in the classroom. Participants felt that having this provision in their schools had enabled children with ASD to have increased tolerance of stress in the classroom and therefore the potential to benefit more from their education.

> *I think he used to get very tense in a classroom situation and, sort of very stressed with noise and a lot of hustle and bustle and from what I, from what I know of what happened in the sessions, there was a, a gradual sort of increase in the, the level of tolerance.* (Mother, participant 8)

> *I think it helps to reduce anxiety, definitely, which then helps their learning. I think it helps us as teachers understand some underlying issues that the children wouldn't otherwise be able to verbalise. So it gives us an insight so then we can adapt their learning experience, umm, I think they're the main things.* (Teacher, participant 4)

> *. . . and gives them that space to work through all of those feelings and those thoughts so that they're able to empty their heads a little bit for an amount of time of those angst and their worries and then it allows them to get them into a better place so that they can learn more in the classroom and I just think if you didn't have that, I just think they would just be overloaded with all of, you know, they just have so much that they're worrying about.* (Teacher, participant 9)

> *. . . the young lad that I actually do support in Year 6, um, it's helped me understand a little bit more about where he comes from, you know, so that when he, when he's had his dramatherapy, he's, you know, we, we then liaise with the team and we get what his issues and problems are, so you're always thinking about them. And you can use it when you are in the classroom.* (Learning support assistant, Participant 10)

6. Families: supporting the whole system

This theme relates to how the dramatherapy service supports not only group members but the wider family, school and community around them. The participants felt that their dramatherapist was like a bridge between the school and the family and that this special role fostered better communication between the two.

> *. . . so it's a really big impact. And also, you know I say, he's more calm, you know, so when he comes home, so, it's like, you know, especially like so after Dramatherapy so like he feels much more relaxed and you know, more positive than other days.* (Mother, participant 7)

> *I know, I think some things that she has now in the class, I know have come because I've spoken to you. And then you've gone off and sort of spoken to them and you*

know, they listen, the school respect your decision. So that's helped me, coz I think, sometimes you know, it helps if someone else is kind of on your side, you know? (Mother, participant 5)

. . . to be honest it's, er, within where I'm working, if I have an issue with toileting, which again can be typical of ASD . . . . Or, erm, anxieties, and I've reached the end of the line of what I can do, I, I would usually come to you and see what's come up in Dramatherapy. (Teacher, participant 4)

I think for, sometimes you're able to form a different kind of relationship with the parents and you're able to have some, sometimes quite difficult conversations with parents and, and because you're a step removed from the school, you can do that and it's much easier for you to do that, rather than the school to do that. So, I think all of those things are really, really important. (Teacher, participant 9)

7. Peers: being included and making friends

The final theme demonstrates how participants reported that dramatherapy groups support service users to develop their social interaction skills and explore their understanding of friendship. Working together in a group creates a sense of shared identity, safety, acceptance and meaningful encounter (Chasen, 2011). Our findings suggest it also promotes the development of peer relationships, which is something that many children on the autistic spectrum really struggle with.

Well he would never ever interact with other children at all but then through Dramatherapy he was able to be around one or two children wasn't he? So that was socially sort of, a massive breakthrough, massive, don't think anything else would have brought him to do that. (Mother, participant 2)

. . . I think, and they're able to form such good relationships, I think, with you and the team, it just means that they, that they're in a very very good place where they can explore those areas which, I think, are quite difficult to them, for them. (Teacher, participant 9)

You know, coz some of them I know do individual drama sessions but a lot of them work in groups and I think that in itself helps them, forms a bond and helps them understand how relationships work and about listening to other people and what sort of feelings others have apart from themselves. (Learning support assistant, participant 10)

Discussion

This chapter presents a thematic analysis of interviews with 12 stake holders (young people with ASD, parents/carers, teachers and other school staff) about the impact of dramatherapy. Seven themes emerged from the data, encompassing using a predictable structure to lessen anxiety and facilitate exploring feelings; using role play and participation to develop confidence, peer relationships and social skills; and supporting the whole system around a child, including families and schools. The findings define the areas where dramatherapy is perceived by our participants to be particularly beneficial for children and young people with ASD. They also reveal overwhelming support from parent/carers and teachers for the use of dramatherapy with this client group, as no negative comments were recorded in the interviews.

There has been little previous research in this area, but evidence is accumulating for the value of dramatherapy in the management of ASD, and other studies have findings that support our results. Chasen (2011) reports anecdotal evidence from parents of children who have attended dramatherapy as part of 'Kid Esteem', saying that they have noticed the skills gained in the dramatherapy are also seen 'in their schools, on playgrounds, at family functions and other social areas of their lives' (p.308). Parents reported a significant positive difference in empathy in Greene's (2012) report on a 10-week dramatherapy intervention with 20 children aged 6–10 years, even though no change was seen in school. Bailey (2009) has suggested that a repeated simple session structure reduces overstimulation and overwhelm, creating the opportunity to increase confidence and reduce anxiety, while others have also noted that the repeated structure of the sessions provides trust and a sense of security that reduces anxiety (Chesner, 1995; Jennings, 1990). Tubbs (2008) recommends using characters and symbols in fairy tales to help children with ASD explore their feelings and thoughts: 'fairy tales provide an imaginative, creative way of teaching morals and encouraging children who may be absorbed in their own sensitive, isolated world' (p.180). It appears that the development of shared play and trust within group work can lead to growing peer relationships and increased self-confidence (Wilmer-Barbrook, 2013; Attwood, 2008; Chasen, 2011). In addition, social skills interventions including drama-based elements are successful in terms of parent-reported assertion/assertiveness and social problems (Lerner et al., 2011).

The strengths of our findings consisted of conducting in-depth interviews with a wide range of respondents, which enabled a full exploration of the impact of dramatherapy in schools. Rigorous analysis, including independent coding and respondent validation of the themes, can ensure the validity of our findings, as both of these methods are acknowledged ways of assuring the integrity of qualitative data (Elliott et al., 1999). Using an interviewer from Roundabout was possibly both a strength and a weakness – a strength, as she already had a good rapport with our participants, which facilitated the interview process, but a possible limitation if her role prevented any negative issues from being raised. However, our previous analysis of written comments after dramatherapy did not reveal any negative statements (Godfrey and Haythorne, 2013), so perhaps such issues would not have arisen in any case. Another limitation was the small number of interviews with children and young people with ASD. Although the children and young people were not the focus of this investigation, the two young people we did interview with their families were reluctant, or unable, to fully engage with the interview process.

This research and other chapters in this book provide inspiring evidence for the value of dramatherapy for people on the autistic spectrum. It is important to listen to the voices of children and young people with ASD who take part in dramatherapy, and to find ways to facilitate their feedback. The growing body of evidence for dramatherapy interventions with this client group suggests a next step might be to test the efficacy of dramatherapy using an experimental design, such as a randomised controlled trial with multi-informant repeated measures, allowing the efficacy of dramatherapy to be evaluated over the short and longer term. In addition, it might be helpful to examine therapy process, to see which therapeutic techniques and environments are most responsible for any changes, and what intensity and frequency is most beneficial to service users.

Conclusion

This chapter demonstrates the endorsement from parents, carers and school staff looking after children and young people with ASD for the use of dramatherapy in schools. They reported that dramatherapy was a positive intervention that facilitated emotional development, peer relationships and social skills in participants, as well as helping to support the wider family and school system around the child. The results of this interview study are encouraging and indicate that further study of dramatherapy treatment is warranted in order to build the evidence base for such interventions in children and young people with ASD.

References

Attwood, T. (2008) *The Complete Guide to Asperger's Syndrome*. London: Jessica Kingsley Publishers.

Bailey, S. (2009) 'Theoretical reasons and practical application of drama therapy with clients on the autism spectrum', in Brooke, S. L. (ed.), *The Use of Creative Therapies with Autism Spectrum Disorders*. Springfield, IL: Charles C Thomas Publishers.

Balten, A. Corbett, C., Rosenblatt, M., Withers, L. and Yuille, R. (2006) *Make School Make Sense. Autism and Education: The Reality for Families Today*, The National Autistic Society, at http://www.autism.org.uk [accessed 08/04/2015].

Barthelemy, C., Adrien, J. L., Tanguay, P., Garreay, B., Fermanian, J. and Roux, S. (1990) 'The Behavioral Summarized Evaluation: validity and reliability of the scale for the assessment of autistic behaviors', *Journal of Autism and Developmental Disorders*, 20, pp.189–203.

Bellini, S. (2004) 'Social skill deficits and anxiety in high-functioning adolescents with autism spectrum disorders', *Focus on Autism and Other Developmental Disabilities*, 19(2), pp.78–86.

Braun, V. and Clarke, V. (2006) 'Using thematic analysis in psychology', *Qualitative Research in Psychology*, 3(2), pp. 77–101.

Carrette, J. (1992) 'Autism and Dramatherapy', *Dramatherapy*, 15(1), pp.17–20.

Chasen, L. R. (2011) *Social Skills, Emotional Growth and Drama Therapy*. London: Jesssica Kingsley Publications.

Chesner, A. (1995) *Dramatherapy for People with Learning Difficulties*. London: Jessica Kingsley Publishers.

Corbett, B. A., Swain, D. M., Coke, C., Simon, D., Newsom, C., Houchins-Juarez, N. and Song, Y. (2014) 'Improvement in social deficits in autism spectrum disorders using a theatre-based, peer-mediated intervention', *Autism Research*, 7(1), pp.4–16.

Crimmens, P. (2006) *Drama Therapy and Storymaking in Special Education.* London and Philadelphia, PA: Jessica Kingsley Publishers.

Elliott, R., Fischer, C. and Rennie, D. (1999) 'Evolving guidelines for publication of qualitative research studies in psychology and related fields', *British Journal of Clinical Psychology,* 38, pp.215–229.

Frith, U. (1989) *Autism: Explaining the Enigma.* Oxford: Blackwell.

Godfrey, E. and Haythorne, D. (2013) 'Benefits of dramatherapy for Autism Spectrum Disorder: a qualitative analysis of feedback from parents and teachers of clients attending Roundabout dramatherapy sessions in schools', *Dramatherapy,* 35(1), pp.20–28.

Goodman, R. (2001) 'Psychometric properties of the Strengths and Difficulties Questionnaire (SDQ)', *Journal of the American Academy of Child and Adolescent Psychiatry,* 40, pp.1337–1345.

Goodman, A., and Goodman, R. (2009) 'Strengths and Difficulties Questionnaire as a dimensional measure of child mental health', *Journal of the American Academy of Child & Adolescent Psychiatry,* 48(4), pp.400–403.

Goodman, R. and Scott, S. (2012) *Child and Adolescent Psychiatry* (3rd edition). Oxford: Wiley-Blackwell.

Grandin, T. (2006) *Thinking in Pictures.* London: Bloomsbury Publishing.

Grandin, T. and Scariano, M. M. (2005) *Emergence: Labeled Autistic.* New York: Grand Central Publishing.

Greene, J. (2012) 'An education psychology service evaluation of a dramatherapy intervention for children with additional needs in primary school', in Leigh, L., Gersch, I., Dix, A. and Haythorne, D. (eds), *Dramatherapy with Children, Young People and Schools.* London: Routledge.

Hill, E., Berthoz, S. and Frith, U. (2004) 'Brief report: cognitive processing of own emotions in individuals with autistic spectrum disorder and in their relatives', *Journal of Autism and Developmental Disorders,* 34(2), pp.229–235.

Jennings, S. (1990) *Dramatherapy with Families, Groups and Individuals: Waiting in the Wings.* London: Jessica Kingsley Publishers.

Jones, P. (1984) 'Therapeutic storymaking and autism', in Dubowski, J. (ed.), *Art Therapy as a Psychotherapy with the Mentally Handicapped.* Conference Proceedings, Hertfordshire College of Art and Design.

Lerner, M., Mikami, A. and Levine, K. (2011) 'Socio-dramatic affective–relational intervention for adolescents with Asperger's syndrome and high functioning autism: pilot study', *Autism,* 15(1), pp.21–42.

Lewis, J. and Banerjee, S. (2013) 'An investigation of the therapeutic potential of stories in Dramatherapy with young people with autistic spectrum disorder', *Dramatherapy,* 35(1), pp.29–42.

Lindkvist, M. R. (1997) 'Movement and drama with autistic children', in Shatner, G. and Courtney, R. (eds), *Drama in Therapy Vol 1: Children.* New York: Drama Book Specialists.

Miller, S. (2005) 'Developing friendship skills with children with pervasive developmental disorders: a case study', *Dramatherapy: The Journal of the British Association of Dramatherapists,* 27(2), pp.11–16.

National Autistic Society (2012) At www.nas.org.uk [accessed 31/05/2015].

Potter, C. and Whittaker, C. (2001) *Enabling Communication in Children with Autism.* London: Jessica Kingsley Publishers.

Sarantakos, S. (2012) *Social Research* (4th edition). Houndmills: Palgrave Macmillan.

Sherratt, D. and Peter, M. (2002) *Developing Play and Drama in Children with Autistic Spectrum Disorder.* London: David Fulton Publishers.

Silani, G., Bird, G., Brindley, R., Singer, T., Frith, C. and Frith, U. (2008) 'Levels of emotional awareness and autism: an fMRI study', *Social Neuroscience*, 3(2), pp.97–112.

Tubbs, J. (2008) *Creative Therapy for Children with Autism, ADD, and Asperger's Using Artistic Creativity to Reach, Teach, and Touch Our Children*. New York: Square One Publishers.

Tytherleigh, L. and Karkou, V. (2010) 'Dramatherapy, autism and relationship building: a case study', in Karkou, V. (ed.), *Arts Therapies in Schools: Research and Practice*. London: Jessica Kingsley Publishers.

Williams, D. (1996) *Autism: An Inside-Out Approach*. London: Jessica Kingsley Publishers.

Williams, D. (1998) *Nobody Nowhere: The Remarkable Autobiography of an Autistic Girl*. London: Jessica Kingsley Publishers.

Williams, D. (1998) *Somebody Somewhere: Breaking Free from the World of Autism*. London: Jessica Kingsley Publishers.

Wilmer-Barbrook, C. (2013) 'Adolescence, Asperger's and acting: can dramatherapy improve social and communication skills for young people with Asperger's syndrome?', *Dramatherapy*, 35(1), pp.43–56.

INDEX

adolescence 72–74, 106, 108, 139
adults: with complex needs 2, 121–134; men with Asperger's 2, 106–118
aesthetic distance 10, 44, 51, 60, 98, 102, 103, 146
agency 53, 55–56
aggression 39, 45, 73
Alonim, Hanna 34
Andersen-Warren, M. 7, 12, 17, 106, 107, 139
anger 110, 116, 126
anxiety 7, 47, 156–157; about relationships 49–50; adults with complex needs 125, 132–133, 134; counter-transference 32; early social behaviour 148–149; externalisation of 49; girls 66, 67, 73, 75, 76; introverted clients 85, 86, 87, 89, 91; loneliness 108, 138; men with Asperger's 108, 117; reduction of 26; session structure 166; stakeholder interviews 161, 162, 164
art 47, 74, 75, 85, 86, 92
Artaud, A. 96
Asperger, Hans 8, 10, 43, 68, 107, 108
Asperger's syndrome 8, 11, 89, 139; definition of 106–107; gender differences 67; impact of dramatherapy 158; men with 2, 106–118; social skills training 157
assessment 6, 77, 147–153
attachment 6, 18, 35, 39, 116, 122
attention deficit hyperactivity disorder (ADHD) 54, 55, 122

'attentional spotlight' 145
attunement 122, 129
Attwood, T. 72, 108, 112
autism 6–7, 8–12, 156–158; adults with complex needs 121–134; definition of 8; diagnosis of 8–9; early social behaviour 137–153; gender differences 67–68; girls 66–77; introverted clients 83, 84–92; non-verbal clients 29–39; as performance 95–96, 100–101, 102; Roundabout dramatherapy 158–166; social skills training 157; Williams on 38–39; working with metaphor 16–27, 41–52; see also Asperger's syndrome
'autistic objects' 17

Bailey, S. 166
Bainbridge, C. 83
Baker, Ava Ruth 67
Bandura, A. 101
Banerjee, S. 11, 26, 75
Barnbaum, Deborah 94
Baron-Cohen, S. B. 16–17, 20–21, 68–69, 74, 97, 108
Barrie, J. M. 32, 39
Barton, M. 50
The Behavioural Assessment of Social Communication (BASYC) 137, 139, 140, 141, 147–149, 152–153, 157
Benbow, Adrian 2, 106–120, 121–136
Bettelheim, B. 43
Bleuler, Eugen 8
Boal, A. 147

body 95, 128, 147
Bogdashina, O. 11, 20, 22, 138, 145
Booker, Mary 11–12, 122
boundaries 7, 38, 45
Bouzoukis, Carol 56
boxes 47
boys 55, 66; diagnosis 67–68; genetic
    hypothesis 69; play with toys 71;
    stereotyping 73–74
brain development 34, 68, 69, 74
Breuer, J. 42
British Association of Dramatherapists
    (BADth) 5, 44, 53, 109, 123–124
Bromfield, R. 74
Brown, T. 7
Brugha, T. 67
Bruyn, S. T. 42
bullying 90
Butler, Judith 95

Cain, S. 83
Callahan, E. 137
Carrette, Jeremy 11, 56, 157
Carveth, D. L. 42
character work 10, 17, 19–20, 27, 41;
    Colourland 24–25; girls 76; introverted
    clients 88; men with Asperger's
    115–116; Pokémon 22–24; school-based
    dramatherapy 60; *The Silky Stranger* 41,
    45, 48–49
Chasen, Lee R. 16, 22, 138; comedy 149;
    dramatherapist's personality 163; 'Kid
    Esteem' 166; mirroring 99, 129; Process
    Reflective Enactment model 7, 11, 12,
    157; rituals 18, 143; role taking 144;
    sensory stimulus 145
Chesner, A. 122, 128
child and adolescent mental health service
    (CAMHS) 58, 77
Clarkson, Petrushka 30
classroom behaviour 161, 164
client reviews 131
Code of Practice 53, 55
communication 8, 9, 11, 68, 137, 159;
    adults with complex needs 125;
    Asperger's syndrome 107; Chasen's
    research 157; common language 20;
    early intervention 138, 153; girls 69,
    70–71; impact of dramatherapy on 158;
    McConnell and Ryser pro-ed rating
    scale 141–142, 151, 152; metaphoric
    50; *see also* language; non-verbal
    communication
complex needs, adults with 121–134

confidence 10, 11, 93, 159; adults with
    complex needs 132, 134; Asperger's
    syndrome 107; girls 72, 75, 76, 77;
    group work 166; impact of dramatherapy
    on 158; introverted clients 86; men with
    Asperger's 113, 114, 117, 118; session
    structure 166; stakeholder interviews
    161, 163
consent 94
containment 6, 17–18, 23, 27, 47–48,
    113–114
conversation 141, 150
Cooley, C. 94
co-operation 159
Corbett, B. A. 157
counter-transference 30, 32, 122
creativity 10, 77, 159

dance 113, 114–115
Davidson, Rosalind 2, 16–28
day centres 124
defences 30
depression 39, 66, 72, 88, 108, 138, 156
de-roling 144
Dewinter, J. 108
diagnosis 66, 67–68, 109
*Diagnostic and Statistical Manual of Mental
    Disorders* (DSM-IV/DSM-V) 8–9, 137,
    140, 141
dialogue 11
Dickens, Charles 96
director's cue 145
disability 94, 95, 124
Dix, Ann 2, 55, 66–80
Dooman, Roya 3, 137–155, 157
double empathy 50
double life metaphor 96–97
dramatherapy 1–3, 4–7, 9–12, 156–158;
    adults with complex needs 121,
    123–134; aims for dramatherapy sessions
    159–160; client's agency 55–56; Code of
    Practice 53, 55; definition of 5, 81; early
    social behaviour 137–153; evaluation 57,
    131, 158, 159; evidence for the value
    of 166–167; girls 66–77; introverted
    clients 84–92; men with Asperger's 106,
    109–118; metaphor and 16–27, 44–51;
    non-verbal clients 29–39; outcomes
    26–27; performance 95–96; play and
    56; Roundabout 158–166; in schools
    54–55, 56–57, 58–62, 90; self-therapy
    93; theoretical bases for 94–95; tools of
    81–82
drawing 47, 85, 86; *see also* art

dreams 34–35
drumming 18, 130, 142, 143
Dunne, L. M. 29

early social behaviour 137–153
education *see* schools
ego development 33
Ellis, Carolyn 94
embodiment 10, 12, 95, 114, 122, 157;
    dramatic landscape 145; embodied
    metaphor 16, 27; EPR paradigm 5–6,
    10, 11
emotional development 7, 133–134, 167
emotional outbursts 29, 31, 35
emotions 10, 27, 156; adults with complex
    needs 129, 130–131; character work 23;
    expressing 8, 11, 18, 22, 158; girls 67,
    70; men with Asperger's 117; reading
    21–22; school-based dramatherapy 59,
    60; stakeholder interviews 161–162
empathy 7, 10, 93, 98; double empathy
    50; girls 70, 71; impact of dramatherapy
    on 139; lack of 8; left brain hemisphere
    69; puppet work 75; from therapist 91;
    women 67; *see also* Theory of Mind
empowerment 5, 53, 82, 85, 93
enactment 10, 47, 49
ending therapy 37, 49
EPR (embodiment-projection-role)
    paradigm 5–6, 10, 11
Erikson, E. 107–108
evaluation 57, 131, 158, 159
'Extreme Male Brain' theory 69
eye contact 34, 36, 61, 99; adults with
    complex needs 124–125, 126, 129,
    131; girls 67, 69, 70; McConnell and
    Ryser pro-ed rating scale 141; men with
    Asperger's 114

fabrics 48, 49, 73
Facebook 71
facial expressions 70, 75, 76, 126, 141
fairy tales 82, 87–88, 166
false belief tests 97; *see also* Sally-Anne test;
    Smarties test
families, support for 7, 161, 164–165, 167
fantasy 110–111, 112
Freud, Sigmund 42
friendships 9, 54–55, 91, 158; anxiety
    about 49; girls 70; McConnell and
    Ryser pro-ed rating scale 141; men with
    Asperger's 116; stakeholder interviews
    161, 165; *see also* peer relationships
Frith, U. 43, 156

Gallo-Lopez, L. 10, 11
games 76, 82, 157, 160
Garner, R. 42
gay men 106, 108, 118
gender 2, 55; characteristics 108; diagnosis
    67–68; men with Asperger's 116–117;
    stereotyping 73–74
genetic hypothesis 69
Gerhardt, S. 33–34, 35
Gillis, J. 137, 147
Gilmour, L. 108
girls 2, 55, 66–77
Gluck, Joel 83
Godfrey, Emma 3, 26, 156–169
Goffman, I. 94
Gould, J. 68
Grainger, Roger 4, 87, 123
Grandin, Temple 9, 74, 92
Greene, J. 7, 139–140, 166
Grimes, J. 83
group work 10, 12, 157, 166; adults with
    complex needs 124, 131; early social
    behaviour 144–153; girls 76; men with
    Asperger's 109–115; Roundabout
    158–166
Growtowski, J. 94–95

Haddon, Mark 41, 107
Hakomi Body Centred Psychotherapy 82
Happé, F. G. E. 43
Hare, D. J. 108
Haythorne, Deborah 1–3, 4–15, 26,
    156–169
Hearst, Caroline 70
Hellemans, H. 108
Henault, I. 108
heuristic research 94
Higashida, Naoki 9, 31, 39, 92, 138
Hodermarska, Maria 2, 17, 25, 93–105
holding 128
Holloway, P. 147
humour 97, 112, 114, 116–117, 149

identity 7, 18, 51, 100, 107–108; *see also*
    self
imagery 74
imagination 10, 35, 68, 71–72, 159;
    Asperger's syndrome 107; girls 75, 77;
    symbolic 113, 114
improvisation 10, 11, 19, 82; girls 73;
    men with Asperger's 110, 111, 113,
    118; musical 20; Process Reflective
    Enactment model 157
indirect approach 44, 51

individuation 29, 35
initiation 139, 148–149, 152, 153
interests 22, 71, 141, 150
International Classification of Diseases
   (ICD-10) 8
interventions 127–131
introversion 81, 83, 84–92
isolation 18, 22, 103, 138; adults with
   complex needs 121–122, 124; character
   work 24; girls 67, 72; men with
   Asperger's 112

Jackson, Jane 2, 121–136
Jennings, Sue 5–6, 10, 11, 17, 81, 128, 142
Johnson, M. 5
Jones, G. 151, 152
Jones, P. 7, 12, 81, 113–114, 121, 137, 147
Jordan, R. 10–11, 16, 24, 151, 152
Jung, Carl 29, 42, 114

Kalyva, E. 74
Kanner, Leo 8, 68
Karkou, V. 12, 75, 157
Kasirer, A. 44
Kenny, L. 3
'Kid Esteem' 166
Kurtz, R. 83

Lakoff, G. 5
Landy, Robert 6, 11, 17, 96, 102, 112, 115
language: action combined with 97;
   girls 69, 75; impairments 43, 45, 68;
   McConnell and Ryser pro-ed rating
   scale 141–142, 150, 151; non-verbal
   clients 122, 125; *see also* communication
Lanyado, M. 74
learning difficulties 11–12, 66, 68, 107;
   adults with complex needs 121–122, 124,
   125–126; men with Asperger's 110, 112
Leigh, L. 55
Lerner, M. 157
Lewis, Jeannie 2, 11, 26, 41–52, 75
Lindkvist, Marian 5, 6–7, 142
loneliness 24, 87, 108, 138
Lord, S. 10

Madders, T. 17
make-believe play *see* pretend play
Mamet, D. 103
Mann, S. 20
Mashal, N. 44
McConnell and Ryser pro-ed rating scale
   140–141, 147, 149–152, 153, 157
Mead, G. 94

medication 59–60, 115
men 2, 106–118
mental health 17, 27; adults with complex
   needs 121–122, 124, 133, 134; loneliness
   108; men with Asperger's 109, 110, 114,
   115, 117
Mesibov, G. B. 115
metaphor 2, 5, 16–27, 29–30, 41–52; aesthetic
   boundaries 6; definition of 42; EPR model
   10; impairment in metaphorical thinking
   41; non-verbal clients 35, 39
Meyerhold, V. 94–95
MIFNE model 34
Milioni, D. 16
'mindblindness' 16–17, 20–21, 27
mindfulness 82–83, 84, 91
mirroring 98, 99–100, 101, 128, 129, 130,
   162
Mitchell, David 9
Mitchell, S. 144
Mittledorf, W. 74
monologue 11
mothers 43; *see also* parents
movement 10, 11, 142, 146, 157; adults
   with complex needs 128–129; dance
   113; girls 75, 77; repetitive movements
   124, 126; Roundabout 160; Sesame
   Method 124
multiple exemplar training 44
music 20, 75; adults with complex needs
   128, 129–130; men with Asperger's 114;
   music therapy 74
mutuality 19, 27

Nash, H. 42
National Autistic Society (NAS) 3, 8, 67,
   106, 107, 122
Nelson, A. 115
neural pathways 34
non-verbal clients: adults with complex
   needs 121–134; children 2, 29–39
non-verbal communication 8, 18, 51;
   adults with complex needs 133;
   McConnell and Ryser pro-ed rating
   scale 150; Roundabout 160
Norbury, C. F. 43

Oaklander, Violet 32
object relations 6
objects 17, 128, 130; *see also* transitional
   objects
OH cards 21
opening rituals 143
Osborn, M. 123, 126

Panek, R. 9
Paquette-Smith, M. 108–109
parents 31, 33–34; feedback from 90, 156,
   159, 160–166, 167; McConnell and Ryser
   pro-ed rating scale 150, 151; meeting with
   37–38; 'refrigerator' mothers 43
Pearson, J. 121
peer relationships 7, 62, 167; girls 72, 73;
   group work 166; McConnell and Ryser
   pro-ed rating scale 141, 150, 151–152;
   stakeholder interviews 161, 165; *see also*
   friendships; relationships
percussion 128, 130, 142
performance 93–94, 95–96, 100–101,
   102, 157
Persicke, A. 44
Peter, M. 10, 139
Peter Pan 30, 33, 34, 39
physical intimacy 101, 102
Pimpas, Ioannis 56
play 6, 11, 29–30, 35, 74–75; dramatherapy
   and 56; dramatic 142–143; free and
   structured 151; girls 66, 71; McConnell
   and Ryser pro-ed rating scale 142; men
   with Asperger's 111–112; non-verbal
   clients 36; play-drama continuum 142,
   153; 'playing space' 46; relationship play
   129; Roundabout 160; school-based
   dramatherapy 59; symbolic 74; *see also*
   pretend play; role play
playfulness 147
Pokémon 22–24
Porter, R. J. 109, 116, 128
Powell, S. 10–11, 16, 24
pretend play 76, 142, 149, 150, 151–152,
   153; *see also* role play
Prevezer, W. 11
privacy 91, 113
Process Reflective Enactment model 7, 11,
   12, 157
projection 10, 12, 20, 93, 157; adults with
   complex needs 122; EPR paradigm 5–6,
   10, 11; girls 73, 77
psychoanalysis 42–43
puberty 72–73
puppets 10, 21, 75, 84, 87; adults with
   complex needs 130; early social
   behaviour 145; healing through 92
Purkis, Janette 71–72

Ramsden, Emma 2, 53–65
reciprocity 141, 150
referrals 109–110, 124, 158–159
reflexivity 60

'refrigerator' mothers 43
relationship play 129
relationships 36, 62, 100, 158, 167;
   ADHD 55; adults with complex needs
   131–132, 134; anxiety about 49–50;
   group work 166; McConnell and Ryser
   pro-ed rating scale 141, 150, 151–152;
   men with Asperger's 116, 117; online
   71; school settings 54–55; stakeholder
   interviews 161, 165; *see also* peer
   relationships; social interaction; social
   skills; therapeutic relationship
relaxation 75, 77, 131, 133, 144, 160
repetitive movements 124, 126
residential hospitals 121
responsiveness 139, 147–148, 149, 152, 153
Reynolds, K. 70
Ridlington-White, Helen 2, 29–40
rituals 17–18, 25, 27, 75, 142, 143
role play 11, 82, 98, 102, 143, 157; early
   social behaviour 146; girls 75, 76;
   healing through 92; impact on social
   interaction 139; men with Asperger's
   110, 115–116, 118; Process Reflective
   Enactment model 157; school-based
   dramatherapy 59, 60; sharing emotions
   22; social skills 162; by therapist 147
Role Theory and Method model 11
roles 12, 17, 27, 96, 122; de-roling 144;
   dramatic play 142–143; embodying
   143–144; EPR paradigm 5–6, 10, 11;
   men with Asperger's 111–112
Romanczykv, R. 137
Rosenblatt, M. 122
Roundabout 156, 158–166
routines 9
Rowe, A. 107, 117
Ryser, G. R. 140–141

Sally-Anne test 43, 46
Sanderson, P. 75
Scariano, M. M. 9
schools 35–36, 54–55, 56–57, 58–62;
   classroom behaviour 161, 164; girls 67,
   76; introverted clients 90, 91; school
   refusal 21, 26; transitions 45, 47, 48–49,
   50, 88
Schore, Allan 30, 34, 35, 38
Scott-Danter, H. 139
Seebohm, H. 147
self 7, 10, 12, 100, 159; adults with
   complex needs 133; body and 128; girls
   77; mirroring 129; performance of 103;
   'True Self' 30; *see also* identity

self-consciousness 101
self-efficacy 93, 101, 102
self-esteem 10, 11, 59, 138, 159; adults
    with complex needs 132, 134;
    Asperger's syndrome 107, 108; girls 66,
    77; impact of dramatherapy on 158;
    introverted clients 85, 86, 88, 90; men
    with Asperger's 117, 118; stakeholder
    interviews 163
self-expression 32, 36–37, 53, 55
self-harm 39, 66, 124, 126, 133
self-regulation 34–35, 36
self-soothing 18, 67, 101, 133
self-therapy 93
sensory materials 128, 130
sensory motor relational play 142, 143,
    148–149
sensory processing 125, 138, 145, 153
Sesame Institute 121, 123
Sesame Method 5, 124
sexual stereotyping 73–74
sexuality 101–102, 108, 116
Seymour, Anna 1–3, 4–15
shame 30
Sherbourne, V. 74, 129
Sherratt, D. 10, 139
Shore, Stephen 66, 74
Siebers, Toby 95
The Silky Stranger 41, 45, 48–49
Sinclair, Jim 50
Smail, M. 143
Smarties test 43, 46
Smith, J. A. 123, 126
social constructivism 94–95
social imagination 68, 71–72, 107; *see also*
    imagination
social interaction 9, 45, 68, 69; Asperger's
    syndrome 107; boys 73–74; early social
    behaviour 137–153; girls 70, 72, 75;
    performance of self 103; play therapy 74;
    see also relationships
social media 71, 107
social skills 7, 9, 11, 138, 156–157, 159,
    166; comedy 149; girls 66, 70, 75, 77;
    impact of dramatherapy on 139, 158,
    167; school settings 54–55; social media
    impact on 71; stakeholder interviews
    161, 162–163; *see also* relationships
song 11, 128, 129–130, 142; *see also* music
Spatula Strategy test 33
Spensley, S. 17
stage directions 145
stakeholder interviews 160–166
stereotyping 2, 73–74

Stone, G. P. 51
stories 10, 11, 12, 59, 60, 61; adults with
    complex needs 128, 130–131; girls 77;
    healing through 92; introverted clients
    86–88; men with Asperger's 110, 112,
    113, 118; Process Reflective Enactment
    model 157; storytelling 157, 160
suicide 39, 108–109
support, for families 7, 161, 164–165, 167
Swanepoel, M. 16
symbols 16, 17, 25–26; archetypal 34–35;
    EPR model 10; non-verbal clients 36,
    38, 39; symbolic play 74–75
Syz, J. 113

Tammet, D. 9
testosterone 69
theatre 4–5, 97
Theory of Mind 9, 25, 83–84, 93, 97–98,
    103; first-order and second-order 43;
    girls 67, 71; 'mindblindness' 16–17,
    20–21; Sally-Anne and Smarties tests 43,
    46; *see also* empathy
therapeutic relationship 6, 18–20, 27, 115;
    adults with complex needs 127, 128,
    133; counter-transference 30; men with
    Asperger's 116; non-verbal clients 36;
    secure attachment 18, 122
therapeutic space 33
'thinking maps' 44
touch 128
toys 17, 71, 130, 140
Tracey Beaker 72
transference 30, 117, 122
transitional objects 17, 18, 31
transitional space 17, 27
transitions 45, 47, 48–49, 50, 88, 143, 152
Treves, Jeni 2, 81–92
Triad of Impairments 8, 9, 68, 69, 83–84,
    107, 156
'True Self' 30
trust 31, 33, 38, 45, 75, 115, 166
Tubbs, J. 166
Turing, Alan 107
Tustin, F. 17
Tytherleigh, L. 12, 157

the unconscious 29, 34, 39, 42, 114

vocalisations 122, 125
voice 5, 53, 55, 57, 85, 91

Wagner, M. 34
warm ups 143

Weider, S. 74–75
well-being 117–118, 159
Whitehead, C. 98
Whyte, E. M. 44
Wickes, F. 35, 38
Williams, Donna 9, 32, 35, 38–39, 71, 115, 138, 145, 148
Wilmer-Barbrook, C. 11, 67, 107, 109, 139, 151, 158
Wilson, Jacqueline 72

Wing, Lorna 8, 67, 68
Winnicott, D. W. 17, 30, 31, 33, 111
witnessing 5, 19, 83, 87, 93, 127
working alliance 61, 62
World Health Organization (WHO) 8

Yalom, I. 82, 84–85
Yaull-Smith, D. 67

Zac, Sister Viktorine 43